Y0-BSL-818
3 5048 00097 5167

MUSSOLINI

BY ANTHONY JAMES JOES

FRANKLIN WATTS
New York | London | Toronto | Sydney
1982

Cover photograph courtesy of: UPI

Photographs courtesy of:
United Press International: pp. opposite title page, 79, 226, 281, 362;
Wide World: pp. 138, 292, 327;
The New York Public Library: pp. 187, 193, 251

Library of Congress Cataloging in Publication Data

Joes, Anthony James.
Mussolini.

Bibliography: p.
Includes index.
1. Mussolini, Benito, 1883-1945.
2. Italy—Politics and government—1870-1915.
3. Italy—Politics and government—1914-1945.
4. Fascism—Italy—History.
5. Heads of state—Italy—Biography.
I. Title.

DG575.M8J58 945.091'092'4 [B] 81-23110
ISBN 0-531-09865-6 AACR2

Printed in the United States of America
5 4 3 2 1

CONTENTS

FOR MY FATHER
AND MOTHER

MUSSOLINI

PREFACE

I have written this book to reintroduce Americans to Benito Mussolini, a man whom most have forgotten, or at best remember only in caricature.

Two views of Mussolini predominate in the English-speaking world. The first of these views holds Mussolini to have been the thoroughly wicked head of an utterly brutal regime, a man of no principle who destroyed Italian democracy, oppressed the poor, persecuted his opponents, glorified imperialism, prostituted himself to Adolf Hitler, and died a deservedly bloody death.

In the second, perhaps more widespread view, Mussolini need not be taken too seriously. From Italy we get opera singers, movie directors, racing cars, and women's fashions—not political ideas. Italy produces not statesmen but Machiavellians, and unsuccessful ones at that. The grisly ending of Mussolini paradoxically strengthens the suspicion that neither he nor his regime were consequential. There is also the swift and catastrophic defeat of Fascist Italy in World War II, an argument against the seriousness of fascism that many Americans, perhaps, find most compelling.

But Mussolini's contemporaries had a different impression

of him. The Italian Socialist party entrusted him with high responsibilities at a very young age. He won copious praise from Bernard Shaw, Georges Sorel, and G. K. Chesterton. Sigmund Freud presented him with a book inscribed "to the Hero of Culture," and Oswald Spengler sent him a set of his collected works. Pope Pius XI pronounced him "a man sent to us by Providence"; in 1931 Gandhi called him "the saviour of Italy." In 1938 John Gunther described him as "the only modern ruler who can be genuinely termed an intellectual"; earlier, David Lloyd George proclaimed Mussolini's Corporate State to be "the greatest social reform of modern times." Nicholas Murray Butler, president of Columbia University from 1902 to 1945, believed that Mussolini's "manifest achievements" would cause Americans to wish to imitate fascism. British Foreign Secretary Austen Chamberlain said that "the more one knows the Italian Prime Minister, the more one appreciates and loves him." Charles De Gaulle–*after* World War II—declared that "Mussolini was a great, a very great man."[1]

Clearly, the difference in the perception of Mussolini between his day and ours could hardly be greater. It is less clear that the passage of time has been all to the advantage of accuracy.

I am very much in debt to many for their help in writing this book. St. Joseph's University provided me with a sabbatical year to put my thoughts together, and many colleagues at that institution have shared their wisdom with me over the years. I am also indebted in special ways to Professor A. James Gregor of the University of California and Professor Domenico Settembrini of the University of Pisa, who both encouraged me in this task and saved me from many errors. I received much good advice and patient help from Robert Levine and Mary Ellen Casey of Franklin Watts, Inc. My wife, Christine Calhoun Joes, has been, in this project as in many things, a tower of strength. Whatever merits this work may possess reflect all this good assistance; its inadequacies are entirely my own responsibility.

INTRODUCTION

The career of Benito Mussolini has importance for us, it seems to me, for at least two major reasons. First, the advent of Mussolini and his followers to power represented a clamorous rejection of constitutional democracy in a large Western country. Mussolini came to power at a very young age; he held onto that power for more than two decades. During those years he won the support of most of his countrymen and the admiration of many distinguished foreigners. However disturbing we may find them, these are facts, and they need to be accounted for, not rationalized away.

Second, and perhaps even more important, Mussolini came to power in a country beset with major and growing crises. Italy was riven by violent class, religious, and regional rivalries; political institutions were rapidly losing their legitimacy; economic development was blocked by seemingly insuperable obstacles. Similar crises afflict many countries today, especially in the underdeveloped or "Third World" areas. In seeking to resolve these questions of political stability and economic growth, Mussolini was "addressing himself to the problems of the twentieth century."[1] How well or ill he succeeded in dealing with this set of problems is fraught with implications for much of the world. And in fact, many underdeveloped nations, facing problems similar to those confronting Mussolini and his Fascists, have produced similar responses: a host of regimes that bear a striking resemblance to Italian fascism have come to power in the Third World. *Mussolini was, in a real sense, the prototypical dictator of our century.*

Over and above these arresting aspects, Mussolini the man provides much to fascinate the student of leadership. In the words of his most assiduous biographer, "Mussolini . . . was in reality a very complex person, and not at all easy to understand."[2] This complexity is reflected in the dual and often contradictory tendencies that, perhaps more so than in most men, characterized Mussolini. He liked to pose as the staid and moral family man, as many official photographs attest; yet his amours, from adolescence to the day of his death (even allowing for exaggeration), were very numerous. Brought up as an antireligious revolutionary, he carried out a historic reconciliation of Church and State very beneficial to the former. Although he knew only too well how to play the vulgar demagogue, he was very much at home in the role of John Gunther's "intellectual statesman." He claimed to have established a new political system in which the State exercised "totalitarian" control, while in fact his fascism always involved a tentative balancing act resting on the most delicate set of compromises. Monarchists and industrialists looked on him as their best insurance against red revolution, but Mussolini, the former Socialist firebrand, sought throughout his career to win the laboring masses to his programs. He glorified the creative possibilities of Darwinian struggle, but was notably sparing of the blood of his enemies. He liked to emphasize the revolutionary and militaristic nature of his regime, yet he more than any other was responsible for the last desperate effort to preserve the European status quo at Munich. Finally, he made Italian nationalism the fulcrum of his mature thought, the foundation of his popular appeal, and the wellspring of his policy, yet he finished his life as the front man for a brutal Nazi occupation of his country.

In light of all this, one might well expect that reflection upon the original Fascist dictatorshp would provide many insights into the political upheavals of our time. But this has not been the case. Two generations have passed since the death of Mussolini, and a number of very high-quality studies of particular aspects of his career or regime have appeared in the United States and elsewhere, especially in the past decade and a half. Nevertheless, it seems true that "the fascism of Benito Mussolini is perhaps the least understood movement of the twentieth century,"[3] and that Mussolini himself is one of its least understood figures. Therefore, the need for a new study of Mussolini that synthesizes for the non-specialist reader the newer scholarship on his life and the Fascist movement which he founded and animated, is so clear that it will perhaps excuse my temerity in undertaking this task.

The purpose of this book is to offer answers to certain basic questions: Why did Mussolini organize the Fascist movement? Why did he come to power? How was he able to hold onto power for so many years? Why did he fall? In searching through the data, I have sought to emphasize those elements I believe most important and helpful for understanding what Mussolini was all about, what his life and career *meant* and *showed.* Thus the book is not a history of Italian fascism, nor a biography of Mussolini in the strictest sense. It is rather a *portrait.* Like all portraits, it is affected not only by the nature of the subject, but also by the interests and needs of the painter, and the concerns and controversies of his own time and place. So it is probably a good idea for me to confess to the reader my own prejudices (at least those of which I am aware) at the start. My favorite preceptors in politics have been James Madison and Alexis de Tocqueville. I believe that constitutional democracy, as that term is generally used in the West, is probably the most civilized and civilizing form of government yet devised. I would prefer to see all peoples everywhere living under that system. It has come to my attention, however, that the world is uncannily unconcerned with my preferences. Most people, now and in the past, have lived under some form of one-man rule, often quite willingly, even insistently. Without doubt, dictatorship is the most salient and characteristic institution of our own time. I hope to persuade the reader that to study Mussolini is to gain particularly fruitful insights into many facets of that institution.

With these purposes, it would be quite useless for me to evaluate Mussolini according to the criteria appropriate to American politicians, to compare Mussolini (to his infinite disadvantage) to a Jefferson or a Lincoln. Instead, I have tried to view Mussolini in the circumstances of his own time and place. It is, further, completely destructive of any effort at understanding human affairs to read history backward, to examine someone's actions and condemn them in light of knowledge that we now possess but which was totally or partially unavailable to that person. Hindsight obscures at least as much as it illuminates. In considering any given policy or decision of Mussolini's, therefore, I have tried to keep before me two questions: How did the world probably look to Mussolini at that specific time? How would the world have looked to me, had it been necessary for me to give advice to Mussolini?

The story of Benito Mussolini is a complex one, with some truly tragic aspects to it. I have done my best to convey to the reader both the complexity and the tragedy of his life. We know that "men are loath to abandon the old clichés and stereotypes that have served them so well, for they make the world around them intelligible, comfortable, and meaningful."[4] Those, therefore, who insist that Mussolini can have but a single dimension, who read this book expecting to find a ritual exorcism, will not be pleased.

PROLOGUE OCTOBER, 1922: THE VIEW FROM THE PALACE

As he gazed through the tall windows of the Quirinale Palace, King Victor Emmanuel might have noted that the long Roman summer had definitely come to an end. The cold rain that had recently fallen had put a chill in the air and marked off the end of a season. And perhaps of an era, who could tell? The king did not like the Quirinale, this ancient residence of popes and kings; he spent as little time here as possible. But now that a decision had finally been made, this was no doubt the most appropriate location in which to consummate it. In a few hours he, Victor Emmanuel III, king of Italy, would formally receive in audience the man he had just appointed to be prime minister, Benito Mussolini.

The rapid rise of Mussolini's Fascist movement had been truly amazing, like a phenomenon of nature, like Vesuvius erupting. A handful of men, none of them very important, had gathered in Milan in the spring of 1919 around the figure of the thirty-six-year-old Benito Mussolini. He had once been a powerful leader of Italian socialism, but his party had expelled him in 1915 because he began to advocate Italy's entrance into the

Great War. In the subsequent three and a half years, fascism had grown into the most vigorous and exuberant organization in the country. Fascism had picked up a lot of support from people embittered by the results of the war. Italy, promised a great deal in 1915 by her allies for entering the conflict, had endured enormous sufferings in the struggle, including 600,000 killed; but after the war she had been allowed to collect very little. The Fascists denounced this "mutilated victory" and the politicians who had allowed it.

But to explain the triumph of the Fascists, the most important key by far lay with the Socialist party. Its policies for the previous decade had been incomprehensible, pitiable, even grotesque. The Socialists opposed the war effort and thus cut themselves off from the sufferings, longings, and exhilarations of their countrymen. After the war they became the largest of Italy's many parties, but they refused to assume office and did everything possible to prevent anyone else from forming a stable government to deal with the nation's problems. Instead, they frightened the whole country with their ferocious revolutionary rhetoric, while gangs of Socialist militants bullied small farmers, insulted priests and army officers in the streets, and literally spat in the faces of wounded veterans. Veterans, indeed, formed the backbone of the new Fascist movement. Many of these were former officers or commandoes, and it was they who, province by province and raid by raid, smashed to pieces the once-mighty Socialist organization. In the 1921 national elections the new Fascist party won three dozen seats in parliament; by the fall of 1922 they claimed one million members, and a party militia of over two hundred thousand. Europe had never seen anything like this—a party organized like an army. And they marched from victory to victory. On October 22, for example, just two days before the opening of the Fascist national convention in Naples, the movement won every seat on the city council of Reggio Emilia, at one time a stronghold of the Socialists.

The Fascists were thus able to demonstrate great strength in the nation. But neither Mussolini nor any other prominent Fascist had ever held ministerial office before, and the elections of the previous year had given them only a relatively small number of seats in the Chamber of Deputies. So the established leaders of the parties and factions in parliament, with their fatal tendency to confuse the Chamber with the nation, refused to recognize the claims of the Fascists to a major share of seats in the new cabinet. Having demonstrated their power, the members of the Fascist movement were eager to see their leaders come to office and implement the party program for national rejuvenation and discipline. The constant stalling, the monolithic resistance from the leaders of the other parties, the offerings of a few crumbs rather than the substance of power, was making them very restless. Mussolini knew that the Fascists must obtain a share of real power soon, or there might well be an explosion that he himself would be unable to control. So the plans were laid for the long-rumored *Marcia su Roma,* the March on Rome. On October 24, Mussolini proclaimed to the party convention in Naples that fascism must and would come to power very soon, either through constitutional processes or revolutionary upheaval.

Besides the impatience of many rank-and-file Fascists, other calculations combined to push Mussolini to an October move. Everyone said that old Giovanni Giolitti, prime minister many times in the past, was maneuvering to head one last cabinet before he died. Mussolini knew well that Giolitti was quite capable of ordering the army to open fire on a Fascist march on Rome, no matter how many decorated war veterans might be in the ranks. Hadn't Giolitti, the last time he was in office in 1920, sent the Italian navy to bombard the city of Fiume, which was being held in the name of the Italian people by the war hero and poet Gabriele D'Annunzio and his followers? In fact, Giolitti was quite old enough to remember when the Italian army had been sent to fire upon no less than the hero Garibaldi and his men at Aspromonte! However, like most other politicians, Mussolini was not in a position to know that Father

Luigi Sturzo, the Sicilian priest who headed the powerful Catholic party, had effectively vetoed a new Giolitti cabinet. The possibility of Giolitti's return to power still loomed as a mortal threat to the whole Fascist party. It was this very danger that prompted the distinguished political scientist professor Vilfredo Pareto to wire Mussolini: "It's now or never." So the mobilization started on October 27, with headquarters in Perugia (right across the street from the prefecture!). The March on Rome had begun.

Watching the slate sky of the late Roman October, Victor Emmanuel could reflect wryly on the way in which his government had reacted to the Fascist mobilization. While the king had been enjoying the waning days of a vacation in Pisa, Prime Minister Luigi Facta wired him that the Fascist danger had passed. Poor Facta! At that very hour Mussolini and the designated leaders of the march—dramatically called by the Latin title of *Quadrumviri,* the "four men"—were sitting in a room in the Hotel Vesuvio in Naples putting the final touches on plans for the mobilization. Victor Emmanuel returned to his capital, reluctantly, on October 27. Hardly had he installed himself in his residence when Prime Minister Facta, having learned that the march was under way, burst in upon the king to announce *his resignation. Porca miseria!* How did this man whom the wits said should be called not *facta* (deeds) but *verba* (words), how did such a man ever get to be prime minister? The answer was obvious. Facta, the sixty-one-year-old provincial lawyer and undistinguished member of the Chamber of Deputies, had been put into office to keep the seat warm for Giovanni Giolitti. Giolitti treated the prime ministership much like a townhouse; when the political weather turned unpleasant, he would vacate it for a while and return to his estate in the country. But Facta had entered his own little game with the Fascists. He—*he!*—had decided that he would be the one to "tame" Mussolini by getting him to accept a subordinate post in a new Facta cabinet. He therefore told Giolitti he might as well remain out of town; if things developed into a crisis, Facta would summon him in plenty of time. Thus Giolitti, the one Italian politician who was a match for Mussolini, was hundreds of miles away during the hours when the March on Rome developed from rumor to reality. Then there was Alfredo Lusignoli, the prefect of Milan. He was supposed to be the government's chief agent in that key city, the center of the Fascist movement. He should have kept the government in Rome reliably informed of what the Fascist leaders were doing and saying. But the Fascists had seduced him with promises of a high post in their new cabinet. Lusignoli was, like Facta, another one of these "Giolitti men." *Madonna!* Poor Giolitti. But that was too bad about him. Victor Emmanuel had never liked Giolitti, and now here he was, an eighty-year-old-man who had formed his first cabinet thirty years ago, trying to slip once again into the bed of power. Yes, Victor Emmanuel might well reflect, it was not just the self-destructive Socialists with their stupid braggadocio and cowardly bullying who had set the stage for fascism; it was also these poltroon politicians with their obscure rivalries and endless intrigues, with their inability to tell the difference between the Chamber of Deputies and the real world. But Mussolini would doubtless give them a lesson or two in practical politics.

The March on Rome proceeded in a most intriguing manner that reflected the influence of a subtle and cynical understanding of the nature of Italian politics. Almost every coup d'etat emphasizes the element of speed. The idea is to take a government by surprise and thus deny opposing forces the opportunity to rally around somebody and organize a counterstrike. But the Fascist march was organized to *avoid* speed. Converging columns of Fascists advanced on the capital city from the north and east with the slow inevitability of a glacier, giving everybody in Rome plenty of time to make selfish calculations. The advance began on the night of October 27-28. In all the cities and towns along the roads to Rome, Fascists occupied telegraph offices, railway stations, and public buildings, usually without a struggle. Army units in many places along the march fraternized with the Fascists, in some cases actually handing over arms to them. It would soon be impossible for the government in Rome to communicate with the rest of the country. The deliberate choreography of the march, like a slow-motion ballet, produced a growing sense of isolation within the government. Meanwhile, Mussolini, like the generals of the Great War, directed the progress of the march from his newspaper offices in Milan, behind the lines. All was proceeding according to plan, in fact better than the plan, and the stakes of the game were consequently rising. Former Prime Minister Antonio Salandra, who had led Italy into the war in 1915 and was now the dominant leader of the conservatives, offered the Fascists several places in a cabinet to be headed by himself. Mussolini rejected the offer. Nothing would satisfy him now but the premiership itself. Mussolini's newspaper *Il popolo d'Italia* issued a warning: "Let them understand that up to the present moment a solution to the crisis can still be found within a framework of the most orthodox constitutionalism, but tomorrow it may be too late." There was a great deal in this for a king to think about.

From the windows of the Quirinale, Victor Emmanuel could see the top of the gleaming white monument that broods above the Piazza Venezia in the heart of Rome. It was called the Victor Emmanuel monument; not, of course, after him, but in honor of his grandfather, the first king of Italy. Thinking about the massive white structure caused the king to remember that he himself was not massive; in fact, he was one of the smallest men he knew of. People always quite unreasonably expected kings to be somehow larger than life and felt cheated if they were not. Victor Emmanuel knew that it was for this reason, in part, that he was not popular with the Italians. When his firstborn son and heir, Umberto, was born in 1904, the city council of Milan actually refused to allow the flag to be flown from the cathedral in celebration. Even his own parents had not especially liked him. He had been given a severe military upbringing, and was allowed to dine with his mother and father only twice a week. They probably blamed themselves for his small stature; the House of Savoy was known for its inbreeding. And so they had married him to a Montenegrin princess, hoping that the infusion of fresh blood would produce a more impressive generation. Unlike his father and grandfather, Victor Emmanuel was no great rider of horses, no dashing collector of mistresses. He was instead a collector of coins. When he became king at the age of thirty-one he knew that people said of him that he was already like a little old man.

Life presents special problems, special denigrations, for small men, even if—especially if—they are kings. Victor Emmanuel could recall a visit to Rome by Germany's Kaiser Wilhelm. The swaggering bonehead had wanted to overawe the Italians with unmistakable evidence of Germanic power, so he brought along with him a picked bodyguard of Pomeranian grenadiers, each one especially chosen for his towering height. Victor Emmanuel had been dwarfed as he walked among them. Instead of being favorably impressed, Italian public opinion was offended at what it interpreted as a deliberate effort to humiliate their king (however unlovable he might be, he was the only king the Italians had). So the kaiser's visit, intended to bolster Italo-German friendship, resulted instead in a diplomatic disaster, and all because he, Victor Emmanuel, lacked a few miserable inches. But—look at Mussolini, a man only a couple of inches taller than his king, yet the world saw in him a strongman, multitudes hung onto his every utterance, vast hosts marched at his command. If nothing else, Mussolini as prime minister would remind an insensitive world that smallness of stature was not incompatible with greatness of soul.

Should the king invite Mussolini to become his new prime minister? Or should the government resist the March on Rome? That is, should he, Victor Emmanuel, sign the proclamation of a state of siege that would direct the Rome garrison to open fire if the marching Fascists attempted to enter the city? That was the heart of the matter.

Why, in fact, should Mussolini be resisted? He had renounced his youthful republicanism and professed loyalty to the royal house. He would provide strong leadership. He certainly knew how to handle these Socialists. Victor Emmanuel hated the Socialists. He could remember as if it were yesterday that dreadful occasion in the spring of 1919 when he was preparing to give an address to the newly elected parliament. The Socialist members suddenly stood up and started singing "The Red Flag." They finally marched out of the chamber, thoroughly disrupting the session and frightening the king half to death. And if Mussolini had tamed these insolent dogmatizers by means of the Fascist party alone, just imagine what he would do to them if he had the powers of the state at his disposal.

On the other hand if, under royal command, the army did fire and the Fascists were scattered, who would benefit from such a denouement except the detestable Socialists? And if the Rome garrison should perhaps be overcome, and the Fascists break into the city in strength—*what then*? What would happen to the monarchy, to the House of Savoy, to Victor Emmanuel himself? Might they perhaps throw him off the roof of the Quirinale? Or shoot him on the very steps of the Victor Emmanuel monument? Or perhaps string him up from Trajan's column? And why would such a dire event have come about? Because the king had ordered the army to fire upon the followers of a man with whom even now Giolitti, Salandra, Facta, and every other politician of note were negotiating, trying to get him to serve in a cabinet headed by one of them! Could a king order his army to shoot, must a king risk his throne and even his life, in a gesture against a man whom the leading politicians of the country might literally at any moment designate as the next prime minister? *Gesúmaria!* It was *too* absurd!

And—question of questions—if the army were ordered to fire on the Fascists, *would it in fact obey*? Most army officers, including generals, were openly sympathetic to the Fascists.

They wanted Mussolini, defender of the veterans, friend of the army, foe of traitors, to come to power and save the nation. Many of the leaders of the marching Fascist columns coverging at that moment on Rome's suburbs were retired officers clad in their old uniforms dripping with decorations. All of the world said that the officer corps was imbued with the old Piedmontese tradition of loyalty to the monarchy. Yes, but the queen mother was an outspoken admirer of Mussolini. And what about the king's brother, the dashing Duke of Aosta, who in 1920 had wanted to be appointed prime minister with dictatorial powers? At this very hour the ambitious duke was hanging around Fascist headquarters in Perugia! With all this sympathy for Mussolini and his followers shown by members of the royal family, who could tell how many officers might have gotten the idea that one could ignore an order to resist the march on Rome and yet still be loyal to the "true" interests of the House of Savoy, a house perhaps to be headed henceforth not by Victor Emmanuel III but by his brother Emmanuel Filibert I, formerly known as the Duke of Aosta? Remember how a couple of years ago whole army units had mutinied in order to help the war hero D'Annunzio seize the town of Fiume? Is that what General Diaz had meant on the night of October 27 when he told the king that "the army will do its duty, but it would be better not to put it to the test"?

On the morning of October 28, acting Prime Miniser Facta (he had not been replaced since his resignation; that was what all the negotiating between Mussolini and the Rome politicians had been about) came to see the king. He had in his hand a proclamation of the state of siege. The cabinet had insisted on it and all that was lacking was the king's signature.

But it was too late. The king declined to sign it. Facta retreated back to the cabinet in confusion.

Two hours later Facta returned. Once more, he requested the royal signature to the proclamation of a state of siege. Once more, the king refused.

The game was up.

For the next few hours, everybody in Rome entered into a mad scramble to get in touch with Mussolini in Milan. The king's aide telephoned him, relaying a royal invitation to come to Rome and form a cabinet. But Mussolini would accept no oral pledges. He was not budging from his newspaper office until he had a written, binding authorization from the palace. At noon on October 29 the required telegram arrived, signed by General Arturo Cittadini in the king's name. In jubilation, Mussolini turned to his brother Arnaldo and exclaimed: "If only our father were here!"

I

THE SETTING

*"One who cannot govern himself
must let himself be governed
by another who can."*

Vico

"Fuori i barbari!"

Pope Julius II

Many students of Italian history maintain that Mussolini's Fascist regime represents an interruption, a "parenthesis," in Italy's normal political development. In this view, fascism was essentially abnormal and accidental, like a careful automobile driver being involved in a crash. Quite to the contrary, I believe it is perfectly clear that Mussolinian fascism did not arrive on the Italian scene like a *diabolus ex machina,* but was deeply rooted in the history of the country. The Kingdom of Italy, from its foundation in 1861 to the investiture of Mussolini as prime minister in 1922, had to confront many serious problems simultaneously. Unification had been carried out by only a relative handful of determined men; under the facade of the new national unity, millions of southerners, Catholics, and peasants remained hostile, sullen, or apathetic, literally for generations. Italian parliamentary institutions, ill-suited to the experience of the population and the task at hand, became increasingly irrelevant and ineffective. Economic retardation, which many believed would be overcome with unification, instead became more pronounced. Italy suffered all the negative aspects of the industrial revolution with few if any of the benefits. In foreign affairs, the kingdom had expected to play an important or even a leading role, but instead compiled a record of hardly unrelieved disappointments, failures, and outright humiliations. Italians turned to fascism in part because the Fascists claimed to know how to reverse this dismal and distressing litany of disappointments, and to realize the *risorgimento** promise of social unity, economic development, and international influence. What follows in this chapter is not an attempt to set forth everything that was going on, everything that was real, in the life of Italy and the Italians. Rather, it is an effort to identify those events, conditions, and tendencies that most clearly contributed to the rise and triumph of fascism.

The half century between unification and World War I was the seedbed of fascism. Many practices for which fascism was later criticized—imperialism, authoritarianism, militarism—were in fact well developed by Italian statesmen during that period. Thus it is worthwhile to dwell at some length on the problems that Italians faced in those decades, especially since Italy has been unique among nations *neither in the nature of her problems nor in seeking their solutions in dictatorship.*

THE UNIFICATION OF ITALY

From Columbus's arrival in America to the Battle of Waterloo, the destiny of Europe was decided by the interplay of a small number of powerful states: France, Spain, England, and Austria, later joined by Russia and Prussia. Italy, in contrast, far from being a united and therefore influential nation, was divided into a number of political units, some independent, some ruled by foreign princes or the Catholic Church, none

*Literally, revival or awakening. This term refers to the struggle for Italian unification from roughly 1815 to 1861.

large enough to count as more than pawns in the game of European power politics.

Italy remained a geographical expression instead of a political power for many reasons, most of them having to do with the fact that Italy emerged out of the Dark Ages and into the era of renewed urban civilization sooner than other areas of Europe. The early resurgence of city life in Italy created a deep-rooted localism, an intense loyalty to one's native city or province. Generations of commercial rivalry and warfare among such leading cities as Genoa, Florence, Milan, Naples, and Rome (the latter ruled by the popes) reinforced this localism. Some of these city-states became rich and powerful; Venice was able to establish a commercial and naval empire with interests on three continents. Italian politics became a superrefinement of the balance-of-power game, the essence of which was the combining and recombining of players to prevent the emergence of any *dominant* player. Unification was thus delayed, and with disastrous results: the combination of economic wealth and political weakness proved an irresistible attraction to those newly-formed large states in the vicinity of the Italians, especially France and Spain. Italian civil wars were soon complicated by foreign intervention and invasion. Italy's politics became colonialized—not unlike eighteenth-century India—and local princes fought against one another with the aid of foreign imperialists. Many Italians, from the time of Dante and Machiavelli, yearned for the unification of their country and the expulsion of the "barbarians." But nobody seemed to know how to bring this about.

An ultimately successful drive toward unification took its impetus from the invasions of Napoleon. The Corsican conqueror carried out many reforms, including the establishment of a small Kingdom of Italy in the north. Although largely wiped out after Waterloo, these innovations nevertheless inspired the movement known as the *risorgimento*.

Post-Napoleonic Italy consisted of seven main political units. In the northwest was the Kingdom of Sardinia, which bore the name of that relatively remote island but was based in the much more important mainland area of Piedmont, with its great cities of Turin and Genoa. Sardinia-Piedmont became the only Italian state that was independent, well-governed, and willing to lead the *risorgimento* struggle. East of Piedmont lay the provinces of Lombardy and Venetia, the richest and most populous area of Italy, including the historic capitals of Milan and Venice. This large area was part of the Habsburg Empire and governed from Vienna. To the immediate south were the "duchies," the historic states of Tuscany, Parma and Modena; life was pleasant enough in these principalities but they were too small to have any weight in international politics, and their rulers were dependent for their thrones on the power of the Habsburgs. Central Italy was the temporal domain of the pope. These Papal States divided the peninsula from sea to sea and were the main barrier, in more ways than one, to a speedy and amicable unification of Italy. Finally, the Kingdom of Naples consisted of the poor and remote southern half of the peninsula along with the island of Sicily. Italian unification, the dream of the *risorgimento,* meant that all these areas, with their different systems of government and economy, with their age-old rivalries and divergent interests, locked into the power webs of the Roman Catholic Church and the Habsburg Empire, would have to be melded into one state and one people.

Of the various plans for Italian unification, three were of great importance. The first was advanced by a Piedmontese priest and politician named Vincenzo Gioberti. Born in Turin in 1801 and ordained a priest in 1825, Gioberti soon got himself into difficulties for his political views (not hard to do in the stifling Turin of the post-Waterloo days). He lived in exile from 1833 until 1848. In that year of revolutionary upheaval and international wars, King Charles Albert recalled Gioberti to Turin to take over the premiership of the Kingdom of Sardinia.

Gioberti was a real Italian patriot, and like Dante and Machiavelli before him, he burned with indignation and shame to see his country the battleground and lottery prize of foreign powers ("barbarians"). He wrote an interesting book whose daunting title, *The Moral and Civil Primacy of the Italians,* well summarizes its message. Father Gioberti thought he had a plan that would both achieve Italian unity and preserve the temporal power of the Roman pontiff, objectives hitherto considered by almost everyone to be mutually exclusive. He called for a federation of all the Italian states under the presidency of the pope. This rather modest proposal foundered principally on the hostility of the Church which, after 1848, adopted a stance of adamantine aversion to any and all schemes for Italian unification of any kind.

Giuseppe Mazzini, a leading patriot of the time, had another idea: revolutionary war—a people's war—to drive the foreigners out and reduce the papacy to submission.

Mazzini was born in Genoa in 1805. He was to make a name for himself among Roman Catholics as a dangerous enemy of religion, but he was deeply religious in his own way. He had a profound sympathy for all poor and oppressed people, believing that men were naturally good and fell into evil because their natural goodness was interfered with or crushed out. He came to view politics as an arena of human redemption (much like many modern "liberation" theologians). The fundamental causes of war were to be found in the selfish rivalries of kings; hence, after the revolution, men would erect a just and peaceful social order based on republicanism and international fraternity. "Liberty, Equality, Humanity" was Mazzini's slogan. With ideas like these he naturally gravitated to the dread revolutionary society known as the *Carbonari* (literally, "charcoal-burners," so-called from their habit of holding nocturnal meetings around campfires).

Slender, with large, somber eyes, Mazzini read a great deal, especially from the Bible, Tacitus, and Byron. In this way, he developed a beautiful writing style, and among the many who greatly enjoyed reading his works was the young Benito Mussolini.

Mazzini's adult life was totally taken up with revolutionary politics. These activities forced him to spend long periods in exile, mostly in Switzerland, France, and England. It was during one of these extensive sojourns outside his beloved homeland that Mazzini founded the society known as Young Italy, a revolutionary organization dedicated to the creation of a united and republican Italian nation. By 1833, Young Italy counted 60,000 members. While in London, Mazzini lived in a grimy lodging house, kept his room filled with tame birds, and earned a precarious living writing literary articles and giving Italian lessons. He also founded the newspaper *Thought and Action.* Like Karl Marx, he spent a good deal of time studying in the British Museum, but he was never attracted to the Marxists, with their dour dialectics and arid atheism. Although reentry into almost any place in his native land meant death if he were apprehended, Mazzini often returned to Italy to stir up or take part in revolts. He was active in Naples and the Papal States, became one of the leaders of the short-lived Roman Republic in 1849, and headed an unsuccessful uprising in Milan in 1853. Although Mazzini's schemes and revolts attracted attention and support over wide areas for many years, he ultimately failed because he could not enlist the support of the majority of the Italians—the peasants—who remained sunk in sullen apathy or were roused to outright hostility against Mazzini by the Church. The people were not interested in a people's war.*

The weaknesses of the plans for unification offered by such men as Gioberti and Mazzini help explain the eventual success of an alternative scheme, that of Conte Camillo di Cavour,

*Even after unification had been achieved, Mazzini never reconciled himself to a monarchist Italy, and continued to be a rebel until the end. He was persecuted by the new government, and although several times elected to the Chamber of Deputies by the city of Messina, he was never permitted to assume his seat. He endured perhaps his bitterest moments when the Italian government he had done so much to create cast him into prison in 1870.

prime minister of Sardinia-Piedmont for most of the decade before 1860.

The distinguished Oxford historian Denis Mack Smith has called Camillo Cavour "the most interesting and important figure in modern Italian history." Born in 1810, he was the younger son of an aristocratic family. As so many young men in his position did in those days, he entered the army, where he was trained to be an officer of engineers. He did not care for army life, nor was he comfortable amid the censorship and hothouse piety that characterized Piedmontese society in the repressive decades after Waterloo. (Besides, the Cavour family had displayed Bonapartist sympathies; Camillo's godmother had been Pauline Bonaparte Borghese.) He therefore resigned his commission to pursue the life of a gentleman farmer, at which he was notably (and surprisingly) successful. Short and stocky, with a large round head and a complacent smile, Cavour, in the typical manner of the Piedmontese ruling classes, was never able to completely master the Italian tongue; he always preferred the use of French, especially in his correspondence. Shortly after entering politics in the late 1840s, he founded a newspaper with the significant title *Il risorgimento.* After becoming prime minister of Piedmont in 1852, he spent the next several years carrying out legal, political, and economic reforms of such magnitude and diversity that little Piedmont took its place as the most well-governed and progressive of the Italian states, a serviceable nucleus around which to construct a united Italy. By 1859, for example, fully one half of the entire railroad mileage of all Italy was located in Piedmont (smaller than the state of Maryland), and the kingdom had also become a haven for political refugees from all over the peninsula.

Cavour steeped himself in the history of England. Above all, he admired its constitution. He was never happier than when sitting in the visitors' gallery of Britain's House of Commons, and (referring to the parliament of his own country), once remarked that "I never feel so weak as when the House is shut."

Although sometimes compared to British statesman Robert Peel, Cavour did not lack Machiavellian characteristics, either. A speculator in financial matters, a gambler in politics, Cavour was in all things an opportunist. Thoroughly devoted to liberalism in theory, in practice he was never above using corruption and deceit to attain his end. This point is vitally important because future generations came to look upon him as the most successful of all Italian politicians, and therefore the one most deserving of emulation. He expressed his philosophy in these terms: "If you must resort to extraordinary measures [i.e., corruption], then do it as quickly as possible, so that the nobility of your objectives makes up for the ignoble methods you employ." Or, more pithily, "if we did for ourselves the things we do for Italy, we would be real scoundrels."

Cavour has often been called the greatest statesman of nineteenth-century Europe (after all, Bismarck and Disraeli could dispose of the resources of great states, which Cavour lacked). Perhaps an essential of political greatness is the ability to recognize facts and use them to achieve one's purpose. At any rate, Cavour certainly grasped that the power of the Habsburgs, the opposition to the Church, and the indifference of the peasantry could not be overcome by the resources of the pro-unification forces; for those Italians who wanted unification and were willing to struggle for it were for the most part confined to the urban middle class, which was both numerically and politically weak. In addition, repeated attempts by Sardinia-Piedmont to expel the Austrians from Italian territory by military force had ended in honorable but total defeat. Italy, therefore, could not be created by the Italians alone; foreign intervention, that perpetual source of Italy's distress, must become the instrument of her deliverance. It was mainly for this reason—Cavour's willingness to play the tough and expensive game of European power politics—that Mazzini never trusted him. Mazzini saw Cavour not as a sincere Italian patriot, but as a schemer for Piedmontese expansion and the aggrandizement of the House of Savoy.* Cavour returned Mazzini's dislike, branding him "the chief of the assassins." But Cavour was able to win many of Mazzini's followers away from him, men like Garibaldi who were, in the last analysis, more interested in national unification than in republican purity. And so Cavour, by sending Sardinian troops to fight in the Crimean War on the side of the British and French, was able to force the postwar Congress of Paris (to the chagrin of the Austrians) to give public and serious consideration to the "Italian question." A couple of years later, by appealing to the imagination of Emperor Napoleon III (and not forgetting to throw in a few tangible inducements), Cavour made an alliance with France whereby Austria was driven out of Lombardy in the War of 1859. With the principal obstacle to unity thus removed, well-organized pro-unification minorities in the duchies and those parts of the Papal States outside the city of Rome carried out relatively bloodless coups d'etat and confirmed the annexation of their respective states to the Kingdom of Sardinia by hasty plebiscites of dubious validity.

These exciting events were exploding in the northern and central regions of the peninsula. Meanwhile, to the south, Garibaldi landed in Sicily with his red-shirted "One Thousand."

Giuseppe Garibaldi was without a doubt one of the most romantic figures in the history of modern Italy, even of all Europe. He had been born in the town of Nice, anciently a possession of the Kingdom of Sardinia-Piedmont, in 1807. As a lad he served in the Sardinian army. He fell under the influence of Mazzini's teaching, joined Young Italy, and participated in several Mazzinian plots. As a result of these involvements he found it prudent to sail off to South America. He fought in various conflicts in Brazil and Uruguay, organizing a band of irregulars known as the Italian Legion.

*Cavour was probably both, alternately and simultaneously.

Returning to Italy to participate in the upheavals of 1848, he battled for the ephemeral Roman Republic, in part because Mazzini was the leader, in part because Garibaldi was a ferocious anticlerical. With his great beard and slouch hat, Garibaldi had a menacing look that belied his usually kind and gentle deportment. When it came to priests, however, Garibaldi yielded to none in his contempt. He once publicly referred to Pope Pius IX as a "cubic meter of dung." With the collapse of the Roman Republic in 1849, Garibaldi could have fled to asylum in Sardinia, but instead he went to the United States. For a while he earned a living as a candlemaker on Staten Island, but Garibaldi was no longer a young man and he longed to return to his homeland. So he purchased a farm on the little island of Caprera, slightly to the north of Sardinia, and there he awaited events.

Sometime after settling down on his rocky isle, Garibaldi decided to abandon his republican dreams and throw his support to Camillo Cavour as the only man who had a serious chance of uniting Italy. This defection was a cruel blow to Mazzini because many of his followers were soon won over to the side of the monarchist Cavour by Garibaldi's example. During May 1860, while Cavour's agents and troops were gobbling up the duchies, Garibaldi suddenly landed (with Cavour's connivance) in Sicily, part of the Bourbon Kingdom of Naples. He had about a thousand men with him. Typically, this large volunteer force contained not a single peasant; most of Garibaldi's troops were lawyers—there were a great many lawyers, often impoverished, in Italy—and university students. (Six decades later, this very class, the educated underemployed, would also pay a major role in the rise of fascism.) In a brief and brilliant campaign, Garibaldi and his thousand Red Shirts conquered the whole island of Sicily, crossed to the mainland and, against impossible and ridiculous odds, soon made themselves masters of the whole Kingdom of Naples. Mazzini tried to convince his old disciple to retain power in Naples as a republican dictator, but the generous Garibaldi wanted to hand over the state to Victor Emmanuel. Garibaldi, however, tried to attach a condition to his magnificant gift: the dismissal by Victor Emmanuel of Prime Minister Cavour. Innocent of statecraft and intrigue, Garibaldi could not understand why his birthplace of Nice had been traded by Cavour to Napoleon III in return for the latter's aid in the War of 1859. This giving away of Italian territory (especially *Garibaldi's* territory) was for the Red-Shirt hero a betrayal of the most fundamental ideas of the *risorgimento.* Therefore, Cavour had to go. Of course King Victor Emmanuel refused this demand, tartly reminding Garibaldi that not only little Nice but also the province of Savoy, the very cradle of the royal family, had been sacrificed for French military assistance. Garibaldi, as all knew he would, turned the Kingdom of Naples over to Victor Emmanuel anyway. Afterward, refusing all emoluments and rewards, Garibaldi sailed back to his rugged and remote island, a true Cincinnatus.* But he swore he would cut off his right hand rather than let Cavour shake it.

Garibaldi's great achievement in conquering the South was tainted by the plebiscites held to register popular approval for the unification of those areas with Piedmont. An honest election would probably have produced a majority in favor of unification, but the plebiscites were anything but honest.

*The world, however, had by no means heard the last of Garibaldi. In 1862, he and some followers invaded the patrimony of St. Peter (today called Lazio), the last parts of the former Papal States still under the rule of the Pope. To avoid diplomatic complications with France and other Catholic powers, the Turin government ordered the Italian army to chase him out. In the so-called Battle of Aspromonte, Garibaldi, the "Hero of Two Worlds," was actually fired at by troops of the new kingdom he had been so instrumental in creating, troops acting to protect the temporal power of the Pope. This was surely one of the very cruelest moments in the story of the *risorgimento.* But Garibaldi forgave again and yet again. In 1866, he commanded some Italian units in the war with Austria (the Seven Weeks War). Four years later he led Italian volunteers fighting for France against the Prussians (a successful commander in a notably unsuccessful war, he won the battle near Dijon). He was also elected several times to the Chamber of Deputies, which he despised. Full of years and disillusion, he died in 1882.

Illiterate peasant women, young boys, even tourists were herded to the polls and told to vote "yes," so that towns and villages known to be overwhelmingly against unification were informed that they had cast a 99 or even 100 percent vote in favor of it. But the poisonous implications of these rigged elections were hard to discern amid the general amazement and gratification that almost overnight a few thousand determined bourgeois had created a new state with twenty-two million inhabitants.

The immediate beneficiary of these dramatic events was Sardinia's Victor Emmanuel II. He had become king in 1849 at the age of twenty-nine, when his father Charles Albert abdicated in the wake of a second unsuccessful war with the Austrian Empire. Educated for the barracks and the saddle, Victor Emmanuel grew up very superstitious and somewhat bellicose. He publicly maintained a mistress, something that in his eyes a real king was supposed to do. His frequent affairs and numerous illegitimate children caused the wits of the day to refer to him as "the father of his country." Women were not his only passion and sport; Victor Emmanuel also thoroughly enjoyed hunting. These hearty pastimes earned him, to his delight, another sobriquet, "the gentleman king," although the French ambassador in Turin informed his masters somewhat churlishly that King Victor Emmanuel told the truth "only on very rare occasions." Intensely proud of his House of Savoy and its Piedmontese heritage, he quite improperly continued to style himself "Victor Emmanuel the Second" after he had been proclaimed first king of Italy.

Perhaps his principal claim to historical recognition is his appointment of Camillo Cavour as prime minister of the Kingdom of Sardinia in 1852. Cavour dominated his king even more than Cardinal Richelieu had dominated Louis XIII, and most of the time Victor Emmanuel recognized with more or less good grace his great fortune in having the smartest politician in Europe as his chief counsellor. The relationship between the two was not always tranquil, however; in one memorable and explosive scene when the *risorgimento* struggle was just about to be crowned with success, the two men had a horrendous quarrel, in the course of which Victor Emmanuel, his great beard and ferocious mustache bristling with royal indignation, called his minister "a rogue" to his face. Cavour resigned. But the king and Cavour knew they needed one another, the quarrel was soon patched up, and Cavour was reappointed prime minister. His Majesty was sincerely bereft at the unexpected death of Cavour a year later.*

THE ROMAN QUESTION

An Italian kingdom had been created, but not completed. The region of Venezia still belonged to the Austrians. More importantly, much more importantly, the pope still ruled at Rome, refused to give it up, and threatened any who would dare lay violent hands on the Holy City with fell spiritual sanctions and the wrath of the whole Catholic world.

The pope at the time was Pius IX, perhaps better known by his Italian name of Pio Nono. Born Giovanni Mastai-Ferretti in 1792, he was subject as a youth to epileptic seizures. Nevertheless, his was to be the longest pontificate in the history of the Roman Catholic Church; it extended from 1846 to 1878. He was to have the further signal distinctions of being the last ruler of Papal Rome, and the first pope whose infallibility was defined by an ecumenical council.

There is a widespread view of Pio Nono that he was a dyed-in-the-rochet reactionary, an early Paleozoic bigot, and this is not entirely inaccurate, especially in regard to the latter years

*Victor Emmanuel would himself die in 1878, at the age of only fifty-eight, of malaria, ancient curse of the unhealthy marshlands surrounding Rome. (They would not be cleared up until the 1920s.) Pope Pius IX, himself not far from the grave, granted the dying Italian king special dispensation to receive the last rites of the Church, even though he was guilty of grave and unrepentant sin in having sent his armies to seize the states of the Church in 1860 and the Holy City itself in 1870.

of his papacy. Yet he did not always possess such a reputation, quite to the contrary; for most of his pre-1848 life, including his career in the Church, he had been looked upon as a Liberal (as that term was understood in Europe of the nineteenth century).* Indeed, his allegedly Liberal views seem to have prevented him from receiving the red hat of the cardinalate until 1840. And at the conclave of 1846 to choose a successor to Gregory XVI, Cardinal Mastai-Ferretti was elected only because Cardinal Gaysruck, Archbishop of Milan, who carried the veto of the Austrian emperor against the dangerous Liberal, arrived, alas, too late. That Pius could have been taken, especially by himself, for a Liberal points up the justice of Metternich's estimate of him: "a good priest, a warm heart, a weak brain." His election to the chair of Peter filled Europe's Liberals with delight in 1846; two years later this same pontiff was forced to flee ignominiously from his capital city by the very Liberals who had cheered him so lustily.

How could a pope—any pope—have been a Liberal in the context of the Italy of the middle of the last century? From a Liberal pope, Liberal Italians expected, even demanded, two things at the very least: first, a constitutional government for the Papal States and second, papal support for the *risorgimento*. No pope, not even one so egregiously lacking in political common sense as Pio Nuno, could have satisfied such expectations. As to a constitution, how could the Sovereign Pontiff, supreme spiritual leader of a universal flock, be bound in any way by laws and decisions passed by a group of middle-class laymen drawn exclusively from one tiny corner of the world and from a party, the Liberals, whose devotion to the

*Liberalism in the mid-nineteenth century was preeminently the code of the rising middle classes. For Liberals, England was the model, Adam Smith the prophet. They wanted limited government, religious liberty, and votes for qualified citizens (i.e., Liberals). They believed in Reason, Science, and Progress—all spelled with capital letters and all euphemisms for the crudest materialism, social Darwinism, and anticlericalism.

truths of the Faith and the prerogatives of the popes were not, it must be said, their most distinguishing characteristics? And as to papal support for the *risorgimento,* what this meant in practical terms to the Liberals was that the Bishop of Rome would pronounce his blessing upon rebellions and wars against the Habsburg Empire. How could a pope, even one so genuinely an Italian patriot at heart like Pio Nono, ally himself with the cause of one nation against that of another, both of them largely Catholic, and still claim to be the universal father of all his children? So of necessity Pius IX quickly, utterly, and bitterly disappointed his erstwhile Liberal admirers. But was not this denouement predictable?

Was not the impossible contradiction of a Liberal pope apparent to all beforehand? No. It was apparent to many, like Metternich, like the seasoned and cynical bureaucrats of the Roman Church, but not to a political naif like Cardinal Mastai-Ferretti. He had to learn the hard way, to his cost, to the cost of Italian unity, and to that of all his Church.

After the upheavals of 1848, Pio Nono could rule in Rome only through the support of foreign bayonets, but he took his revenge on his tormentors, in a manner of speaking. He became an intransigent defender of the Temporal Power; never, never would the Roman pontiff recognize the loss of his states in central Italy. He hurled excommunications and anathemas at all who presumed to lay profane hands on the territories of the patrimony of St. Peter. All of modern Europe, all of contemporary civilization suffered his disdainful rejection in the Syllabus of Errors, thrown down at the world's feet in 1864. This document, which can most charitably be described as ill-advised, has been a source of embarrassment to Catholic apologists ever since. At the time of its issuance it evoked every reaction from ridicule to consternation. What, asks the Roman Catholic historian E. E. Y. Hales, must have gone through the mind of President Abraham Lincoln when he read that the pope had condemned "progress, liberalism, and modern civilization"?

During Pio Nono's seemingly endless and endlessly troubled pontificate, the total centralization of churchly authority within the hands of the Roman professional clerical bureaucracy reached its consummation, a tendency that had been growing since the days of the Council of Trent. The dramatic climax of this process occurred at the first Vatican Council, which convened in December, 1869. At this grand ecclesiastical convocation, the first in the history of the Church of Rome to which Catholic secular rulers had not been invited, the doctrine of Papal Infallibility was voted and proclaimed (against the tenacious opposition of nearly one hundred bishops). It was the supreme triumph of ultramontane *romanità* at the very hour when Rome in fact ceased to be papal.

Among the many unfortunate policies pursued by Pio Nono was forbidding Italian Catholics to participate in the affairs of the new Italian kingdom. The inevitable result of such a prohibition was that Italian political life fell completely under the direction of men who were, to say the least of it, not punctilious in their solicitude for the dignity of the Church in general and of Pius IX in particular. One consequence of this, not really vastly important but vastly revealing nonetheless, was that when Pius finally died in 1878, a mob of enlightened Liberals attacked his funeral procession, seeking to desecrate the body and throw it in the Tiber. The enterprise failed, but its lack of success owed nothing to the Roman police who, during this revolting spectacle, stood aside watching. Such a scandalous dereliction of duty moved even the sturdily Anglican Mr. William Gladstone to express to the Italian ambassador his "amazement and disgust."

However lamentable his personal or intellectual shortcomings may have been, there was nevertheless much merit in the view of Pio Nono and his advisers that possession of the city of Rome was absolutely vital to the survival of the Catholic Church. This may seem an absurdity today, because the idea of a pope exercising temporal power is alien to us. It did not seem absurd then, because the idea of the pope *not* exercising temporal power was outside the experience and memory of all. The pope was spiritual father to a vast flock that extended from Manila to Munich, from Bogota to Brussels. The major non-Catholic powers of the world—Great Britain, Germany, Russia—ruled over important Catholic minorities. If the pope lost his territorial sovereignty and lived on Italian soil under the protection of Italian law, then he conceivably could one day become (or be made to appear by the Church's opponents) a tool of Italian foreign policy. The implications of such a possibility were catastrophic for the internal unity of the Church; therefore the pope refused to yield and called upon Catholic Europe to help him against the aggression of the new Italian state. The Emperor Napoleon III heeded this papal call and sent a French garrison to Rome, less for love of the pope than from a desire to please the powerful French Church.

Yet to the triumphant statesmen of the *risorgimento,* it was equally obvious that Rome had to become the capital of their new kingdom. No other city in Italy could begin to compare with Rome in historical and sentimental importance. An Italian kingdom without Rome would be a body without a heart. Besides, if not Rome, then which other city would be the capital? Turin, Naples, and Florence all had impressive claims to capital status if the choice had to be made, and such a choice would stimulate regional rivalry and outrage regional pride. Hundreds had been killed in riots when the capital had been shifted from Turin to Florence in 1865. It should be borne in mind that in these very years of the 1860s when the new kingdom was just finding its legs, its leaders could observe the much older unity of the United States of America being tested in a cruel civil war, generated by regional hostility. Thus, for overwhelming reasons of sentiment and practical politics, it had to be Rome.

Cavour, who might have been able to work out an eventual compromise, died almost simultaneously with the proclamation of the new kingdom. And so the "Roman Question" poisoned the politics of the new Italy, and indeed of all Europe:

Napoleon III's support of Papal Rome helped make impossible an otherwise perfectly desirable alliance among France, Italy, and Austria. Thus Napoleon had to face Bismarck without allies in the Franco-Prussian War of 1870.

Upon the defeat of the French, the Italian army forcibly occupied Rome (which was followed, of course, by the usual 99 percent favorable plebiscite). Pius refused recognition of the deed, excommunicated all those involved with the seizure of his city, proclaimed himself the "Prisoner of the Vatican," and settled down to await the collapse of this godless and usurping regime. He also forbade good Catholics to participate in the affairs of this impious and impermanent state. The Pope's loyal subjects could be *né eletti né elettori* (neither office holders nor voters). Italian politics was thereby deprived of the services of many men of probity, and of a Catholic political party that could have added a needed conservative element to parliament and helped integrate the peasantry into the life of the nation.

It was no little thing to create the Kingdom of Italy in the teeth of so much opposition, so much apathy, so much history. The men who did it—Gioberti, Mazzini, Garibaldi, and above all, great Cavour—are justly renowned. But from the moment of its appearance on earth, the new state bore those unmistakable marks which told the story of its conception and forecast the trials of its future: the politics of elite minorities working their will through violence and electoral chicane.

NORTH AND SOUTH

The conflict between Italian State and Roman Church was the most emotional and glamorous of the kingdom's problems, but it was not the most fundamental; it could be, and one day would be, resolved by the signing of a piece of paper. Much more intractable (and much more insidious because harder to grasp and easier to ignore) was the vast disparity between the northern and southern parts of Italy, a disparity equally serious in its political, economic, and psychological aspects.

The Southern Question was only dimly perceived in the heady atmosphere of unification in 1861, but it was to be a millstone around the neck of Italy's economic development, a source of political corruption, and an obstacle to national integration decades after the resolution of the Roman Question, indeed decades after the death of Mussolini and the destruction of his Fascist regime.

Italy is about the size of the state of Arizona, or the combined states of New York, Pennsylvania, and West Virginia. Within this relatively small geographical framework there are many social variations, many Italies, speaking many different and often mutually incomprehensible dialects. Northern or continental Italy is a great plain drained by the Po River, longest river in the country. Here are orderly Turin, wealthy Milan, exquisite Venice, bustling Genoa; Padua, whose university has been called the seat of the modern scientific revolution, and somewhat farther south, Bologna, with the oldest university in all Europe. From sub-Alpine Piedmont came Camillo Cavour, Agostino Depretis, and Giovanni Giolitti, the three politicians who did most to shape pre-Mussolinian Italy. The Milan-Genoa-Turin industrial triangle contains the bulk of Italian industry and most of its enterprising middle class. This part of Italy is by far the most prosperous, most "European"; it is also perhaps the least representative. It is a long distance between the urban bustle of Milan and the dusty remoteness of the hill villages of Basilicata—a distance of centuries. It is in the southern parts of the country that one realizes the truth, that Italy is an overpopulated country with little good farmland and few mineral resources. Under the superficial aura of a happy people eating lots of pasta and laughing in the sun, Italy is, as she has been, a land of hard and often desperate toil, where many live in real deprivation, "on a barren soil, in the presence of death."

It is tempting to say there there are two Italies, north and south, the one worshipping money and looking to the future, the other worshipping power and transfixed by the past. But even within the south itself, which may be defined as beginning at Rome and including the islands of Sicily and Sardinia, there are many variations. The south means Rome, capital of an empire, of the Catholic Church, of united Italy, the womb of Western civilization, a city in its historical richness and architectural achievements unmatched in all Europe. The south also means little-visited Abruzzi, mountainous home of hardworking and devout peasants. The south is Naples, where sophistication and squalor exist closely packed together, where Giovanni Battista Vico and Benedetto Croce reshaped the intellectual contours of Europe, and where children to this very day die of polluted water. The south is impoverished Sardinia, so remote that its people employ a system of pronunciation that has long died out in the rest of Italy; and Sicily, too hot and too dry for good crops, too often invaded, too long misgoverned and exploited by outsiders, with its western side the classical home of Mafia justice and moonlit assassinations.

The pre-unification south, called the Kingdom of Naples, was long ruled by a Spanish branch of the Bourbon family, that did its very best to keep new ideas and new ways out of the realm. Bourbon rule was light and paternalistic, with low taxation (the whole kingdom's bureaucracy was half the size of little Tuscany's alone!) and no conscription; but there were also no schools, no health services, few roads and practically no railroads (in 1860, Sicily had no railroads at all).

The *risorgimento* burst upon the somnolent southern kingdom in the form of Garibaldi and his Red Shirts. Unification meant a draft to fill the ranks of the new army, high taxes to pay for the wars of the *risorgimento.* Unification meant war against the Church; the Bourbon Concordat that regulated relations between the kingdom and the Church was renounced by the new Piedmontese overlords, church property confiscated, religious orders suppressed, monasteries closed, threescore bishops thrown into prison, and religious marriage deprived of legal sanction. These and other blessings of reform that arrived in the portfolios of the condescending northerners shocked and alienated almost everybody. A special agent dispatched from Turin reported back that:

> *a unitarian party does not exist at Naples. I would dare to assert that there are not twenty individuals who want national unity, and these are . . . people who have government jobs. [Unification] came about because of middle class hatred of the Bourbons, and because of admiration for Garibaldi. . . . You would be mad to think that the people want to be ruled from Turin, or that they are reconciled to the destruction of their former system of local government.*

Disappointment and anger turned into violence. After two years of unification, the south was in a condition approximating civil war. One hundred thousand regular troops, commanded by Piedmont's best generals, were required to pacify the country. The troops visited bloody atrocities upon Sicilian villagers, who in turn rose in wrath in 1866, invaded the city of Palermo and overcame the regular garrison there. More men and women were killed in these hideous struggles than in all the military engagements of the *risorgimento,* and malaria claimed even more lives than the fighting. Rebellion would die down, only to flare up again. In 1894, Sicily was again put under martial law and groaned beneath the weight of an army of occupation fifty thousand strong.

Economic decline accompanied the violence. The Kingdom of Naples for years had tried to encourage the growth of certain industries by providing tariff protection. But free trade was enlightened doctrine at Turin, and so southern tariff walls were destroyed, and so were nascent southern industries, buried under a mass of imported goods from northern Italy and Europe. Cavour had wanted special legislation to help the south, but his successors believed (conveniently) that honest administration and laissez-faire economics would do the job, and so the north-south gap was permitted to widen. No prime minister before 1901 had even thought it worthwhile to visit the south; eventually even major political leaders would suggest that the kingdom's hard-won unity should be broken up, that Sicily or even the whole south should be granted independence. It was too poor, too ungovernable, a drag on the rest of the country.

On the other hand, it should be noted that the south, with 37 percent of the Italian population in 1861, had 7 percent of the national railway mileage in 1861, and 32 percent in 1875. In the 1870s the south contributed 30 percent of the national taxes and received 46 percent of public works appropriations.[1]

Wherever the blame should be laid, degeneration continued. In the 1880s, two-thirds of the inhabitants of the city of Naples could not be sure of their next day's employment. As late as 1900, when unification was forty years old and Benito Mussolini was seventeen, 90 percent of draftees from Sicily were found to be illiterate or physically unfit for service.

The principal response to these conditions (besides armed rebellion) was emigration. Beginning in the 1880s, southern Italy began to send a flood of her young men and women to other European countries, and to the United States, Brazil, and Argentina. Mostly illiterate and unskilled, they helped to build railroads, dig tunnels, construct houses, and harvest crops. The tide continued to swell. In 1913 more than 900,000 Italians left the homeland that could not provide them with either steady work or enough to eat.

INSTITUTIONAL PROBLEMS

Another obstacle to the emergence of stable and orderly politics lay in the attitude of both elite and masses toward government. The common man's view of the state and its servants had been formed through centuries of evasion, defiance, and rebellion against clerical, Habsburg, and Spanish arbitrariness. Even in relatively well-ruled Piedmont, Lombardy, and Tuscany, there was no tradition of local self-government to furnish large numbers of people with priceless lessons in applied political science. Things were worse in the south, where government had long been in some ways a kind of racket.

For their part, the elite national bourgeoisie who had made the new government were no band of Jeffersonian democrats. In the days of struggle before 1860, writes the historian Denis Mack Smith, "the party of Cavour was in general ignorant and frightened of the common people, and preferred to impose its will with the aid of diplomacy, rather than to rouse this sleeping giant and give it ideas above its station." Instead of a constitutional convention being called to work out a new framework of government for a new Kingdom of Italy, the constitution of Piedmont was simply imposed by Cavour's heirs on the rest of the country. This Piedmontese document established a constitutional monarchy in which the king retained wide executive powers, especially in foreign and defense policy. A Senate, appointed by the king, had powers equal to the Chamber of Deputies, chosen by an electorate severely restricted by property and income qualifications. Right from the start, the masses were excluded from political participation (not that many of them were really interested). Defects in the constitution became more apparent after the capital was finally established in Rome; now the great days of the *risorgimento* were over, and the pulse-quickening poetry of the glorious, if brief, national liberation struggle was succeeded by the dreary and disappointing prose of a narrow and artificial parliamentary system. One can only speculate if things would have been different in the long run had the permanent capital been established not in baroque and bureaucratic (i.e., southern) Rome but in a more businesslike, more European Milan, or Turin.

Like the founding fathers at Philadelphia, the leaders of the new Italy were confronted with the problem of whether the kingdom should be tightly centralized, or should allow substantial amounts of regional autonomy. Arguments in favor of regional powers were impressive. After all, Tuscany, Naples, and Lombardy had their own traditions of jurisprudence and administration suited to local conditions; besides, it was insulting simply to sweep all these laws and practices and institutions away and replace them with imported Piedmontese articles. After all, *what had occurred in 1860-1861 anyway?* Had the Italians been unified, or had the non-Piedmontese majority simply been swallowed up by annexation into a Greater Piedmont?

On the other hand, given the newness and fragility of the Italian kingdom, given the wide regional diversity in custom, economy, and even language that would certainly exert centrifugal influences, given the widespread indifference or even hostility to unification in the southern half of the country, was not Napoleonic centralization the only way to bind the country, its regions, and its peoples together and prevent the new nation from eventually dissolving into its components? These arguments were most persuasive to the Piedmontese, and it was the Piedmontese throne, army, and civil service that controlled the levers of power. Centralization thus became the order of the day. It produced the worst of all possible worlds, destroying local institutions, ignoring local customs, outraging local pride, yet failing to bridge the gap between the various regions. Victor Emmanuel, although the first king of Italy, continued most insensitively to call himself "the Second," and the first all-Italian parliament, meeting at Turin in 1861, was officially styled the eighth. Thus, from the first days of unification "the idea was beginning to gain currency that the Piedmontese had all along . . . acted with a disingenuousness and Machiavellian lack of frankness, and that one of their chief aims from the start had been to exploit national feeling simply for the purpose of provincial self-aggrandizement."[2]

After his untimely death in 1861, Cavour's lieutenants and heirs, known as the Historical Right, governed the country for fifteen years.* During this time they won Venetia from the Austrians, worked out a modus vivendi with an officially implacable Church, established and preserved the national credit (through a savagely regressive system of taxation), and planted the new government finally and firmly in Rome. This was all achieved against great odds. Nevertheless, many serious cracks continued to exist and to deepen under the facade of the political structure, and the chances that they would be repaired in time were gravely reduced when the Historical Right fell from power in 1876.

Most supporters of the new Kingdom of Italy were loosely grouped together in the middle-class and anticlerical Liberal party. Severe suffrage restrictions, plus the virtual abstention of devout Catholics from political life, gave the Liberals a near monopoly on parliament and government. The party was broadly divided into two wings. The one called the Historical Right and led by Cavour's lieutenants ruled the country for the first decade and a half of its existence. The second wing, the Left, was more "radical" in the context of the period, standing for an activist foreign policy and aggressive anticlerical measures. Although led by the Piedmontese, Agostino Depretis, the Left was disproportionately southern, and has been described as less a political party than an accumulation of grudges.

Depretis was born in 1813, and became leader of the Left in 1873. He served as prime minister three times between 1876 and 1887, the year of his death. Depretis had earned the dislike of Cavour, although he was moderate both in his policies and in his personal demeanor. In foreign affairs, Prime Minister Depretis led Italy into the Triple Alliance with Berlin and

*Cavour's death at age fifty-one may well have been opportune for his own historical reputation, but for Italy his loss was catastrophic, comparable perhaps to what the death of George Washington a few months after his first inauguration would have meant to the Americans.

Vienna. In domestic affairs, Depretis was almost totally concerned with putting together and keeping together a majority in parliament behind his various cabinets. Thus, although of unimpeachable personal honesty (even as prime minister he continued to live in an apartment one hundred steps above street level) his name has become inextricably linked with the degeneration of Italian political life after 1876. Vilfredo Pareto observed that Depretis headed the most dictatorial regime possible in a parliamentary system. The main tools employed by Depretis to ensure the possession of power by his party were *trasformismo* and electoral corruption.

Depretis coined the term "transformism" to describe a practice that had existed since the days of Cavour; the practice consisted of combining moderate and centrist elements in parliament, of whatever party or tendency, to exclude extremists of all types. While Depretis did not invent the practice, he developed it into a science or, rather, a way of life. For Depretis, the object of transformism was governmental survival, the instrument was governmental patronage. As Depretis "transformed" members of parliament into his faithful (if temporary) supporters, parties, even factions, ceased to stand for anything much; parliamentary life degenerated into a contest over the distribution of favors.

Even more than transformism, however, the really distinguishing characteristic of the Left after 1876 was its conception of the ballot box as a receptacle to be stuffed. Electoral chicanery had certainly not been unknown before 1876; witness the plebiscites of 1860–1861. Under the Left, however, it attained many refinements, especially in the south. Known opposition voters would be detained by the police right before polling day, and the working of the jury system in those parts made it almost impossible to bring even notorious lawbreakers to swift justice. Consequently, "governments in Italy never lost elections, though electoral victory rarely guaranteed them a stable majority."[3] Depretis's management of the 1876 elections, held shortly after he became prime minister, was so effective as to amount to overkill: the entire south returned a mere four opposition deputies. That election considerably lowered the quality of men in the Chamber of Deputies, and parliamentary life never really recovered.

In summary, almost every cabinet after 1876 rested on a "transformed" majority, a temporary patchwork of personal and regional factions held together not by principles but by a passion for patronage. Controversial issues tended to be avoided, while ministers changed on the average of once a year—a game of musical chairs that evoked boredom or contempt from many citizens. The basis of this system was the large number of southern seats totally at the mercy of government pressure or electoral fraud. It is important to grasp the major consequence of all this: after 1876, long-term, principled, and effective opposition to the cabinet, *any* cabinet, largely disappeared. *Italy was in effect a one-party system decades before anybody had heard of Benito Mussolini.*

Cabinets after 1876 also came to rely more and more on outright coercion of the opposition and other undesirable elements. The Ministry of the Interior established the practice of internal exile, sending troublesome (that is, critical) citizens to remote villages to reflect on the vagaries of this life. Labor agitators found themselves whisked away to penal colonies. Unfriendly newspapers were often banned if their editors could not be bribed. The waning days of the century witnessed a paroxysm of governmental repression. Prime Minister Crispi dissolved the Socialist party in 1894, suspended parliament for months at a time, authorized taxes by royal decree, and in 1895 used the police to elect a Chamber overwhelmingly friendly to himself. Three years later, serious riots in Milan were used by Prime Minister Luigi Pelloux as a justification for closing down parliament, shutting many universities, arresting certain deputies, dissolving the Socialist city council of Milan, and suspending hundreds of newspapers throughout the country.

The first decade and a half of the twentieth century was so completely dominated by the ringmaster of parliament, Giovanni Giolitti, that the period takes its name from him, the Giolittian Era. Born in 1842, Giolitti began his governmental career as a civil servant in the Ministry of Finance. He soon entered electoral politics, and between 1892 and 1921 he served as prime minister for a total of ten years, the record up to that time. He organized his last cabinet when he was nearly eighty years old. In his autobiography published in the 1920s, Mussolini wryly identified Giolitti as the man "of whom it may be said that he made the premiership a profession." (Mussolini, however, was to serve as premier for more than twenty years.)

Giolitti was in a sense the Italian Gladstone, a durable Liberal, the grand old man of pre-Fascist Italian politics. A tall, reserved, and dispassionate Piedmontese, he corresponded not at all to the stereotypical, flamboyant, chest-thumping Italian politico. His clarity of speech and economy of expression often reminded his listeners of another Piedmontese politician, Camillo Cavour.

During the supremacy of Giolitti (1903-1914), government repression declined, but parliament did not function much better than before. Actually, Giolitti perfected the techniques of "parliamentary dictatorship" created by Depretis. Giolitti had widened the suffrage considerably but this, in his view, merely rendered electoral manipulation and *trasformismo* all the more necessary to produce the right kind of majority. Mussolini's father once recounted indignantly how a number of cows in his village were registered to vote, "by name."

Historians have labeled Giolitti cynical, pedestrian, and opportunistic, and he certainly displayed all these traits. But Giolitti was far more than just another political boss. He keenly observed his environment and realized that he was helping to govern a nation that was experiencing serious changes and was afflicted with profound and explosive problems, some old, some new. He did what he could to alleviate the conditions of the lower classes in a poor country; it was not, in fact, very much, nor did he have the type of personality that could have rallied the masses to him. A real conservative, Giolitti well understood the necessity of reform. "I deplore," he observed in 1892, "as much as anyone the struggle between the classes, but let us at least be fair and ask who started it." He insisted that "the friends of order have a duty to persuade the working classes, and to persuade them with deeds, not words, that they have more to hope for from the present order than from dreams of the future." Giolitti had a grand design, nothing less than the eventual reconciliation of the Catholics and the Socialists to the constitutional system. He actually made a good deal of progress toward his objective and he might have made more, but the outbreak of world war interrupted his plans.*

The extension of voting rights under Giolitti plus the accumulating problems of a society that was beginning to industrialize, raised the level of political interest and political passion, but neither of these could find any real outlet in the parliament. The Chamber of Deputies remained, as it had begun, a tight little world of its own, staffed with captive deputies and captained by virtuoso bosses like Giolitti. The hero Garibaldi (called *duce* by his admirers) had thrice resigned from parliament and was loud in his preference for dictatorial methods. Many Socialists, furthermore, were hostile to "bourgeois" parliamentary institutions on principle, and filibustering and fistfights in the Chamber robbed its members of dignity in the public eye. Meanwhile, academic critics like Gaetano Mosca and Vilfredo Pareto, leveling acute attacks on the corruption and demagoguery that they held to be the essence of any parliamentary system, helped undermine the very intellectual foundations of the political order.

*Like Giolitti, Mussolini would also seek to incorporate the Socialist and Catholic masses into the political order; like him, Mussolini had enjoyed some real successes along that road when he too saw his plans smashed by the coming of a world war.

Italy's parliamentary institutions, designed for a society with a much larger middle class, were neither popular nor effective. The introduction of universal manhood suffrage in 1919, rather than a new beginning, was the death knell of parliamentary government. Italians had long been divided into three mutually hostile blocs: Liberals, Catholics, and Socialists, none of whom were committed to constitutional democracy *per se.* Manhood suffrage simply extended this paralyzing division from the piazza into parliament. Thus the tension-reducing and benefit-increasing functions of government ground almost to a halt at the very time when Italy was facing profound problems of readjustment from World War I.

THE ECONOMY

The Giolittian Era was something of an economic revolution, with industrial production increasing 87 percent from 1901 to 1913. Italy's economic development on the whole, however—between the occupation of Rome by royal troops in 1870 and by Fascist legionnaires in 1922—was painfully slow. Despite important centers of industry in Lombardy and Piedmont, the country remained overwhelmingly agricultural and therefore overwhelmingly poor, for in rural Italy there were too many people trying to live on an unyielding soil. The most popular explanation for Italy's retarded industrialization is lack of raw materials, especially iron and coal. There is a lot of truth in this, but by no means the whole truth, for a similar lack of many essential resources did not prevent the leaders of Meiji Japan from turning their country of peasants into a major industrial power between 1868 and 1918. No, the major obstacle to economic development must be sought in the absence of wise governmental leadership, both before and after unification.

For two hundred years after 1559, the power of Spain was predominant in Italy, and Italian interests were subordinated to those of Spain. A lot of energy and wealth were wasted in internal warfare and conspicuous consumption by princes of

State and Church. As the nineteenth century dawned, "political demarcations, guild restrictions, tariffs, discriminatory taxes, tolls and imposts, a proliferation of monetary and measuring systems, lack of communications, impassable or nonexistent roads, absence of credit facilities, hazards of trade, and brigandage collectively placed a blight upon all remaining forms of enterprise by effectively freezing initiative. The market was reduced to the locality, often not extending beyond the confines of the commune."[4] Many of these conditions, instead of being swept away by state action, remained in existence after unification.

The cabinets of the Historical Right were obsessed by the need for "sound currency" and a balanced budget. As Benedetto Croce, their most distinguished apologist, views it, "it was necessary to give the lie to those, both in Italy and outside, who held that Italy, having been aided politically by ability and fortune, would split on the rock of finance, or would at least lose credit and arouse distrust in the financial world." Under longtime Finance Minister Quintino Sella, "economy to the bone" became the battle cry. In other words, large scale investment in economic development was not being carried on. The last accomplishment of the Historical Right was to present a balanced budget in March 1876, but to bring this about Italians had become "the most heavily taxed people in Europe," with numerous taxes falling on the basic staples of the poor.

At the same time, many important politicians lacked knowledge of or interest in economics, or were positively hostile to industrialization. Consequently, the power of the state was not employed for planned, long-term intervention to build up sectorial strengths, compensate for weaknesses, and channel capital into the most prudent and rewarding areas. Instead, piecemeal legislation conferred favors on special clienteles, often to the serious detriment of the national interest.

Toward the end of the century, the appearance of militant

labor and socialist organizations among the volatile and numerically weak proletariat introduced messianic expectations, political strikes, and revolutionary rhetoric, all of which clouded the economic picture, undermined morals, and discouraged investment. In light of all this, it is no wonder that "the private per capita wealth of the richest and most advanced areas of northern Italy in the second half of the [eighteen] eighties was still very much below one half of the contemporary figures for France as a whole."[5] Of course, the standard of living of the peasant and the landless agricultural laborer was much lower. For them, unification had meant higher taxes and the draft; their only contact with the Kingdom of Italy was through the policeman and the revenue agent. Many peasants suffered from pellagra—the result of eating too much flour—but the flour yield per acre in Italy was only a third of that of England. Rural life for many, especially in the south, was a Gethsemane of illiteracy, bandits, inadequate water, and malaria (the countryside, even around Rome, was full of mosquito-breeding marshes, and King Victor Emmanuel died of malaria in 1878). As late at 1922, whole areas of rural Italy—millions of men, women, and children—had not been integrated into national life, indeed had hardly been touched by the modern world.

FOREIGN REVERSES

Regimes unpopular or ineffective at home sometimes recoup their position by successes, or apparent successes, in foreign affairs. But here, as everywhere else, the record of post-unification Italy was one of failure, frustration, and even disaster.

The events of 1860-1861 had brought together most Italian-speaking areas into one kingdom, but important territories still remained outside, most notably Rome, under the pope, and the large northeastern region of Venetia, still ruled by Vienna. In 1866 the Austro-Prussian or Seven Weeks War occurred, in which Prussia and Italy were victorious over the Habsburgs.

As her reward, Italy received coveted Venetia, but even these fruits were bitter, as Benedetto Croce explains:

> *How great was the eagerness, the confidence, the enthusiasm, the rejoicing in 1866 on the declaration of the long-expected and hoped-for war against Austria for the liberation of Venetia! The effects of the disillusionment which followed were all the more serious, awaking as they did only recently discarded criticisms as to the paucity of military prowess among the Italians of modern times.... Even now that they were united they had failed to win glory; rather, they had been beaten, both by land and sea, by an enemy inferior in numbers, while their ally Prussia had achieved much that was also an earnest of things to come; moreover, Prussia had won the war and concluded the armistice, without reference to her ally, whose incapacity she despised and whose loyalty she even dared call into question, so that Italy must perforce receive Venetia, not direct from Austria, but as a gift from Napoleon III to whom Austria had entrusted it.*[6]

Even with the occupation of Rome four years later, Italian unification was not complete, for the cities of Trent and Trieste and their hinterlands still remained in the hands of the Austrians. Italy would not finally possess these areas until the end of World War I.

Italy, an old civilization and a young nation, displayed the cynicism of age in domestic politics and the touchiness of adolescence in foreign affairs. The proclamation of Rome, imperial Rome, as the new capital in 1871 evoked many memories and seemed to call for new deeds of glory. A country with Rome as its capital would have to be mighty. Victor Emmanuel proclaimed: "Italy must not only be respected, she must make herself feared." In an attempt to give flesh to such bellicose sentiments, after 1860 over a third of the Italian budget was devoted to war preparations.

But nothing went well. The defeat of France by Prussia in

1870, partly caused by Italy's refusal to help (the "Roman Question" again*) was looked upon in many circles as a defeat for the whole "Latin race." The other powers emerged from the Congress of Berlin in 1878 with colonies, bases, and prestige; Italy had only "clean hands." A bitter shock came in 1881 when France annexed Tunisia, site of ancient Carthage, a land of great sentimental, economic, and strategic interest to Italy. Rebounding from this unexpected blow, Italy became a partner in the Triple Alliance. "By joining Germany and Austria in 1882 Italy hoped to secure her back door while she fished for colonies and improved her international position."[7] Nearly sixty years later Mussolini would use identical logic to justify another German alliance.

But since the Triple Alliance failed to bring forth the expected gains, by 1894 the president of the Senate was moved to declare that the only thing holding Italy together was the army. In 1896 came the worst calamity thus far, the massacre of several thousand Italian and native troops by the Abyssinians at Adowa. Shocked and humiliated, Italians bitterly recognized that in spite of fulsome rhetoric and the expenditure of vast sums of money, their country was in fact one of the great powers only by courtesy.

At the beginning of the new century, Italy was becoming surrounded and isolated in what she liked to look upon as "her" Mediterranean. France had long ago taken Algeria and Tunisia, and was moving on Morocco. Britain was established in Malta, Cyprus, Gibraltar, and Egypt; across the Adriatic the Austrians were about to take Bosnia. Italy must act soon or be completely shut in. Many believed that what the country needed was a good, successful war, not only to establish her control of the central Mediterranean, but also to consolidate

*Napoleon III had alienated the Italian government by keeping a French garrison in Rome to maintain papal rule over the city, just as he had previously alienated French Catholics by assisting Italian unification at the Pope's expense in the first place.

her national unity. Thus, when the Italo-Turkish War broke out in 1911, an act of naked aggression in which the Italians seized Libya from the "sick man of Europe," it was welcomed and defended even by eminent intellectuals like Benedetto Croce and Gaetano Mosca.

The brief war had profound consequences. It dealt a final blow to the already ailing Triple Alliance, because Germany had invested much effort and money in Turkey and deeply and loudly resented Italy's mauling of her protégé. Then, by confirming what had long been suspected, that Turkey was in a state of advanced military decomposition, the war provoked the Balkan conflicts of 1912 and 1913, overtures to the World War I. And so arrived the hour of supreme trial for Italy and for all Europe.

The Kingdom of Italy began its life beset with many conflicts and disparities: between Catholic Church and Liberal State, between north and south, between bourgeoisie and peasantry, between parliament and people, between national aspirations and national capabilities, and between Italy's economic health and that of her neighbors. A half-century later, when the lights began going out all over Europe, none of these problems had been solved, indeed many had become worse. The cracks and flaws of Italian society would be partially papered over in the emergency of World War I, only to reappear at the war's end more alarming than ever. Out of the postwar maelstrom fascism would emerge and march to power—under the leadership of Benito Mussolini.

II

EARLY DAYS IN THE ROMAGNA

*"In my life
I have never had a friend."*

**Benito Mussolini,
1943**

THE ROMAGNA

In 1883, Victoria was in the forty-sixth year of her seemingly endless reign, and Chester Alan Arthur was doing much better as president of the United States than anybody had a right to expect. Karl Marx would die that year; Darwin had died the year before. Lenin was thirteen years old, Bertrand Russell eleven, Winston Churchill nine, Albert Einstein and Josef Stalin four, Igor Stravinsky and Franklin Roosevelt one. Clement Attlee, Edouard Manet, John Maynard Keynes, and Joseph Schumpeter would all be born in 1883, and on July 29 of that year in the hamlet of Predappio in the province of Forlì, Alessandro and Rosa Maltoni Mussolini became the parents of a son, whom they named Benito.

The province of Forlì is located in the region of Italy called the Romagna. Lying along the Adriatic coast, the Romagna is a rugged, mountainous area dotted with old, ruined castles. The place was often a battleground, invaded by Lombards and Byzantines and contested by the armies of popes and emperors. The government of the region, usually in the hands of ecclesiastics, was never very good and often was wretched. At the time of Benito Mussolini's birth, most of the inhabitants were sharecroppers and rural day laborers, hardworking, poor, and malnourished men and women who planted and harvested wheat, corn, vegetables, and especially grapes. The Romagnoles had been hammered by their history and their mountains into a tough and volatile people, celebrated for their fascination with political affairs, a fascination that amounted to a passion. They liked their politics heavily spiced with violence, so much so that the Romagna was a perennial center of armed rebellion.

This taste for combative politics was in large part a result of the influence in the region of one of the most romantic figures in the pages of revolution, the anarchist Mikhail Bakunin. Born in Russia in 1814, the son of minor nobility, Bakunin was trained to be an artillery officer. He soon developed the habit of going AWOL, and so was forced to resign his commission before his career had really started. He traveled to Berlin in 1840 where he was exposed to the revolutionary faith, which he embraced with what would be a lifetime's dedication. His declaration that "the passion for destruction is a creative passion" pretty well summarizes his political philosophy. After wandering through Switzerland and Belgium, Bakunin settled for a while in Paris where he met both Karl Marx and journalist Pierre Proudhon and witnessed their titanic and embittered struggle for the soul of the revolutionary movement. He also got a good taste of Parisian street fighting during the upheavals of 1848. His first major manifesto was entitled *An Appeal to the Slavs*, in which he proclaimed his faith in the peasant tradition of violent revolt. He came to know the prisons of Austria and later those of his native Russia, but managed to escape Siberian exile (not very difficult to do in those lax Tsarist days). He later found his way to the United States and eventually, in 1861, to London. From there the much-traveled evangel of anarchy finally made his way into Italy where he stayed for several years, refining his creed of a society of perfect liberty to be ushered into existence by violent revolution. He also built up a network of secret revolutionary societies. Before his death in 1876, Bakunin had attracted enough attention to cause Marx to have him and his followers expelled from the First International. (This continuing conflict between Marxists and anarchists split and weakened the European revolutionary movement for years.) Bakunin's teachings eventually made their way into Spain where they found ground even more fertile than in Italy; indeed by 1936 the anarchists were actually the largest of all the Spanish revolutionary groups, a circumstance that contributed in no small way to the defeat of the republic and the triumph of Franco.

Bakunin hated Germans (for example, Marx), centralization of government, any subordination of anybody to authority; he loved Slavs deeply, and peasants most of all. His simple gospel, austere life, and patent sincerity won him many followers in Italy. And there were also Italians who, even if they did not fully and formally embrace his creed, even if they were not proper so-called Bakuninists, still felt a deep sympathy for the teachings of the romantic Russian with his bristling beard and compelling vision. Especially in the Romagna, men would call themselves in all good faith the disciples of Karl Marx and still display all their lives the unmistakable stigmata of anarchism. One such man was Alessandro Mussolini, the father of Benito.

It was once thought essential that the biography of every Roman Catholic saint contain evidence that its subject had been in some way of royal descent. In the same manner, some of Mussolini's less sagacious admirers sought to explain his undeniably uncommon gifts and abilities by turning him into a descendant of ancient nobility. Alas for their efforts, Mussolini never lent himself to this kind of legitimization-through-ancestry. In fact, in the autobiography of Mussolini published for the English-speaking world (mainly drafted by his brother Arnaldo and edited by Benito Mussolini himself), he states with bland truthfulness that "I came from a lineage of honest people. They tilled the soil. . . ." Mussolini's father, Alessandro, was a blacksmith of peasant heritage. Benito describes him as a heavy man with strong and fleshy hands. Alessandro was a strict disciplinarian who believed in a generous amount of corporal punishment, especially in the case of unruly Benito, explaining "better a blow today from your father than two blows tomorrow from a stranger." (It is not entirely clear to what extent young Benito was impressed with the force of this maxim.)

Although he had had no formal schooling, Alessandro Mussolini was far from being an ignorant man. He wrote numerous articles for local Socialist newspapers, helped at one time to create a cooperative, and in later life served as a vice-mayor and town councilor.

As a youth, Alessandro's heart had been captured by the teachings of Mikhail Bakunin. In later years he drew away somewhat from the doctrines of the Russian anarchist and became an ardent member of the Italian Socialist party. Indeed, he would one day be known as the "father of Predappio socialism." Despite this affiliation and despite the fact that Alessandro appears to have read most, perhaps all, of an Italian translation of volume one of *Das Kapital*, his socialism continued to display a definitely populist, even anarchist, influence. He was distressed by the sectarianism of so many Italian revolutionaries, seeking instead to reconcile and draw together in harmony all those who rejected the old established order. In 1891, for example, when Benito was eight years old, his father wrote: "What is socialism? This question is asked by the masses who are ignorant of this noble idea and are frightened by the powerful and mysterious word that echoes resoundingly from one end of the world to the other. Socialism, we answer, is open, violent, and moral rebellion against the inhuman order of things as now constituted. It is knowledge and the excelsior that illumine the world. It is reason that supplants faith. It is free thought rebelling against prejudice. It is free love taking the place of a legal contract. It is free agreement among all men to live a truly decent life. It is true justice that reigns sovereign over all the earth."

Another time, protesting the necessity of so many Italians to seek work and a home overseas, Alessandro declared: "And to think that if bourgeois Italy should plough and put into cultivation the immense area of uncultivated and marshy land that we have in Italy, bread would certainly not be lacking to any of its workers and Italy could still rightly boast of its being called by the beautiful name of the garden of Europe."

Many years later, the son of Alessandro Mussolini would indeed drain the marshes.

Alessandro's father, Luigi, had once spent time in a papal prison, and the anticlericalism of the father was magnified in the son. Alessandro was one of the very few men in Predappio who stayed away from Mass even on Christmas. He named his eldest son Benito after Benito Juarez, the revolutionary scourge of the Mexican Catholic Church and the conqueror of Maximilian. "O priests," he would write, "the day is not distant when you will cease to be useless and false apostles of a deceitful religion and when, leaving behind obscurantism and falsehood, you will embrace truth and reason, and you will throw your cassocks in the purifying flame of progress to put on the honored blouse of the workingman, very happy to understand and to pursue with us a high mission of life."

Alessandro would read to Benito at the table after supper, often from *Capital* or *Les Miserables.* The Mussolini household also sheltered copies of the Socialist party national daily newspaper *Avanti!* ("Forward!") as well as volumes by Manzoni and Dante. Benito paid close attention to the radical teachings of his blacksmith agitator father, teachings transmitted by deeds as well as by words. Vigorous and impassioned, Alessandro Mussolini was arrested several times for political agitation; once he smashed a ballot box to protest the government's tampering with the voter registration rolls. And his sparsely furnished house and meager larder often provided food and shelter for Socialist comrades in trouble with the authorities of their own communities.

With their blacksmith father so busy at politics, so generous to friends, and so often in jail, the Mussolini family was poor, their living conditions spartan. Benito's childhood house was a gloomy affair, with damp crumbling walls covered with moss. The house, an austere rectangular shape, held three rooms, one of which served as a schoolroom for local children. Entrance to the family dwelling area was through the classroom and the kitchen did double duty as the boys' bedroom. When the winter was especially cold and fuel especially hard to obtain, there would be days with little or no fire in the hearth.

The main family meal was usually served at midday and consisted only of vegetable soup. On Sundays a pound or so of meat might be added to the pot. The evening meal was normally based on wild salad greens (usually chicory) that grew plentifully in the surrounding area. On many days there was no salt, no oil, no bread, or a heartwarming glass of red wine. Undoubtedly as a direct result of this austere regimen, all through his life Benito Mussolini remained a spare eater, almost a vegetarian.

Benito's maternal grandmother, Marianna Maltoni, often stayed for extended visits with the Mussolinis. She kept busy caring for the children while mother Rosa taught school, gathering vegetables for the evening meal, and protecting Benito from the wrath of his father which he often provoked by some boyish transgression.

The living standards of the Mussolinis in Predappio were certainly spare enough, but poverty is a relative concept. Conditions were probably made more bearable by the knowledge that the Mussolinis were certainly no worse off than most inhabitants of the Romagna, and certainly better off than many, especially the unfortunate landless day laborers.

When his father died in 1910 at the age of fifty-seven, Benito wrote of him: "Of worldly goods he left us nothing; of spiritual goods he has left us a treasure." His father had "a rectangular mind, a wise spirit, a generous heart. He wanted," Benito wrote, "to make mankind true of heart and sensitive to fraternity. Many were the speeches and articles about him after his death; three thousand of the men and women he had known followed his body to the grave. My father's death marked the end of family unity for us, the family."

Benito's mother, Rosa Maltoni Mussolini, was born in 1858 in a small town in the province of Forlì. Her father was a veterinarian and Rosa was a teacher's college graduate. The household in which Benito grew up was unusual in the Romagna in that standard Italian, rather than dialect, was normally spoken within it.

The young Rosa Maltoni, with rich black hair, a determined jaw and a demure air, had come to Predappio to teach school. One day she found in the notebook of one of her pupils a message from the local blacksmith, Alessandro Mussolini. An exchange of letters followed, then visits. Eventually, in January, 1882, the couple was married, in (at Rosa's insistence) the local parish church. Although deeply attracted to the atheist blacksmith, Rosa herself was a devout Catholic. She was never successful in overcoming the ferociously antireligious principles of her husband, but Alessandro made many concessions, beginning with the church wedding and including the baptism of their infant son Benito. On the wall of the Mussolini family's modest living room a portrait of the Virgin Mary hung beside that of Garibaldi.

Rosa was very tolerant of her husband's bitter anticlericalism, his endless political activities that interfered with breadwinning, and his indulgent attitude toward often parasitical party friends. But she never accepted for a minute the proletarian status of her family. Although she was a poor woman, she had definite aspirations for her husband and especially for her children (one reason why everyone in the house had to speak proper Italian).

In Rosa's eyes, the clearest need of the Mussolini household was more money. She was well thought of as a teacher in the district and one day, summoning up all her considerable courage, she wrote to her superiors asking for a raise in her meager stipend. "Your Excellency may see for yourself," she wrote, "that this year the economic hardship in this little village is at its height, owing to the reduced yield of the crops and the total failure of the grape harvest, the only produce of these places. And it is precisely for the above-mentioned reasons that my poor family is in such strained financial circumstances that we are forced to cut off the studies of a little boy of ours, twelve years old [Benito], who is now at the Royal Normal School at Forlimpopoli and who according to his teachers promises to amount to something."

No raise, alas, was forthcoming in answer to this appeal, but Benito stayed in school anyway.

Benito took after his father more than after his mother, and in later life he often acknowledged the paternal influence while saying very little about his mother. Yet all the evidence indicates that Rosa was a good woman and a good mother, and her son Benito once wrote that "to offend her was my worst fear." At her death the twenty-three-year-old Benito wrote that "from me has been taken the one dear and truly near living being." His mother "had toiled and hoped too much and died before she was yet forty-eight years old. She had, in her quiet manner, done superhuman labors." Many people marked her passing; even for a funeral-attending age and society, her burial rites drew together a very large number of mourners.

Benito was the firstborn of the Mussolini family of Predappio, followed in 1885 by a brother Arnaldo and in 1888 by a sister Edvige.

Arnaldo and Benito always went to different schools, sharing only their summer vacations together. Perhaps because of this absence of schooltime competition, they soon developed a warm relationship. After graduating from school Arnaldo, like his older brother, went to Switzerland for a while but finally settled down in the Friuli region of northeastern Italy. When during World War I the area was invaded by the Austro-Germans, Arnaldo was forced to abandon his house, and so he joined the Italian army. After the war, Arnaldo took a position with his brother's newspaper, *Il popolo d'Italia*, and when Benito became premier Arnaldo was entrusted with the editorship. Their relationship became especially close then, and Arnaldo's total loyalty to his older brother made him indispensable. Yet, while Benito and Arnaldo resembled each other physically, they differed in many fundamental ways. Alessandro Mussolini had named his second son after Arnaldo da Brescia, a rebel against papal power; however, unlike his father and brother, Arnaldo grew up to be a devoutly religious man. Soft-spoken, self-effacing, and full of common sense, Arnaldo often took care of those duties that Benito found distasteful, such as sending money for the care of the future prime minister's illegitimate children. Arnaldo Mussolini died on December 21, 1931, nine years after the March on Rome. His death left a gap in Benito's life that was never filled.

From his younger sister Edvige, Benito often borrowed money to go out on dates. He was never overscrupulous about paying her back, but she did acquire through this process of lot of girlfriends. While he was a soldier serving on the Austrian front Mussolini wrote many letters to his sister, who was now married. After the death of Arnaldo, Premier Mussolini had Edvige's husband transferred to a job in Rome so his sister could be near him. She became his confidant, her advice being especially sought in such delicate family matters as finding a suitable husband for the prime minister's daughter. Edvige was often approached by the families of political prisoners, and she was apparently able to obtain clemency for many of them (not, in fact, a very difficult thing to accomplish during the long Mussolini regime).

SCHOOL DAYS AT FAENZA

Margherita Sarfatti, Mussolini's friend and biographer, observed that "the childhood of a great man is never really happy. The necessary subordination to his elders is in conflict with the craving for supremacy inherent in his nature." However that may be, there is no doubt that young Benito was a lonely and restless boy, spending many long hours wandering by himself in the hills around Predappio. In spite of his relatively free life in those days, Mussolini felt himself closed in. "There in Predappio one could neither move nor think without feeling oneself to be at the end of a short rope." The vastness of the freedom he actually enjoyed was soon to be made manifest to him.

In September 1892, when Mussolini was nine years old, his mother sent him to a Catholic boarding school run by the Salesian Fathers in the town of Faenza, twenty miles from Predappio. She wanted her restless and headstrong son to receive discipline. At first, Alessandro had been militantly opposed to the whole idea; he wanted his firstborn son near him, and certainly not in the hands of the priests. But Rosa, as always in matters of this nature, had her way, and the young and apprehensive Benito went off to Faenza.

Called Faventia by the Romans, Faenza had since the fourteenth century been the manufacturing center of a highly prized earthenware known as faenza majolica. Most of the town's fifteenth-century walls were still intact, and it boasted a population of forty thousand. It also had a boarding school conducted by the Oblates of Saint Francis de Sales—popularly known as the Salesians.

Giovanni Bosco had founded the Salesians in 1855, a teaching order devoted to the education of boys, whose principles of pedagogy were very advanced for that time. Children were to be studied, not merely directed; there was to be a great deal of physical exercise and hardly any corporal punishment. As a symbol of his enlightened intentions, Bosco (who eventually himself became a saint in the Roman Calendar) named his new organization in honor of Saint Francis de Sales. De Sales had been the Catholic bishop of Protestant Geneva during the Counter-Reformation. During those troubled days he authored *An Introduction to the Devout Life*, considered by many to be a spiritual classic. De Sales won many converts from Protestantism to his Church, through his eloquent preaching and a life devoted to charitable works. He was especially interested in improving the education of the poor.

In spite of all this promising heritage, the Faenza school was a complete disaster for young Mussolini. Perhaps the experiment was doomed from the very start, given that Benito was disinclined to accept discipline by nature. Nor could he have been expected to adapt himself easily to the dramatic change involved in being taken away from the free life of the Predappio hills and placed in the restrictive life of a clerical school, which however enlightened, was rife with hothouse piety and talebearing. Alessandro had, moreover, undoubtedly sought to put his son on guard against letting the priests fill his head with a lot of superstitious nonsense. On the other hand, the exalted principles of Giovanni Bosco must have provided a standard at which to aim rather than an accurate description of everyday life at the school. Benito, being the son of a well-known subversive and anticlerical, surely required constant surveillance.

Poverty had never meant very much at Predappio, because all were poor. But this was not the case at the Salesian school of Faenza. Dining facilities for the students were segregated according to social class, and Mussolini, along with the other poorest boys, had to take his meals at the lowest table where inferior food was set out. It should be noted that this sort of blatant discrimination was by no means peculiar to either Italian or Salesian schools. Nevertheless, the experience seared the young Mussolini. Forty years later, Prime Minister Mussolini recounted the story in an interview: "At table we boys were divided into three groups. I always had to sit at the bottom and eat with the poorest. Maybe I could forget the ants in the third-class bread, but that we children were divided into classes, that still burns my soul." This situation confirmed all his father's teachings about the senseless humiliations exacted from the defenseless by an unjust and pitiless society. As Ernst Nolte, a particularly perceptive student of fascism, observed about this matter, "there is no reason why rage at injustice should not become a legitimate starting point for lasting socialistic feelings."

Benito felt denigrated and isolated and he soon got into trouble. He threw an inkpot at a teacher who had struck him with a ruler (behavior not in accordance with Don Bosco's principles). On another occasion, he cut the hand of a fellow student who had angered him. For this offense, young Benito was forced to spend most of the night locked in a courtyard where he was chased and nearly bitten by one of the watchdogs. Eventually readmitted to his room, he awoke the next day with a raging fever and became delirious. As further punishment he was demoted, and forced to live in isolation from his classmates for several days.

Young Mussolini found the punishments meted out to him all the more objectionable because they were administered calmly and deliberately, without the human contact involved in anger and hot blood. And it can be particularly devastating to a child when he is assured by an adult that he has offended not only man but God as well, and that possibly eternal punishment awaits him from an all-seeing and all-remembering God, a God transformed into a particularly remote and horribly inescapable prefect of discipline. In the hands of neurotics the sublime teachings of Christianity may be twisted into a system of terror for children: "Even if we can't see you God does!"

Young Benito was finally expelled from the school in 1894. However generous the heart of Giovanni Bosco, however praiseworthy the intentions of his followers at Faenza, they failed miserably with Benito Mussolini and thus altered the course of human history. Benito never got over his days at the school; he would remain full of resentment and rebellion all the rest of his life, against the Church, against Italian society, against the international order. The Faenza experience surely goes a long way to account for Mussolini's inability, until the day he died, to form any real friendships—with the exception of his younger brother Arnaldo.

FORLIMPOPOLI

In the wake of these disastrous events, Alessandro Mussolini at last had his way. Benito was placed in a state school in the town of Forlimpopoli, a small community several miles southeast of Forlì. The institution was named for the poet Giosuè Carducci. Mussolini was to remain in the school for almost seven years, although he was temporarily expelled for indiscipline in January, 1898. At the Carducci school the general atmosphere was less oppressive, the instructors were more tolerant, there were no discriminations based on social class. Mussolini flourished scholastically and socially. Those subjects he liked or wished to learn he learned easily; he did especially well in geography, history, and Italian. His ability to grasp essentials quickly impressed many of his instructors, and was to remain a characteristic of his throughout life.

He continued to borrow money from his long-suffering sister Edvige and used it to buy books and newspapers. He would often climb to the roof of an abandoned church where he knew he could find undisturbed quiet for his reading. The attention of the young Mussolini was not totally taken up with books, however. During his schooldays at Forlimpopoli the larger world outside the turbulent Romagna shook with terrible and tragic events. When Mussolini was thirteen, Italian troops were massacred at Adowa by the armies of the Abyssinian Emperor. Two years later Milan erupted in riots during which hundreds were killed and wounded. In 1900 Umberto of

Savoy, second king of united Italy, was assassinated by the agent of a group of Italian immigrant anarchists based in the United States. These tumultuous events stimulated within the boy a desire to play an active role in political affairs. He attended a number of meetings of the local Socialist organizations, and as the son of Alessandro Mussolini, the ardent comrade-blacksmith of Predappio, he was warmly welcomed. At the age of seventeen the intense, dark-eyed young Mussolini, still hardly more than a boy, saw his name mentioned in a real newspaper: *Avanti!*, the national daily of the Socialist party, praised a discourse on Giuseppe Verdi delivered at a town hall meeting by "comrade student Mussolini." And so the ink entered his blood.

Political activities, however, did not unduly interfere with his studies. At the end of his training at the Giosuè Carducci school, Mussolini was awarded the diploma of elementary school teacher, with honors.

The easiest way for a son of the poor to make his way in the world was to become a schoolteacher, and that is what the eighteen-year-old Mussolini decided to do. He applied for a teaching post in Predappio but was turned down. He had no better luck with an application (which perhaps revealed his deeper desires) to be appointed secretary of the commune of Predappio, a sort of town clerk. With no opportunities at home, he accepted a temporary teaching post in the Po River valley. And so, in any meaningful sense, his days as a Romagnole came to an end.

His principal biographer, Professor Renzo De Felice, holds that the influence upon Mussolini's life of the romantic and passionate Romagna has been overdramatized; he insists that Mussolini's later career in Milan (from 1912 to 1922) was a much more decisive period of his development. This is undoubtedly true with regard to his intellectual growth. But his emotional makeup, his fundamental orientation to the world, were surely influenced profoundly and permanently by the teachings of Alessandro, the poverty of the Romagna, and the humiliations of Faenza. By the time he was twenty years old Mussolini displayed that Romagnole combination of rebelliousness with an admiration of power, a pugnacious cynicism along with the search for a sure faith, that was to characterize him until the day of his death. And to the end Mussolini retained a deep attachment to his native region, and returned there often after he had become head of the government.

III

THE SOCIALIST

"Let us not forget that Mussolini was a Socialist party leader."

Palmiro Togliatti

"In a sense all European dictators of the present day are the children of the Communist Manifesto."

Alfred Cobban
1936

GUALTIERI EMILIA

In February 1902, having learned some German and a good deal of French, nineteen-year-old Mussolini took up his teaching duties in Gualtieri Emilia, a small town along the Po River. His appointment was as a substitute teacher, for which he was to receive a salary of 56 lire a month, 40 of which went for his board.

Thirty-five pupils, first and second graders, were handed over to his care. Many of the children came from impoverished families, a circumstance that presented the novice schoolmaster with special problems. "How," the birthright Socialist teacher wrote to the mayor of Gualtieri Emilia, "can we expect a clean sheet of paper from a boy who because of dire circumstances has to do his homework in a stable?" Remembering those terrible days in the Faenza school, Mussolini also expressed his views on scholastic discipline: "The teacher must forestall and remove the causes of evil in order not to have to resort to painful repression," an enlightened maxim which he usually tried to follow.

The region of Emilia is today an integral part of that area known in Italian politics as the "Red Belt" because of the consistently large vote its inhabitants give to the Communists and the Socialists. Even in Mussolini's days as a schoolteacher there the Socialists had made great strides, and many towns had a Socialist mayor and town council. Gualtieri Emilia was one of these towns, and on one occasion Mussolini made a well-received political speech there at a mass meeting attended by the mayor and numerous other municipal dignitaries. But Mussolini was not at all impressed with the mellow character of Emilian Socialism. The followers of Karl Marx in the Emilia region were always organizing dances, at least so it seemed to the young Romagnole teacher, who did not participate. Every Socialist activity or meeting or demonstration also required, it seems, the dutiful consumption of heroic quantities of good Emilian red wine. This kind of activity was by no means edifying to the slim and austere revolutionary from the Predappian hills (although it must be admitted that he succumbed to the general levity of the region at least to the extent of learning to play the violin).

But even the most austere young revolutionaries have been known to have their weaknesses, which may explain why Mussolini's contract was not renewed, why he left Gualtieri Emilia after the end of the term. Some of his biographers, including hostile ones, have tried to explain the brevity of Mussolini's sojourn in that town on the basis of a political disagreement that he had had with the mayor. But that was not the case, or at least not the main reason, as Mussolini himself, always the most honest of all his biographers, affirms.

Mussolini had become involved with the wife of a citizen of Gualtieri Emilia who was away in the army. Tipped off by an informant, the deceived husband returned to town and tossed his wayward wife out of the house. Mussolini promptly set her up in lodgings where he could visit her every evening after school ("she always waited for me at the door"). This was just a trifle too gamey even for the freethinking and wine-guzzling

Socialists of Gualtieri, and so the critical young Romagnole was advised that there would be no teaching position for him in the future.

Mussolini did not hold a grudge. Or perhaps he did; at any rate he found a reason, after he became prime minister, for revisiting the little town of Gualtieri Emilia. Right after his smashing electoral triumph of 1924, the long official limousine with the former schoolmaster in the back seat roared into the little town that twenty years before had found him unworthy. It has not come down to us how many of the administrators who had given Mussolini his walking papers were there to witness this denouement, or what they thought of it.

With no real prospects in Italy after his teaching position was terminated, and with compulsory military service looming every month a little larger on his horizon, Mussolini decided to leave his native land for a while and set out for the Swiss border.

SWITZERLAND

Mussolini was just turning twenty years old when he took his train ride through the magnificent Alps, and he was deeply impressed with them. "I stood at the window for almost the whole of the journey" to Lucerne, he later wrote to a friend. "The night was splendid. The moon soared above the immense mountains, all white with snow." Upon alighting from the train, he read in a newspaper that his father had been arrested back in Forlì province for participation in "electoral disorders."

"My stay in Switzerland", he wrote later, "was a welter of difficulties." This is quite an understatement. His first weeks in the land of the Swiss were in fact Zolaesque: he often went hungry; he was arrested for vagrancy; he slept under bridges; he even contemplated suicide. "The only piece of metal I had in my pocket was a nickel medallion of Karl Marx."

He supported himself throughout his stay in Switzerland

(which was to last almost two years) with a variety of jobs. Soon after his arrival in the country he was taken on as a common laborer in a construction crew, working eleven hours a day to earn enough money to buy some roasted potatoes. On the first day at this job, Mussolini later recalled, he noticed a large clock atop a nearby public building. He looked at that clock often, but the hands, so it seemed to the young man, never moved. He quit that job when his boots wore out from carrying heavy loads over the gravelly paths of the construction site. While in Lausanne he worked as a wine merchant's delivery boy, supported mainly by the tips of patrons. The hotels he could afford were dirty, so he often slept in the open. (Throughout his later life, even when he was prime minister, a bed with clean crisp sheets remained for him the symbol of true luxury and comfort.)

He naturally gravitated toward local organizations of the Swiss Socialist party, many sections of which were made up largely of Italian immigrants. As an educated and vigorous young man, he quickly acquired a great deal of influence on these mainly unskilled and very poor manual laborers.

He was elected secretary of a local labor union, and was chosen as a delegate to a labor union convention in Lausanne in November 1902. Soon he was making speeches to Italian Socialist organizations all over the republic and was elected one of the representatives to the Eighth Congress of Italian Socialists in Switzerland. He became a noted figure in the politics of his host country. On one occasion, when the Swiss authorities wanted to expel him from the country (which would have meant his arrest on the other side of the frontier as a draft evader), the Italian Socialists in Switzerland set up such a clamor that the order for his deportation was canceled. (Mussolini had, however, made a brief return visit to his native province legally, in October 1903; his father had wired him that Rosa was dying, but by the time Mussolini arrived back in Predappio his mother had recovered.)

Traveling the country, working at odd jobs, making speeches

While in Switzerland, Mussolini's fierce anticlericalism and socialist militancy won over the working class but did not endear him to the Swiss authorities.

and friends, and perfecting his French, Mussolini's days were filled with activity. He nevertheless found time for an affair with the mysterious "Eleonora H.," a Polish medical student in Geneva. Not much is known about this woman except that her charms caused Mussolini to go far out of his way to visit her on more than one occasion.

It was during these Swiss days that Mussolini established his reputation as a vociferous anticlerical (the Italian term is *mangiapreti*: literally, "priest-eater"). Alessandro's teachings and the dreadful experience at Faenza are a sufficient explanation for Mussolini's orientation to this subject, but there were political reasons for his antireligious attitudes and activities as well. The principle of tolerance for organized religion was on its way to becoming established doctrine among the reformist wing of European Socialism (those elements to which Mussolini referred with great contempt as the "spaghetti Socialists"). So his assumption of the posture of an anticlerical militant was in part one aspect of his general repudiation of the softening or "bourgeoisification" of the old-time revolutionary creed taught to him by his father Alessandro. Nor were Roman Catholics the sole object of his antireligious passion; Mussolini engaged in a public debate with a Swiss Lutheran pastor on the existence of God, during which the fiery young man from Predappio demonstrated his command of all the pseudo-scientific "proofs" of turn-of-the-century militant atheism.

Mussolini had also developed a taste for polemical writing. Less than a month after his arrival in Switzerland he published an article in the journal of the Italian Socialists of that country, *L'Avvenire del lavoratore* ("The Future of the Worker"). He wrote numerous other pieces for various organs, including *Il proletario*, an Italian-language weekly printed in New York City. Mussolini's writing style was clear, incisive, and tinged with revolutionary fervor that won the admiration of his impoverished working-class readers.

His combination of inflammatory writings, labor agitation, and foreign birth got Mussolini into frequent trouble with the

Swiss police, and more than once he went to prison for brief spells. (It must of course be borne in mind that for a Socialist activist, being sent to bourgeois prisons was hardly a disgrace; far from it.) Margherita Sarfatti writes that the future *Duce*'s prison experiences taught him patience; they also seem to have taught him to detest close spaces. When serving on the Austrian front during World War I, for example, Mussolini preferred to face bombardment in the open rather than seek shelter in tightly packed caves and trenches. And once, when he was visiting the famed Isle of Capri, he caused many eyebrows to be raised when he refused to enter the Blue Grotto.

Renzo De Felice, author of the most magisterial biography of Mussolini, holds that the Swiss experience was fundamental to the formation of the young Italian. One of the most important contributions those months in Switzerland made to Mussolini's development was the planting—very deep and almost unnoticed—of disturbing thoughts in the mind of the young Socialist, thoughts on the subject of the relative importance of class and nationality. Classic Marxist social analysis, of course, taught that patriotism and nationalism were spurious devices whose purpose was to delude and divide the exploited workers. The workingman, said Marx, had no fatherland; workers of the world, unite! Mussolini, a birthright Marxist, unquestioningly accepted this keystone of the Marxian epistemological arch. It was during these very days that he wrote: "Some of the economic conclusions of Marxism may perhaps be erroneous, but the sociological conclusions are valid. Against the new theory of collaboration and cooperation of classes, there stands firm and unshaken in its Marxist foundation the theory of class struggle." But the nature of Swiss Socialism called the accuracy of this doctrine into question. First of all, the Socialists in Switzerland were divided and organized along national lines, the most important segments being the German and the Italian. German-Swiss Socialism tended toward compromise and legalism. The Italian wing was heavily influenced by the events of Milan in 1898, in which scores of demonstrating workingmen had been killed in the streets and hundreds more imprisoned. The more radicalized Italian Socialists, many of them educated in the harsh school of the manual laborer, were often immigrants, men who had journeyed north in search of work and who helped build the St. Gotthard and Simplon tunnels, with much loss of life. Mussolini gradually became aware that these simple men, Socialist true believers every one, were looked down upon and held in contempt not only by the comfortable and smug Swiss bourgeoisie, but also by the German-speaking sections of the Swiss Socialist party itself. The latter would often fail to support their Italian co-partisans in their bitter strikes and struggles for improved wages, a pattern of action that puzzled and angered Mussolini to the extent that he was driven to declare that in Switzerland there was no true Socialist movement at all. These early and disquieting lessons on the relative importance of the struggle among *peoples* as opposed to the struggle between *classes* would be remembered and magnified, with enormous consequences, in the not far distant future.

VILFREDO PARETO

While he was in Switzerland, the young Mussolini also came into contact with the ideas of the distinguished economist and political historian Vilfredo Pareto, who was teaching at the University of Lausanne. Mussolini attended his classes; "Pareto was giving a course of lectures in Lausanne," he wrote some time later, "on political economy. I looked forward to every one." Pareto himself wrote years later that "Mussolini was for some time in Lausanne and attended my courses, but I didn't know him personally."

Pareto was born in 1848 in Paris, although his family was of the Ligurian nobility (from the region around Genoa). He graduated from the Turin Polytechnical Institute, but his interests turned from engineering to political problems, and he sought a seat in the Italian Parliament in the elections of 1882 (without success). Pareto was left a handsome legacy in 1898; henceforth financially independent, he spent most of the remaining part of his life as a professor at the University of Lausanne.

For Pareto, the theories of Marxism were "demonstrably false." This, at first glance, should have been more than enough to earn him the passionate animosity of the young Mussolini. Pareto, however, offered an analysis of history and society that was so congenial to Mussolini's developing thought that the young Romagnole was drawn to the expatriate professor from the first encounter, and remained a vocal admirer of his ever after.

One of Pareto's main concepts was that rationality plays a very limited role in human affairs, especially in great historical movements or upheavals. Men do not so much use reason to plot their course, they employ it rather to justify—to *rationalize*—courses of action that are attractive to them on other, prerational grounds. Another Paretan fundamental thesis was the social inescapability of rule by an elite: firmly implanted in the Machiavellian tradition, Pareto stressed that the principal and decisive division in any given society was normally not the one between social classes but the one between the elite which ruled and the mass which was ruled. This division into elite and mass was for Pareto a universal and necessary law. Democracy—the participation in the decision-making process by all, or by great numbers of citizens—was a delusion, a trick used by the elite to pacify the mass whom they thereby controlled. The Marxists were just another set of contestants in this eternal struggle for power. The leaders of the Socialist movement were not, as they thought or claimed, the tribunes of "the people," nor would "the people" rule if and when the Socialist leaders came to power. Instead, socialism was the protective cloak of a would-be elite that sought to mobilize the mass in an effort to eject the present ruling class and take its place. The Marxists hoped, by exacerbating and justifying the envy of the rich by the masses, to satiate their own desire for power. But under no circumstances was the state going to "wither away." After the Marxist revolution, as before, there would be rulers and ruled. No revolution ever had, no revolution ever *could*, put "the people" into power; revolution only replaced one elite with another. (It is said that this critique of Marxist revolution cost Lenin many sleepless nights.)

Although the revolutionaries' slogans about equality were hollow, Pareto did not reject revolution; in fact, he tended to teach that revolution was often good for society. Revolution occurred, taught Pareto, because within every ruling elite unworthy elements eventually accumulate, elements that do not wish to, or know how to, hold onto power. A sure sign of elite decay is that entrance of outsiders into the elite is rendered more and more difficult by the erection of artificial barriers, such as birth and social refinement, that have nothing at all to do with the art of wielding power. On the other side, individuals appear among the masses who, although they were born outside the ruling group, display all the characteristics that should entitle them to membership in a ruling elite, especially a taste for and an understanding of power. (This is Pareto's democratic side: natural aristocrats, natural rulers may be born anywhere, even in log cabins, like Lincoln.) Thus, a revolution normally occurs because vigorous elements among the masses find themselves held down by a degenerate ruling class. Revolution can only succeed if the ruling class no longer understands how rule is to be maintained. The resulting "circulation of elites" provides a sort of political blood transfusion that reinvigorates a society. But no revolution, however beneficial, ever changes the basic *structure* of a society—the fundamental elite-mass dichotomy.

This idea of politics as a struggle among elites appealed strongly to Mussolini precisely because he had just about abandoned the idea that the Socialist revolution would ever come to Italy by the spontaneous uprising of "the people." The revolution required a hard and dedicated elite that would know how to mobilize the untutored masses by an appeal to the powerful nonrational urges that animated them. Mussolini's writings of the early 1900s (for example, his article in the *Avanguardia socialista di Milano* of October 1904) are filled with appreciative references to Pareto's ideas. For young Mussolini, Pareto's theory of elites was "the most extraordinary sociological conception of modern times." Pareto eventually came to know Mussolini and to reciprocate his admiration. In 1922, after Mussolini had become prime minister, Pareto, then a septuagenarian but still intensely interested in political events, accepted appointment to the Italian Senate, at the urging of his former student.

THE ARMY

Perhaps the primary reason why Mussolini decided to go to Switzerland was to escape the draft; every male citizen of Italy was legally required to give two years of military service, and Mussolini's class (those born in the year 1883) would soon be due. The records at the Royal Prefecture at Forlì for April 28, 1904, show Mussolini absent without justification when his class was called up. "Italy needed bread and she was bled white instead by an army and a navy," Mussolini wrote in those days. (But the day was coming when he would see a direct link between a powerful army and navy and the ability to obtain bread for the nation.)

Then everything changed in September 1904. King Victor Emmanuel II, in anticipation of and thanksgiving for the birth of Crown Prince Umberto, issued a proclamation of amnesty to all draft evaders who would consent to clear their records and serve in the armed forces. This was a golden opportunity for Mussolini to remove his name from the list of those who would be imprisoned if the Italian authorities ever laid hands on them, an opportunity for him to be able to live and work openly again in his own country. So Mussolini returned to Italy, presented himself to the authorities and was assigned, in

January 1905, to the 10th Regiment of Bersaglieri (marksmen) stationed in the city of Verona.

A small, pleasant city, the setting for Romeo and Juliet, Verona was on the Adige River along the Brenner Pass road. Conquered by the Venetians in 1405, Verona had done very well under the rule of that tolerant commercial empire. Perhaps its most illustrious son had been the painter Paolo Veronese. "Verona, where my regiment was garrisoned," Mussolini wrote, "was and always will remain a dear Venetian city, reverberating with the past, filled with suggestive beauties." Forty years into the future Verona would be the scene of the last important political drama of Italian fascism. The lovely town also suffered severely during World War II at the hands of both the Germans and the Americans.

"I liked the life of a soldier," wrote Mussolini several years later, "and I can say that in every regard I was an excellent soldier." Actually, his service, which ended in September 1906, has left behind it precious little in the way of records beyond a letter to his captain thanking the latter for a sympathetic note on the death of Mussolini's mother (who had succumbed to meningitis in February 1905). Nevertheless, for a draft evader, a known antimilitarist, and a prominent revolutionary Socialist to have served in the military for almost two years without having gotten into any trouble must be seen in itself as quite an achievement of a kind, and an indication of the complexities of Mussolini's personality.

INTERMEZZO

After he left his Bersaglieri regiment Mussolini took up another teaching post, this time in an elementary school in Tolmezzo, a little town on the eastern slopes of the Alps. It was not a good experience: the town was dull (not too dull for the usual romantic involvement, however), it seemed to be raining all the time, the pay was very low, and the children were driven to indignation at the very suggestion of classroom discipline. One of the few bright spots in the depressing and humid episode came in April 1907 when Mussolini was awarded a diploma by the University of Bologna, entitling him to teach high-school French.

Mussolini left damp and dreary Tolmezzo in August 1907. He had another job, this time in a private high school in the town of Oneglia, on the Italian Riviera. Nothing could have contrasted more dramatically, more pleasantly, with Tolmezzo. Mussolini loved the area, did well at his teaching, and began publishing articles for the local Socialist newspaper. But the Riviera was not "Red" Emilia; Mussolini's standard brand of revolutionary socialism was a bit too indigestible for the authorities at Oneglia, and his contract was not renewed.

In the wake of these disappointing experiences, it appears that Mussolini finally came to the conclusion, at the age of twenty-five, that teaching was not the career for him. He would turn full time to journalism and politics. Without immediate prospects, however, he returned to his birthplace at Predappio where he quickly got into serious trouble. A rural strike was bitterly raging, and young Benito Mussolini was arrested for having threatened one of the leaders of the effort to break the strike. The local prosecutor decided to make an example of his case and Mussolini found himself sentenced to three months in prison. The excessive judgment was appealed and Mussolini's appointed time in jail was reduced to twelve days.

In the fall of 1908, shortly after his release from jail, Mussolini published a long essay about the theories of Friedrich Nietzsche entitled "The Philosophy of Force," in *Il pensiero romagnola*, a weekly put out by the Republican party in Forlì.

Nietzsche (1844–1900) had been a professor of philosophy at the University of Basel until ill health forced him to leave in 1879. By 1889 he was hopelessly insane. His writings, nevertheless, influenced an entire generation. Nietzsche looked upon Christianity, with its glorification of meekness and compassion, as the revenge of the Jews upon the Roman Empire. Like

Georges Sorel, Nietzsche rejected the pseudo-civilization of the nineteenth-century bourgeoisie, and also the "slave mentality" of Christianity that undergirded it. But Nietzsche did not look to the proletarian class for the redemption of this degenerate society, as did Sorel, but to what he called "supermen"—heroes who would smash through custom and deceit and establish new and more virile values.

Nietzsche enjoyed a certain vogue in leftist circles in the first decade of the twentieth century and Mussolini, who prided himself on being acquainted with the latest intellectual currents, knew Nietzsche's writings well. In fact, having perfected his knowledge of German while in Switzerland, Mussolini was able to read the original German editions of the philosopher's works. Mussolini was strongly attracted to the idea of "supermen" who would overthrow falsehoods and mediocrity, the bourgeois and Christian order. Nietzsche's emphasis on the need for willpower, activism, and rebellion evoked a sympathetic response from the young Romagnole. And, in dramatic contrast to the sterile, reductive approach of the orthodox Marxists, Nietzsche's open contempt for scholastic straitjackets caused Mussolini to see in him the clear intellect of the true *mediterraneo*. In his *Philosophy of Force*, Mussolini declared that "the superman is a symbol" of social regeneration—that liberation of man so longed for by all contemporary revolutionaries. This essay was well received in Nietzschean circles, and the philosopher's own sister Elizabeth would, some years later, acclaim the March on Rome. For his part, Mussolini remained an admirer of Nietzsche to the end of his life. In 1943, when the *Duce* of fascism was being held prisoner by his king, Adolf Hitler sent him a beautifully bound forty-two volume set of Nietzsche's collected works.

TRENT

During most of 1909 Mussolini was living and working outside his native country once again. The twenty-five-year-old ex-schoolmaster had been offered the position of secretary to the local *Camera del lavoro* (a sort of labor union) in the town of Trent, across the Austrian frontier. Included in the position was the editorship of a small weekly, *L'Avvenire del lavoratore* ("The Future of the Worker"; this was not the same paper that Mussolini had contributed articles to while he was in Switzerland). Mussolini accepted the position and crossed into Austria-Hungary on February 6, 1909, to take up his new duties.

The Austro-Hungarian Empire was, like the Habsburg family that ruled it, a relic of former glories. The Austrians, through direct or indirect rule, had been supreme in the Italian peninsula after the defeat of Napoleon at Waterloo in 1815. The wars of the *risorgimento* had all been, in one way or another, directed against the Austrian hegemony: the unification of Italy in 1860 was a definite signal that the days of Austrian power were waning. Her crushing defeat at the hands of Bismarck's Prussia in 1866, as a result of which she was expelled from German politics and lost the rich province of Venetia to Italy, was shortly thereafter followed by the unification of Germany under Prussian leadership. Outplayed, overmatched, too often defeated, bypassed by history, the Austrian Empire (after 1867 called Austria-Hungary, or the Dual Monarchy) settled down to a long period of slow and genteel decay. By 1910, Austria had a large population (fifty million as compared to Italy's thirty-five million) and was held together by Habsburg tradition, an efficient civil service, and a decent army. It was, however, the weakest of the great powers, except for Italy. Austrian power was constantly being corroded by the acid of nationalistic passion.

The Austrian Empire was an ethnic patchwork quilt, put together in the days when young princesses brought provinces with them as part of their dowries. The dominant groups in the Empire were the Germans (Austrians) and the Hungarians, but these two together made up less than half the total population. The balance was composed of increasingly restive and resentful Slavs (Poles, Czechs, Slovenes, Slovaks, and Croats), along with significant Romanian and Italian minorities. Many of these desired to be united with their ethnic kindred across the frontiers of the Empire, or to set up their own new nation-state. Russian expansionism, in those days known as Pan-Slavism, further disturbed the fragile stability of the Austrian state. It was becoming clear to many that the seething ethnic rivalries and hatreds could not be contained much longer, that the last days of the House of Habsburg were at hand. And indeed the assassination of Franz Ferdinand (heir to the Austrian throne) by a Slavic nationalist in the summer of 1914, would be the signal for plunging Austria and the whole of Europe into the disastrous civil war whose first installment extended to 1918. And as if to embody the entire political situation of increasing senescence and approaching demise, Emperor Franz Josef of Austria was seventy-nine years old and had been ruling for sixty years when young Benito Mussolini arrived in the town of Trent.

Trent had a long history. Called by the Romans Tridentum, it had been a military colony on the road to the strategic Brenner Pass. The Council of Trent had unfolded within its walls, that series of assemblies (1545-1563) of bishops and theologians that so dramatically changed the traditional face of the Catholic Church and did so much to assure the permanent division of European Christendom into warring Catholic and Protestant camps. The Trent that Mussolini came to was larger than Faenza, and was the capital of a region called the Trentino. A mountainous land of cold winds and sheltered valleys, the Trentino possessed the vital Brenner Pass, the corridor leading from Teutonic Europe into Latin Europe. Full of green forests and devout Catholics, divided linguistically and culturally between Germans and Italians, the Trentino, along with the area at the head of the Adriatic Sea around Trieste, made up what was called *Italia irredenta* ("Unredeemed Italy"). All good Italian patriots longed for the day when these "unredeemed" Italian-speaking areas would be united with the motherland in a complete and permanent union. (Both Trieste and the Trentino would in fact be annexed to the Kingdom of Italy after World War I had shaken the Habsburg edifice to pieces.)

When Mussolini made known his acceptance of his appointment in the Trentino, the local Socialist newspaper declared that "the selection could not be better.... He is a cultured young man, and to the great advantage of our movement, he has a thorough knowledge of the German language." Mussolini found Trent more congenial than Forlì; among other advantages it had an excellent municipal library. Nevertheless, as in his student days he often went without food to save what little cash he had to buy books. He lived in a room in the poorest quarter of the town and subsisted on corn meal mush and beans. Eventually his Socialist comrades became so embarrassed at his impoverished appearance that they bought him a new suit. Incorrigible, Mussolini crumbled up the hat that went with it, so as not to "look too much like a bourgeois."

Under his vigorous direction, the reputation of *L'Avvenire del lavoratore* grew, along with its circulation, which rose from 1,600 to 2,400. Among his contributions to the *Avvenire* was the publication in installments of his translation from the German of *My Youth*, the anonymous memoirs of a German working girl. It was also during this time that he wrote his spicy historical romance, *The Cardinal's Mistress.*

Young Mussolini made a profound impression on many of his comrades in the Trentino. Antonio Piscel, an attorney and a leader of Tridentine socialism, described Mussolini as "a young man of great intelligence and very broad culture, a facile writer, a very talented polemicist, and a proud, indomitable character." During his stay in Trent, Mussolini also developed his oratorical abilities, prompting the first descriptions of his powerful voice as "beautiful."

But he had critics as well. Mussolini in the Trentino was like an anticlerical bull in a field of red vestments. In the columns of his paper he castigated the Vatican as a "den of intolerance." He was sued for libel by more than one priest, and Mussolini lost several of these cases, paying fines or visits to the city jail.

The local magistrate, one Signor Tranquillini, was a loyal servant of the Habsburgs and often censored Mussolini's writings and decided libel cases against him, especially if a priest was involved. The root of the problem was that, to Mussolini's endless outrage, the Catholics of the Trentino were not only, like Catholics everywhere, "servants of superstition and intolerance"; worse, they were antinational, that is, pro-Austrian. Many devout Italian-speaking Catholics in the Trentino were indeed less than eager to be united with the Kingdom of Italy, which they viewed as the despoiler of the papacy and a veritable cesspool of liberalism and antireligion. France, under the control of Dreyfusards, Masons, and Jews, was for all practical (i.e., political) purposes lost to the Church; Spain, Portugal, Belgium all counted for little in European politics; Ireland and Poland were under the rule of non-Catholic powers. Thus Austria-Hungary was the last of the great powers still faithful (more or less) to the Roman Church. In gratitude for this allegiance, the Italian clergy of the Trentino and their numerous followers gave their loyalty to the Vienna government with only the slightest twinge of conscience. It was in this complex context that the young socialist Mussolini engaged in bitter polemics with the principal lay leader of Tridentine Catholicism, another young man by the name of Alcide De Gasperi. More than three decades after these Alpine encounters De Gasperi was, after Mussolini's death, to rule Italy as the first of her Christian Democratic prime ministers.

Perhaps the most important dimension of Mussolini's experience in the Trentino was the growing influence exerted upon him by Cesare Battisti, a leading Socialist of Trent. Battisti owned and edited two newspapers, the daily *Il popolo*, and the weekly *Vita Trentina*, to which Mussolini contributed several articles. Battisti was convinced that in the Trentino the class struggle was overshadowed by the rivalry between Italians and Germans. In his protest against the inferior position of the Italians in the Trentino, Battisti urged that the region's Italian bourgeoisie and Italian proletariat came together in a defense of Italian cultural and political rights. In taking this position, he was foreshadowing what was to become the quintessential doctrine of Mussolinian fascism. When the World War I broke out, Battisti fled the Trentino into neutral Italy and urged Italians to begin a "sacred war of liberation" of their co-nationals in unredeemed Italy. He joined the Italian army, was captured by the Austrians in 1916, and was hanged as a traitor.

According to Margherita Sarfatti, Mussolini's intimate collaborator as well as biographer, Mussolini's months in the Trentino were crucial because they finally awakened within him those sentiments of nationalism that had been dormant ever since his return from Switzerland. There is much to recommend this view because, as was the case in Switzerland, in the Trentino the German population looked with contempt upon the Italians. This was nowhere truer than within the ranks of that bulwark of international brotherhood, the Socialist party.[1] "Workers of the world, unite!" had been the cry of Karl Marx. Instead of adhering to this watchword, Swiss and Austrian socialism were characterized by "certain exclusive attitudes" that "have no reason to exist. Even the Italian tongue, much despised Italian," Mussolini complained in Trent, "has the right of citizenship in the meetings of workers and civilized peoples." The prejudices of Teutonic Socialists had at last made Mussolini realize that "I am desperately Italian. I believe in the function of Latinity."

Mussolini had hitherto experienced what it was like to be looked down upon because one was poor. What his Swiss experience had first suggested was now confirmed in the Trentino: one was also looked down upon because one was Italian. The conviction began to grow within him that the revolution had to do much more than punish the greedy and insensitive bourgeoisie and put an end to their crude injustices within Italy. The revolution also had to make the Italians a modern people, respected by the other peoples of Europe. The Socialist revolution must complete the work of the *risorgimento* and bring unity, dignity, and true independence to the Italians.

Inevitably, Mussolini's anticlericalism, antimilitarism, antimonarchism, his editorial and platform vehemence, and his generally unsavory reputation in establishment circles led to his expulsion from Austria. Mussolini's arrest and the subsequent order for deportation aroused ardent protests from Socialist representatives in the Vienna parliament, and the threat of a general strike in the town of Trent. So the authorities took Mussolini to the smaller town of Rovereto, where it was much less likely that the tracks into Italy would be effectively blocked by protesters. When Mussolini and his escort arrived at the border post on Sunday, September 26, it was one o'clock in the afternoon, but the train was not scheduled to leave for Italy until seven that evening. The official in charge of the place, a Hungarian baron, gave Mussolini liberty to walk around the town freely in exchange for his word of honor not to escape. Mussolini returned in time to catch the train into Italy, and he was to recall that act of kindness by the baron for many years thereafter.

Shortly after his second return to his native country, Mussolini began work on what was to become a long treatise, *Il Trentino Veduto da un Socialista* ("The Trentino as seen by a Socialist"). In this essay, which Renzo De Felice says is one of the very best things Mussolini wrote in his life, the clericals are excoriated for having "denied the Fatherland," because among other things they voted in favor of war supplies for an Austrian army that could be used against Italy at any moment. But the political and cultural rights of the Trentine Italians were menaced not only by Austro-Hungarian imperialism but also by a radically exclusivistic German Socialism. The economic situation of the Italians in the Trentino was too underdeveloped to permit hope for serious proletarian resistance, not to speak of a proletarian revolution. The Kingdom of Italy was too weak to free them by force of arms. There was only one course left open: the "unredeemed" Italians of the Austrian Empire could not be mobilized in their own defense by appeals to their economic interest but by appeals to their sense of nationality and national grievance. Thus nationalism—a new nationalism of the deprived classes—would be revolutionary in its effects. And so here was born another major theme of the fascism to come: national solidarity linked to social renewal.

SYNDICALISM

Of all the intellectual currents with which Mussolini came into contact during the first decade of the century, most important of all were the ideas of the revolutionary syndicalists, to which he formed a lasting attachment. The syndicalists had emerged, especially in Italy, as a sort of proletarian elite guard that distrusted and challenged the parliamentary-reformist wing of socialism. Among the major leaders of the movement were Georges Sorel and Robert Michels.

Sorel, born in France in 1847, had been trained as an engineer. Like Vilfredo Pareto, he turned eventually to the consideration of political problems, and gradually emerged as the principal theoretician of revolutionary syndicalism. In Sorel's view, the Europeans had sold all their values and prostituted themselves to the bourgeois gods of materialism. He wanted a revolution to regenerate and cleanse Western society. The instrument for the salvation of decadent European civilization was the proletariat: as a class it had nothing, and therefore had no stake in the continuation of the corrupt social order. Sorel wanted, or rather needed, the proletariat to be hard and revolutionary. It was precisely because of this that he hated those intellectuals who sought to use the socialist movement as a vehicle for advancing themselves by dominating the proletarian parties. Above all, he was the vociferous foe of what he saw as a mushy humanitarianism that was sapping the vitality of the socialist movement from the top down.

Robert Michels (1876-1936) was born in Germany. His most influential work, *Political Parties*, was published in 1911. It was a study of the distribution of power within the German Socialist party. In this book Michels advanced his concept of

"The Iron Law of Oligarchy," with which his name has been ever after associated. For Michels, all intelligent political action was determined by the recognition of a few fundamental principles. Men have a natural desire and tendency to belong to a group; man is a social being, he wants and needs group membership and support. Modern society is characterized by group competition. This competition takes place on an international level, between states, and on a subnational level, between interest groups of various sorts. Because man-in-his-group lives in a world of strenuous competition, he needs organization, discipline, and solidarity to survive. The key to group cohesion is not economic interest but psychological need. Group survival, therefore, requires leadership gifted in the arts of maintaining loyalty and cohesion; group survival requires elite direction. This is one reason why all large and successful groups offer evidence of the existence of an "Iron Law of Oligarchy," the invariable direction of the group's affairs by the few. Another reason for the universal phenomenon of oligarchical control is this: most people, the majority of the members of any group, are normally inert. Through lack of time, interest, intelligence, or expertise, most members of the group are unavailable for the direction of affairs, or even for meaningful participation in decision-making. This makes the task of ruling elites considerably easier than it might be. Besides, many dominant minorities (elites) successfully camouflage their control behind the myth of democracy, the myth that the leaders are really chosen by the membership and are responsive to its will. Ultimately, however, political direction always remains the affair of a minority.

Applied to Italy, Michels' concept had obvious implications. Italy was a loser in the competition among nations, she was a "proletarian" nation, poor and oppressed. Her salvation would only be found in an enlightened ruling elite that would know how to gather up her scattered resources, win the adherence of the masses, and reassert her interests in the international arena.

In Italy, leading syndicalist theorists and publicists like

Paolo Orano, Angelo Olivetti, and Sergio Panunzio demanded, like good Marxists, the industrialization of Italy and the triumph of the bourgeoisie that this would entail. They rejected—again like good Marxists—Italian parliamentary politics because they viewed the Chamber of Deputies (correctly) as an arena and a marketplace where selfish and retrograde groups fought for and sold governmental favors while being, at the same time, unwilling or unable to foster the industrial development of the country. But the syndicalists were "the first Marxist heretics of the twentieth century." They were heretics because they were suspicious of Marx's cloudy metaphysics, they resisted "enslavement to fixed dogmas," and rejected the mechanistic repetition of rigid Marxist formulas. They sought solutions to the very real problems in the world in which they lived. They therefore jettisoned unusable and irrelevant ideas like economic determinism and the inevitability of revolution and laid stress instead on the moral and creative dimensions of social conflict (solidarity, sacrifice) and the psychological foundations of successful struggle (the Will, the Myth).

All these ideas were profoundly attractive to Mussolini, so much so that "the most important influence upon Mussolini's development," in the opinion of his biographer De Felice, "was exercised by revolutionary syndicalism."[2] The young Mussolini was well acquainted with syndicalist ideas. In 1909 he wrote approvingly of Sorel's concept of the Myth—a compelling vision to evoke action and sacrifice from the usually dormant masses—and this key Sorelian notion deeply influenced Mussolini in his turning away from standard mechanistic Marxist determinism. When Mussolini was in jail in 1911 and 1912, he spent most of his time reading Sorel's works. He was to write some years later that "all that I am I owe to Sorel." Mussolini was also familiar with the teachings of Michels; in a review published in *Il popolo* in September 1909, he called Michels "a noted German revolutionary socialist and a great friend of Italy and the Italians." Michels was to live out his life as a university professor in Fascist Italy, full of admiration for Mussolini and loaded with honors by the regime.

LEADER AT FORLÌ

Mussolini returned from the Trentino to the Romagna at the end of September 1909. Shortly after that, the Socialists of the province at Forlì chose him to be their executive officer, with the understanding that he would also found and edit a weekly newspaper. Mussolini accepted and took up these responsibilities in January 1910.

Forlì, capital of the province of the same name (most Italian provinces are small and are named after their chief city), was a good-sized community and the center of a fertile agricultural district. Called Forum Livii by the Romans, Forlì was one of the fortresses captured by Cesare Borgia, the model for Machiavelli's *Prince*. Socialism in Forlì was of little influence when Mussolini assumed office. With only about 1,300 members, the Socialist party was inferior in size and élan to the local Republicans, and was generally moribund. Mussolini immediately began to breathe new life into the organization. He was a whirlwind of initiative, starting up and running a new weekly, reorganizing and revivifying the party structure, sparring with the Republican competition, and preparing the provincial party organization for the approaching national Socialist Congress to be held in Milan. He also undertook (characteristically) the leadership in a movement to build a workers' library in the town.

Forlì was a peripheral city, not a major metropolis, but Mussolini soon became recognized as the semi-official spokesman for socialism in the entire region of the Romagna, a hotbed of social protest from time immemorial. Indeed, from his leadership post in Forlì, Mussolini was to rise swiftly (actually in only a few years) to the first rank of the leadership of Italian socialism. In this regard (if in no other), the career of Mussolini might be compared to that of William Jennings

Bryan, another impecunious lad who became the head of a minority party in a fairly remote region steeped in rural protest, and rose in a short time by endless labors and irresistible oratory to national prominence. (Unlike Bryan, Mussolini would actually arrive one day at the chair of national power.)

Mussolini's rapid rise does invite some reflection. The pattern had established itself before he was even twenty-seven years old. Wherever he went—to Switzerland, to Trent, to Forlì—the young man swiftly advanced to the first rank of his party, and by the time he was thirty he would be the most notable personality in Italian Socialism.

About five-feet-six-inches (Napoleon's height), he had a "fine, massive, compact head . . . the eyes are searching, storing up, and brooding . . . the body is of the short, athletic type . . . there is something altogether tigerlike about him."[3] His capacity for sustained hard work, his intensity and sincerity of manner, his attractive speaking voice, and his growing effectiveness as a writer exerted a kind of magnetism over people, enabling him to exact a deep loyalty from individuals and hold sway over audiences.

Among Mussolini's principal responsibilities was the founding and editing of a weekly for the Forlì Socialist party; the name he chose for it was *La lotta di classe* ("Class Struggle"). The previous weekly put out by the Socialists of the province had collapsed several years before, but in 1910 there were over two hundred Socialist weeklies being published in Italy. Nevertheless, in a very short time Mussolini had turned *La lotta* into a publication that attracted national attention. His hand was involved in every aspect of the paper's production, and at times it seemed as if he actually lived on the premises.

In the pages of *La lotta* Mussolini deplored that the city library, an up-to-date and well-stocked facility, was frequented only by professors and students, while the bulk of the population wasted its time and energy in "taverns, dances, brothels, and sports." The consciousness of the Forlì Socialists clearly had to be raised, dramatically and rapidly. The revolution so longed for was not going to produce itself, it would be produced by men and women who understood what they were about, and why. The revolution was not going to solve mere economic problems, but moral ones; the revolution must produce a higher human type, more disciplined, more productive, more civic-minded, more intellectually oriented. Workers, out of the taproom and into the reading room!

Over and over again Mussolini thundered forth his essential message to the readers of his newspaper. The class struggle was real, and it was war. The bourgeoisie, aware of its interests, organized in its own defense and, employing all the powers of the State, waged daily war upon the interests and even the persons of the masses. Therefore, the proletariat had to reply in kind, with dedication, discipline, and organization, under the leadership of its vanguard elite.

But if the elite did not know where it was going, how could it lead the proletariat to its destiny?

For Mussolini, the birthright Socialist, it was not only the Socialists of Forlì province who were wanting. Italian socialism as a whole was in need of renewal, from top to bottom. The fundamental truth of socialism, the fundamental truth of human existence, as Mussolini insisted over and over again (despite the disquieting doubts generated by his days in Switzerland and the Trentino), was the class struggle. But this truth was slowly fading from the vision of Socialists, especially those of leadership rank. Everywhere Mussolini's gaze turned, he saw the perversion of the party by the "well-fed Socialists of the new era." Too many Socialists were in the party for the wrong reasons, essentially for entertainment or as a hobby or to call attention to themselves or to get themselves elected to the Chamber of Deputies. How could socialism ever accomplish its historic task with such material? And so the editor of *La lotta* addressed himself not only to the task of conversion of outsiders to the Socialist faith but to the purification of the Socialists themselves; his self-imposed task was to stir up the faith of the strong and drive out the weak and the false. "To quantity we prefer quality."

More and more in the pages of *La lotta* the increasingly syndicalist cast of Mussolini's thought became visible. Socialism was not something "scientifically correct but [is] a beacon of hope and change and purification. Socialism," he wrote, "is not a business or a political game or a romantic dream, much less a sport. It is a force for moral elevation, individual and social, it is perhaps the greatest dream which has agitated collective humanity. It is certainly the dearest hope of millions and millions of men who suffer and who want not to vegetate but to live." The triumph of socialism was not "inevitable." It required organization and willpower and fighting spirit. In the last analysis, what was required to build the new civilization was not ballots but barricades.

In later years Mussolini and his Fascists were to be severely criticized in many quarters for their frank acceptance of force as a determinant in human affairs, especially in international disputes. Yet Mussolini's dedication to the efficacy and legitimacy of force was equally frank and sincere when he was a leader of socialism; in fact *he was able to rise to the leadership level of Italian socialism precisely because of his appeal to the legitimacy and necessity of force*. Mussolini had learned the role that force plays in human affairs from the sufferings and teachings of his own father, the blacksmith pamphleteer and self-taught Socialist of Predappio. His experiences in the school at Faenza, among the immigrants in Switzerland, and the Italians of the Trentino had vividly revealed to him the treatment that awaits those who could not or would not defend themselves. Besides, for Mussolini, violence was a means of developing commitment; becoming involved in violence forces one to examine and be sure of one's beliefs.

And in taking this stance he was squarely in the tradition of the *Communist Manifesto* and *Capital*. Phrases like "proletarian revolution" and "dictatorship of the proletariat" do not call to mind a leisurely game of badminton. From the Commune of Paris to the Petrograd coup, from the crushing of Budapest to the invasion of Czechoslovakia and Afghanistan, the disciples of Karl Marx have proclaimed the right of the enlightened to impose the truth on the unenlightened, whatever the numerical proportions between the two groups might be. Mussolini was never more truly the follower of Marx than when he appealed to violence as the ultimate arbiter of history.

THE CRISIS OF SOCIALISM

The death of Friedrich Engels in 1895 brought European socialism to a crisis that had long been brewing. This crisis was not to be resolved until after World War I; its resolution would involve the disintegration of the classical Socialist movement and the rise of both Leninism and fascism.

At the turn of the century European socialism prided itself on its achievements which, in its own view, were principally the elimination of the possibility of major war. Socialist congresses and conventions proclaimed the triumph of Socialist internationalism and the consequent permanency of peace. The theory was that modern war between major European powers would require both the draft and greatly increased productivity to supply the materials of war for the vastly increased armies. But the masses, under the leadership of Socialist parties everywhere, organized into powerful Socialist trade unions in all the major industrial centers of Europe, would refuse induction into the armies and refuse to produce the weapons of war. It was inconceivable that French proletarians would fight and kill German proletarians, that Czech proletarians would spill the blood of Russian proletarians. No, the next time the guns went off they would not be aimed at enemies across the border but at enemies *within* the borders of each country. Workers of the world, unite! The myth of international Socialist solidarity would be the first and most resounding casualty of the First World War.

Underneath the serene surface of Socialist self-congratulation, however, disturbing controversies simmered. The crux of the problem was this: Marx had insisted that the spread of industrialization and the consequent growth of the proletariat would be accompanied inexorably by the deepening of proletarian poverty and alienation ("immiseration"), and the increasing dedication to the proletariat to the revolutionary cause. But this had not in fact happened. The countries that were most industrially advanced—England and Germany—had the largest and best organized but also *least revolutionary* Socialist movements. Those countries where the Socialists were the most revolutionary—Russia and Spain—were also the places where the economy was the most retarded and the Socialist movement was weakest. The most powerful Socialist parties in the world had continued, in effect, to preach revolution but had been practicing accommodation to the established order.

There were, in general, two main schools of thought within socialism as to how this divorce between theory and practice should be resolved. The first called for the accommodation of Socialist vision to reality; the second demanded an imposition of Socialist vision *upon* reality.

The leading advocate of the first course was the German Socialist Eduard Bernstein (1850-1932), whose major work *Evolutionary Socialism*, published in 1898, suggested that Socialists bring their preaching into line with their practice. The age of the great revolutions was over, Marxist mythology had outlived its usefulness, and Socialists should accept what they had in fact become—namely social reformers. Parliament, the press, and the ballot box were the weapons through which to introduce the new and just society.

Among advocates of the second course were V. I. Lenin and Benito Mussolini; they insisted that Socialists should in fact practice what they preached, namely class war and social revolution. Both Lenin and Mussolini had begun to realize that Marx was wrong about the inevitability of the proletarian revolution. The cataclysm would not come about spontaneously, but needed the guidance of a dedicated revolutionary elite. The immediate implications of this position were very important: in classical Marxism the revolution would be supported by the great majority of the people; the subsequent "dictatorship of the proletariat" would be brief and essentially democratic because it would be essentially desired by most people. But in the Leninist-Mussolinian model, the revolution would look more like a coup. It would be carried out by a well-organized and highly disciplined minority. The subsequent dictatorship would therefore be long and severe, not a dictatorship *of* the proletarian *majority* but a dictatorship *for* the proletarian *minority* under the leadership of the revolutionary party. In the nineteenth century, Marxists had substituted "class" for "nation," and in the first years of the twentieth century some of them wanted to substitute "party" for "class." With each substitution, more people would be excluded from the revolutionary category. Once again "truth" would have to be substituted for "numbers," "quality" for "quantity."

SECESSION AT FORLÌ

From the time the Italian Socialist party held its first congress at Genoa in 1892, it had indulged in raucous schisms over dogmatic hairsplitting. This was not the sort of characteristic that would appeal to men like Mussolini. Neither were other trends that began to emerge. To many Socialist leaders the term "Italy" included hardly more than the Po Valley; the center and especially the south of the country, with its impoverished masses of peasants, were conveniently forgotten. Worst of all from a revolutionary viewpoint, the party's reformist wing was exercising increasing influence. The reformists were led by men like Claudio Treves (1869-1933) and Filippo Turati (1857-1932), men of privilege and education, who assumed the leadership of the untutored masses almost as a matter of right. (Mussolini would one day have to fight a saber duel with

Treves, who had challenged him to such a contest, staggering evidence of Treves's "nonproletarian style.")

Mussolini deplored mechanistic reliance on economic determinism to do the revolutionaries' work for them. He instinctively distrusted the reformist leaders because they were middle-class intellectuals, plausible men with soft hands. Most of all he rejected the tendency of the reformers to compromise with the system and wage their class struggle in the halls and committees of the Chamber of Deputies. To Mussolini the whole socio-political system of the nation was thoroughly rotten, and above all the Chamber was "the great circle of corrupters and corrupted."

At the October 1910 Socialist Congress at Milan, the lean and youthful Mussolini had seen the well-fed and middle-aged leaders of the reformists carry all before them; socialism seemed to have lost its way, the salt had lost its savor. No longer could the evidence be denied: there was no real revolutionary party existing in Italy. One would have to be created. The healthy and combative elements of Italian Socialism would have to be gathered together in a rejuvenated and rededicated Socialist party made up not of dull reformist accommodation but of pristine revolutionary faith.

Mussolini set forth these plans at the Forlì provincial congress in April 1911. Of the thirty-eight sections of the provincial party, twenty-seven voted to support Mussolini and his walkout; no section explicitly rejected Mussolini's proposal, such was his personal influence over his fellow Socialists in his native province. Within a few months the new party could claim forty-four sections, not counting women's and youth organizations. Mussolini could boast with truth that there were few if any regions in Italy that had as strongly organized a Socialist party as the secessionists at Forlì.

But the revolutionary secessionist movement did not spread. It remained dominant in, but generally limited to, the province of Forlì. Meanwhile, another national congress of the Socialist party was approaching (this one to be held at Modena); leaders of the party's left wing felt that the absence of Mussolini and his radical cohorts would seriously undermine their position and strengthen the hand of the reformers.

Mussolini now faced a real dilemma. To ask for readmission to the old party would, to say the least, imply failure and submission. To remain outside the party risked isolation, stagnation, and the defeat of the radicals at the Congress of Modena. Mussolini seemed to have gotten himself into an inescapable trap.

At precisely the right moment, however, a *deus ex machina* appeared in the form of Prime Minister Giolitti, who decided to lead his country into a war against the Turks.

THE WAR FOR LIBYA

While Mussolini had been busy building up his organization at Forlì, pressures had also been accumulating in Rome for a war with Turkey. Prime Minister Giovanni Giolitti was no classical imperialist, but he knew the desires of many of his countrymen for war, a good little war to solidify national unity, which was considered by many to be all too brittle. Besides, Britain and France had extended their control over almost the entire southern shore of the Mediterranean. The taking of Turkish Libya would be Italy's last opportunity to avoid being completely closed out of this strategic area, and indeed from the entire colonial sphere. Without Libya, without *someplace*, Italy would find herself completely locked up inside the Mediterranean. Thus the quintessentially skeptical and pacific Giolitti led his country into a war of aggression against a tottering Turkish Empire, a war that would accelerate the slide into world conflict.

The Turks had fallen far since the great days of the conquering sultans, who had built up the vast empire when their neighbors in Europe had been relatively weak. Successive rulers had paid very little attention to economic development in their dominions, but instead relied on ever-increasing taxation to meet ever-increasing expenses. Furthermore, a number of recent sultans had been, quite simply, of very poor leadership material. Things had reached such a state that in the century after Waterloo the shoring up of the collapsing Turkish state became a cardinal point of British foreign policy; propping up the Turkish "sick man of Europe" meant keeping the Russians out of Constantinople and hence out of the Mediterranean, away from Suez. The great Cavour himself had been able to put Italian unification on the agenda of Europe by intervening in the Crimean War between Russia on the one side and Turkey and her British protectors on the other.

Despite some occasional attempts at reform, Turkey's estate continued to deteriorate. Finally, in July 1908, a group of young, German-trained army officers of intellectual bent—the original "Young Turks"—carried out a coup, took control of the realm, and announced a comprehensive program of fundamental reforms in Turkey. The Young Turks were eventually to fail in their enterprise; they could not solve the tangled problems of an empire half in Europe and half in Asia, made up of people speaking many languages and practicing many religions. Things had already been turning somewhat sour under the new regime when the Italians declared war on September 29, 1911.

The formal war was short. Turkish resistance soon collapsed, even though the soon-to-be-great General Mustafa Kemal had been sent to Libya to assist in operations against the Italian invaders. Peace was made within a year, although guerrilla fighting continued deep in the wilds of interior Libya for a long time. Though successful from the military point of view, Italy's brief war was to unleash incalculable consequences, both at home and abroad. The war showed that in spite of the Young Turk revolution, the Ottoman Empire was still in a state of military and political decay. The sick man of Europe was about to expire. Emboldened by events, Greece, Serbia, and other Balkan states started their own war against Turkey the next year, with a second Balkan War in 1913 as well. Thus, if the assassination of Franz Ferdinand at Sarajevo in June 1914 was a firebrand thrown onto the powder, the firebrand had been lit in Libya. Italy's attack on Turkey strained relations with Berlin as well, because Kaiser Wilhelm's government had been devoting a good deal of effort toward building up its Turkish ally, having in effect replaced Britain as the sick man's physician.

MUSSOLINI AND THE LIBYAN WAR

In Italian domestic politics the effects of the Turkish War were to be, in their own way, equally momentous. Giolitti had been working quietly for many years to domesticate the Italian Socialists. His grand design included bringing some of the reformist leaders into his cabinet eventually, thus "transforming" the Socialists from enemies of the Italian establishment into merely the left wing of the parliamentary system. When the war came, several of the reformist leaders inside socialism were of a mind to support Giolitti, men like Treves and Bissolati. There was a similar movement among the syndicalists as well; while some of them looked upon the war in Libya as a dangerous distraction from the Austrian danger, other revolutionary syndicalists approved of the war because the acquisition of Tripoli would be an aid to Italian industrialization and a stimulus to Italian national consciousness.

Benito Mussolini, however, came out vociferously against the war and called it an imperialist outrage. There is nothing surprising in this; as a birthright Socialist and leader of the revolutionary wing, Mussolini could hardly have been expected to support the "ruling class" as they spilled the blood of the masses in order to grab off the riches of foreign lands. But Mussolini's opposition to the war, and especially to Socialist support for it, was based on rather more complicated reasons. Mussolini certainly had no aversion to violence per se (neither had Karl Marx). The problem was that the imperialistic violence of the Italian ruling class was a waste of blood and energy. Italy's rulers were too incompetent, too backward-looking, too selfish to be able to use any gains from foreign wars and overseas empire for the improvement of the whole nation, or for even a substantial part of it. Appeals to patriotism and nationalism were not evil in and of themselves; Mussolini had seen how nationalism could become an instrument of revolution in the Trentino. The problem was that the persons and circles who employed the terms patriotism and nationalism were enemies of the working class through their greed, and indeed enemies of the whole nation through their incompetence. Thus the duty of real Socialists was clear: oppose the wasteful war, oppose the arch-seducer Giolitti. The fact that so-called "reforming" Socialists, men like Treves and his coterie whom Mussolini detested, not only did not actively resist the war but actually spoke of supporting it, proved how deeply they had been corrupted, how alien from the Socialist gospel their attitudes had become. For several years Mussolini had dreamed of taking control of the party away from these milk-and-water Socialists, these nonrevolutionary revolutionaries; fate had finally thrust the necessary instrument into his hands, in the shape of the Turkish War.

But before Mussolini could work out the doom of the reformers, he had his own part to play in the antiwar agitation at Forlì. Because of his incitement of the proletariat to strikes and sabotage, he was arrested and put on trial before the tribunal of Forlì. In an address that made a deep impression upon all his auditors, Mussolini hinted at the campaign he was about to launch against the reformers. "I say to you, gentlemen of the Tribunal, that if you acquit me you will do me a favor, because you will restore me to my work and to society. But if you condemn me you will do me an honor because you find yourselves in the presence not of a malefactor but of a proclaimer of ideas, of an agitator for conscience's sake, of a soldier of a creed which calls for your respect in that it bears within itself the vision of the future and the great strength of the truth." His oratory notwithstanding, Mussolini was found guilty and sentenced to twelve months in prison (his time was later reduced to five months).

IN PRISON AT THE ROCCA

The medieval citadel of the city of Forlì was known as the *Rocca*. It was dark and damp, with no hint of modern plumbing. Even for the austere twenty-eight-year-old Mussolini, veteran of several prisons, these were dour circumstances. But a few rays of sunlight did penetrate the gloom: the traditional good relations between Italian jailers and their prisoners prevailed, and this meant among other things that Mussolini could have a hot dinner brought in from time to time. He received frequent visits from his new wife Rachele. Best of all, perhaps, he had the companionship of Pietro Nenni, who had been arrested along with Mussolini after the antiwar disorders in Forlì province.

Pietro Nenni was eight years younger than Mussolini, his fellow Romagnole. Nenni was a rebel from a very early age, first against the Catholic Church and the harsh discipline of the orphanage where he was raised, later against the whole social system. He joined and later became leader of the Republicans of Forlì. In the Romagna the Republicans were the party of the sharecroppers, while Mussolini's Socialists championed the landless day laborers. Nevertheless, Mussolini and young Nenni became good friends, and stood shoulder to shoulder in many skirmishes with the detested establishment. Nenni would eventually leave Italy after his onetime friend Mussolini became prime minister. He would go to Spain during that nation's civil war to fight for the Communists. Fleeing to France just ahead of the victorious Franco's forces, Nenni eventually fell into the hands of the Germans, and his life was saved only through the timely intervention of his former cellmate in the Rocca. After World War II, Nenni emerged as the head of the Italian Socialists. During the heyday of Stalin, at the cost of serious schisms, Nenni held his Socialists in an ironclad alliance with the Italian Communists. This collaboration was broken only after the Russian invasion of Hungary in 1956 had left absolutely no room for doubt in anyone's mind about the nature of Kremlin-style communism. Always behind the times, always fighting yesterday's battles, always outmaneuvered, first by De Gasperi's Christian Democrats, then by Saragat's Social Democrats, then by Togliatti's Communists, Nenni had reduced his Socialist party to a mere shadow of itself by the time he resigned as leader in 1969.

But who in 1911, in those dim and chilly cells in the Rocca, could have foreseen all these things? Mussolini and Nenni often stayed up together all night talking about books (Mussolini was reading a great deal of Sorel in those days). And although he often complained to Nenni that he missed his family and his violin, Mussolini the alumnus of the jails of three countries (the Swiss Republic, the Empire of Austria and the Kingdom of Italy) was a model prisoner. So he had been in Switzerland and the Trentino, so he would be later in the days following the fall of his regime. Prison had a calming effect on him, helping him focus on what he had to do. Besides reading and discussing books, Mussolini was writing a number of things. During his stay in the Rocca he wrote a brief autobiography, *My Life from 29 July 1883 to 23 November, 1911*. He also produced a very interesting (from the point of view of future events) short work called *John Huss the Truthteller*. This brief book, to be published in 1913, dealt with the Bohemian precursor of the Protestant Reformation in a very sympathetic way. John Huss (1369–1415), a professor at the University of Prague, became caught up in the Great Schism, the scandal of the "three popes" which rocked Europe during the fourteenth century. He was charged by the Austrian rulers of his homeland to abjure certain false teachings; Huss held that, since they were not in fact his teachings, he could not abjure them. So he was burned at the stake. Mussolini, in his study of the unfortunate professor, underlines the importance of a growing national sentiment in Bohemia that underlay much of the theological controversy in which Huss was involved. He suggests to the reader that such sentiment could play an important role in the mobilization of popular protest, a discovery he had made a few years previously during his sojourn in the Trentino.

THE CONGRESS OF REGGIO EMILIA

Mussolini was released from the Rocca in March 1912, and immediately began making preparations for the next national party congress, scheduled to meet in July. The first thing to be done was the restoration of his Forlì organization to full communion with the Socialist party at large, and a reconciliation was quickly accomplished in April. Now all was ready. By becoming increasingly parliamentary and bourgeois, the Socialist party had lost its way in so-called reformism. This must be reversed. The insufferable bourgeois intellectuals who presumed to speak for the proletariat and who would sell the party—*his* party by birthright—to a self-serving Giovanni Giolitti, these so-called reformists must be unmasked and expelled permanently. "The proletariat must be psychologically prepared for the use of liberating violence," thundered the disciple of Sorel from his base at Forlì.

The Socialist Party Congress, destined to be one of the most important affairs of its kind in Italian history, opened on July 7, 1912. The site was the city of Reggio Emilia, center of a fertile valley not far from the town of Gualtieri Emilia where Mussolini had once been schoolmaster. Formerly the seat of the illustrious Este family, rulers of Modena, Reggio Emilia had now achieved another kind of celebrity as the center of the Parmesan cheese industry. Mussolini wanted to rid his party of its reformist wing on ideological grounds; the expulsion of at least some of the reformers would also, not incidentally, increase his weight within the party. At Reggio he would achieve his long-desired aim.

Mussolini settled on Leonida Bissolati as the target of his purge effort. Bissolati (1857-1920), slim, aristocratic, a rather verbose romantic with old-fashioned manners, was the prince of the reformers. He had been the first editor of the party national daily *Avanti!* Giolitti had actually invited Bissolati to join his cabinet, and although the latter refused, he supported Giolitti's war in Libya. (Bissolati would go on to serve in the government of Italy during World War I.) The reformer whom Mussolini most detested on personal grounds was Turati, with his long, flowing beard and delicate ways; Turati had long ago snubbed the young Mussolini as being insufficiently educated. But Bissolati was much more exposed politically, and so it was against him that Mussolini launched his attack. Mussolini had traveled quite a path since his days as a rock carrier and agitator in Switzerland. Before the assembled leadership of Italian socialism he now stood, young, slim, dark eyed, and poorly dressed, a revolutionary who had suffered exile, imprisonment, and expulsion, the implacable evangel of the true revolutionary gospel, the foe of all comfortable compromises, the son of Alessandro and the student of Sorel.

His oratory stunned and swept the delegates. "When the wise surgeon," he roared, "realizes the futility of any other cure and wishes to avoid gangrene, he resorts to amputation." Turning to the arch reformer Bissolati, Mussolini pointed to him dramatically and exclaimed in Latin: *"Ex ore tuo, judico"* (out of thine own mouth I judge thee!)

The Congress was a complete triumph for Mussolini. Bissolati and several others were expelled; Turati and Treves, while remaining within the party, had suffered a rout. There is a rich irony in those events of the Reggio Congress. Mussolini himself was, in less than three years, to embrace Bissolati's teaching that the proletariat must be integrated into the nation, and that Italy must practice imperialism in an imperialistic world so that its people might survive. If Mussolini and his admirers had not caused Bissolati to be cast out in 1912, he himself would almost certainly not have been expelled in 1914 for preaching the very same program. Lenin and Mussolini shared the belief in the inadequacy of mere economic issues for mobilizing revolutionary forces; both embraced elite leadership and the necessity of violence for settling deep conflicts. Lenin himself approved of Mussolini's actions at the Reggio Congress. But the expulsion of the far-seeing Bissolati in 1912 made possible, even necessary, the expulsion of the far-seeing Mussolini two-and-a-half years later. These twin events together deprived Italian socialism of its best leaders, both moderates and revolutionaries. And it was this double decapitation of socialism that in turn made it possible for Mussolini and his blackshirted followers to win a complete victory over the Socialists after World War I.

All this was to come. For Mussolini, the most important immediate results of the Reggio Congress were that he unquestionably emerged as the dominant figure in the party, and that in December 1912, he arrived in Milan to take up his new duties as editor-in-chief of *Avanti!*

MILAN

Milan, heart of the Po valley, was in many ways a unique city. Its center was radial, with streets extending like the spokes of a wheel in all directions. Its cathedral, the proudest achievement of Italian Gothic, was the third largest church in all Europe, held 20,000 worshippers, and had taken 500 years to build. From its top one could easily view the majestic Alps glowering upon the fertile plains of Lombardy. The proud La Scala theater tugged like a magnet at the hearts of opera lovers in all lands. The city had fascinated Stendhal, and some of the finest passages of Alessandro Manzoni's *I promessi sposi* record scenes and events within its walls.

A number of Europe's cities can rival Milan's history in

terms of years, but few can do so in terms of pageantry. Here Saint Ambrose, "the flower of Latin eloquence," had been elected Bishop in A.D. 374, and in this city the holy bishop had converted the great Augustine himself. Here Ludovico Sforza (1452–1508) maintained the most magnificent renaissance court in all Europe. Sforza subsidized Leonardo da Vinci, earned the hatred of Machiavelli, disputed control of Lombardy with France and Spain, and ended his days in a French dungeon. The Habsburg Empire took possession of the city in 1706. Napoleon made Milan the capital of the short-lived Kingdom of Italy in 1805, but it was handed back to the Austrians after Waterloo. The entrance into the city of victorious Victor Emmanuel in 1859, at the side of his ally Napoleon III, was one of the dramatic highpoints of the entire *risorgimento*.

But the Milan of 1912 had much more than rich history and splendid buildings to boast of. It was a vigorous and bustling city of one million inhabitants, the financial and industrial capital of Italy, and for many (especially for Milanese) it was the *moral* capital as well, far superior to bureaucratic, somnolent, clerical, sterile, *southern* Rome. In this humming economic and social hive Mussolini was to make his home for the next decade.

For a while Mussolini lived the life of a bachelor in Milan, although he had been head of a family of his own for quite some time. Rachele Guidi had been outstanding in the neighborhood of Forlì for her hair, which was very light in color. Her family was very poor; her father died when she was seven-and-a-half, and Rachele had to leave school and go to work. Some time after the death of his wife Rosa, Alessandro Mussolini moved into the city of Forlì and opened up a small inn. Nina Guidi, Rachele's widowed mother, soon obtained a job at the establishment, and thus Rachele and Benito met. She went to live with Benito in 1910, without benefit of a marriage ceremony (after all, what does a rising young Socialist militant want with a lot of bourgeois ceremony?). The first of her five children, a daughter Edda, was born in September 1910. She was also to bear Vittorio in 1916, Bruno in 1918, Romano in 1927, and Anna Maria in 1929. When he became editor of *Avanti!*, Mussolini left Rachele and Edda at home in Forlì while he went to live in Milan, about a hundred and seventy kilometers away. After a while, his visits home became less frequent. So one day Rachele packed up Edda and a few belongings, and arrived unannounced on Mussolini's doorstep, informing him firmly of her intention to move in.

Benito Mussolini was never famous for an addiction to material comforts, and life in the little apartment was not luxurious. The Mussolinis had a bed, Edda's crib, books and newspapers, and a kitchen table. Mussolini spent a great deal of time at that kitchen table, furiously producing articles and book reviews for *Avanti!* and shouting at Edda for making so much racket. Little by little they acquired some decent furniture; Mussolini wanted to buy what Rachele said she needed all at once, on credit, but Rachele would not hear of it. Cash on the barrelhead, that was her fundamental principle of domestic economy. At first the countrywoman Rachele did not like Milan; it seemed to be all confusion and rushing and noise. People were not very friendly, they had no time for anybody or anything. But as time passed she came to know the city's narrow lanes and broad avenues, and grew accustomed to the urban pace. She discovered special markets where food prices were low, watched her husband advance in Socialist prominence, and went to an occasional show with Mussolini on his press pass. In 1915, with the husband going off to the war, the Mussolinis went through a civil marriage ceremony (to please Rachele they finally had a church wedding in 1925). During 1923, when Mussolini lived in Rome as Prime Minister (who knew for how long?) he would call his wife on the telephone at their Milanese apartment every night. In one of his autobiographies Mussolini described Rachele as a "wise and excellent woman" of patience and devotion.

In fact, patient she would have to be, because her husband was not only prominent, he was also promiscuous. How could it have been otherwise? The mores of Mussolini's society permitted, even expected, married men to enter into extramarital relationships. The lonely little boy of remote Predappio, the isolated outcast of the Faenza school had grown up into a militant Socialist, the scowling foe of all canting priests and hypocritical bourgeois, and he found that he was attractive to many different women, peasant or sophisticated, Italian or foreign.

One of these women was Ida Dalser. Mussolini probably first encountered her in Trent. They ran into each other again in Milan, in late 1913 or early 1914. Ida was the proprietress of her own beauty parlor, and Mussolini undertook to set her up in an apartment. One day, indignant over Mussolini's constant refusals to marry her, she marched to his office, and stood under the windows of *Avanti!* shouting invective. Some who claim to have been eyewitnesses report that Mussolini became enraged, grabbed a pistol from somebody, and ran down the steps determined to put an end to both Ida and her abuse. At the last moment he was dissuaded from his impetuous course by some fellow journalists; even in Italy, shooting one's mistress could lead to tiresome legal complications. The affair went on. In 1915 Ida bore a son whom she called Benito. Mussolini recognized the child as his own and made provision for his support, leaving the details to his brother Arnaldo. Ida kept up a barrage of letters to Mussolini demanding marriage. Finally, she (an Austrian subject) was interned in 1917 as an enemy alien; possibly Mussolini had grown tired of reading her repetitious letters and ungallantly pointed out Ida's nationality to the authorities. After the war she went back to Trent (now an Italian city), but the letters began again. Eventually Ida wound up in a mental institution where she spent several years; she died in 1935. As to what happened to her son Benito, the record is not clear. He probably died like his mother in an insane asylum in 1943, although there are those who believe that Benito Dalser was killed in a naval encounter during the Second World War.

Then there was Leda Rafanelli. She was among other things a Moslem and a novelist, and in 1946 published a book in Milan called *A Woman and Mussolini.* Leda first met Mussolini in Milan in March 1913. She was very impressed with him, and subsequently wrote a highly flattering article about him that appeared in an anarchist weekly. She invited Mussolini to her apartment and he accepted. Leda was taken by surprise, however, when the man who showed up at her door was not the fiery revolutionary but a rather nervous and shy newspaperman in a dark suit with a bowler hat in his perspiring hand. "We shall read Nietzsche and the Koran together," Leda told him.

Leda wore oriental perfumes and she liked to make oriental coffee for Mussolini. The novel-writing Moslem was deeply interested in spiritual and transcendental ideas, which could not possibly have been of less concern to her nervous newspaperman. Nor would Mussolini let Leda read his palm, although (or perhaps because) she assured him that she was very skilled at this art. The relationship tapered off after a while; after all, Mussolini was simultaneously seeing not only Leda but also Ida Dalser and Margherita Sarfatti (not to mention his patient wife Rachele). Besides, Leda became disenchanted with Mussolini once he began advocating Italian intervention in the war; Leda found war not to be transcendental.

Angelica Balabanoff, another of Mussolini's female friends, had been born to privilege in Russia. As a young girl, she embraced revolutionary opinions and left home at the age of seventeen to take up a life of voluntary exile. She studied and traveled for a while in Germany and Belgium. Like many Russian revolutionaries, including her friend Lenin, she turned up in Switzerland to bask in the civil liberties of the despised bourgeoisie. She spoke very good Italian and spent a lot of time evangelizing the Italian immigrants there. She and Mussolini first met in Zurich in March 1904. Short, blond, and hunchbacked, Angelica was older than Mussolini and in a way she took charge of him, lending him books and helping him improve his German. Passionately devoted to the teachings of Karl Marx, Angelica had other passions as well; she entered into liaisons with an extraordinarily large number of Italian Socialists. Margherita Sarfatti, whose testimony in this matter cannot be called completely disinterested, states that Angelica had no sense of the beautiful and was not overly fastidious about personal cleanliness. Angelica became, along with Mussolini, a member of the executive committee of the Italian Socialist Party in July 1912, following the watershed Congress of Reggio Emilia. She was also an assistant editor of *Avanti!* Her relationship with Mussolini was utterly shattered when he embraced interventionism at the end of 1914. Shocked that he could dare change his mind on anything so important as the meaning of the war without consulting her, humiliated that her judgment had been betrayed and her influence publicly repudiated, Angelica became from that time forward Mussolini's most vitriolic critic. Her memoirs, published in Berlin in 1927, sizzle with denunciation of the former comrade who had scorned her.

Certainly the most important and lasting relationship that Mussolini developed with another woman in his Milanese days was the one with Margherita Sarfatti. Margherita was beautiful, blond, and Jewish. The daughter of a Socialist professor at the University of Venice, she was the wife of a prominent lawyer. Her husband would help clear Mussolini in 1915 of charges that he had embraced the interventionist position because he had been bought by "French gold." In her valuable biography of Mussolini she describes the editor of *Avanti!* as brave, youthful, modest, and compelling. She asked him if she could help out at the newspaper. Since she was knowledgeable about modern painting, Mussolini found her a job as an art editor. She taught him to be neater in his appearance (it was under her tutelage that Mussolini took to wearing spats). She also taught him to have some appreciation for literature and modern art; like so many others, she attested that he was a very apt pupil. After he came to power, Mussolini found Margherita another position, this time as editor of *Gerarchia* ("Hierarchy"), the philosophical journal published monthly by the Fascist party. In 1924, Margherita became a widow; after that, Mussolini would on occasion spend the night at her home. Rachele found out about one of these nocturnal visitations and she went back to Forlì very upset, but soon enough she calmed down and returned to her wayward husband. Mussolini learned to confide in Margherita Sarfatti as he could in no man since the death of his brother Arnaldo, and his friendship with her lasted for twenty years.

THE EDITOR OF *AVANTI!*

By December 1912, twenty-nine year old Mussolini had become a member of the inner leadership circle of the Socialist party, and in a very special way. Milan was the heart and vanguard of the industrial revolution in Italy, *Avanti!* was the banner and symbol of Milanese socialism, and Mussolini was the editor and dynamo of *Avanti!* This was a far cry—a cry of delight—from being editor of the weekly *Lotta di classe.*

Mussolini was the first editor of *Avanti!*, indeed the first front-rank Socialist leader, who was himself the son of a Socialist. Along with this distinction of a true working-class background, Mussolini brought to the Milanese daily the passion that had breathed life into the *Lotta* at Forlì. Margherita Sarfatti, his intimate collaborator, writes that when she first came to see Mussolini in his offices at *Avanti!* he reminded her of Savonarola, so tireless and determined was he to cleanse and rejuvenate his party. During his two years as editor, the circulation of the paper rose from 28,000 to close to 100,000. Mussolini opened the columns of *Avanti!* to distinguished syndicalist spokesmen like Sergio Panunzio, and he also founded a small theoretical weekly, the *Utopia.* He would remain essentially a journalist all the rest of his life, with a journalist's passion to read newspapers as well as write them. Like most journalists, he acquired a lifelong proclivity to equate newsprint with reality; if it was in the headlines it must be true. His output of editorials, articles, and reviews was prodigious, and his days and nights were filled with activity and satisfaction. His collected works, consisting in no small part of his writings while in charge of *Avanti!*, would eventually fill forty volumes.

In the steady stream of expository and polemical articles flowing from his pen, Mussolini quoted the writings and appealed to the authority of Karl Marx, to whom Mussolini liked to refer as "the father and teacher" and "the immortal teacher." Two aspects of Mussolini's Marxist faith stand out most sharply: a passionate dedication to the class war and an unshakable belief in the final, cataclysmic march to power of the proletariat under its natural leaders. And it is in these two beliefs that Mussolini's shattering criticisms of his party originated.

All over Europe, in the eyes of the editor of *Avanti!*, the Socialist parties had become flabby and complacent, and that is where the trouble lay. Most contemporary Socialists preferred to give a literal and dogmatic interpretation to Marx's teachings, so that for them the revolution of the oppressed *had* to happen, and therefore European Socialists had little more to do than deliver heroic declamations in congresses and cafés. The practical effect of this dogmatic determinism was that socialism everywhere was slipping and sliding toward reformism, and mere seeking after incremental improvements in the system, and this of course amounted to *acceptance of and a strengthening of the hated system*. This was a grave error; the proletariat had no real friends or allies in the bourgeois world: "We are alone!" Besides, good student of Sorel that he was, Mussolini viewed the proletariat not merely as an oppressed class, but as the instrument through which degenerate bourgeois society, Italy included, would be swept away and a whole new edifice built upon the ruins. Reformism, accommodation, all these boiled down to the *preservation* of the system, the preservation of backward and poverty-stricken Italy, and the concomitant corruption of the Socialists. "We want," Mussolini proclaimed, "to force the Socialists to be Socialists and the bourgeois to be bourgeois." Time and again, in the pages of *Avanti!* and in *Utopia*, Mussolini demanded that Italian and European socialism turn again in the direction of revolution.

History would not unfold nor would the revolution happen by themselves. An elite body of carefully selected leaders must *make* it all happen. "The class struggle is fundamentally a struggle between minorities," he declared. The proletariat needed to be rallied by dedicated men who had proven their abilities. The supremacy of the leadership over the party must be complemented by the supremacy of the party over allied organizations such as trade unions. The principle of leadership was essential and decisive, because "the masses are not dynamic but static." In a few years, of course, this set of propositions would be universally known as "Leninism," but they formed the heart of Mussolini's political thought both as a Socialist and as a Fascist.

Mussolini accepted the consequences of his teachings. *Avanti!* published ferocious editorials in the spring of 1914 against the killing of some peasants by royal troops in the south. Mussolini was put on trial for sedition. He not only accepted the responsibility, he demanded it. "All the thunderbolts should fall on my head alone," was his defiant statement to the courts. (He would similarly take upon himself total responsibility for events in another context in January 1925.) "I will say to you that you should acquit us, not because we have not committed the offense, but because we *have* committed it, and because we promise to commit it again!" He was acquitted.

In the fall of 1913, the busy editor stood in the national elections as Socialist candidate for parliament at Forlì. In his view, elections were by no stretch of the imagination the means by which the proletariat could solve its problems. Rather, election campaigns were a means of passing judgment on the bourgeoisie and measuring the progress of Socialist strength. Mussolini was defeated by the Republican candidate in a heavily Republican area. In the country as a whole, only fifty-three Socialists were elected to a Chamber of Deputies of over five hundred. But the Socialist party did make gains, and the elections were generally viewed as signaling the approval of the working class and its sympathizers for Mussolini's policy of intransigence toward the system.

The vigorous young editor of *Avanti!* attracted attention and admirers everywhere. The School of Socialist Culture in Milan invited Mussolini to give a series of lectures on the meaning of socialism. In February 1914 in Florence, he delivered an address on "The Historical Value of Socialism" that was favorably commented upon by such intellectual lights of the bourgeoisie as Giuseppe Prezzolini and Gaetano Salvemini. Salvemini would soon enough become one of Mussolini's most embittered critics, but in May 1914 he wrote that "Benito Mussolini has been the man who was necessary and irreplaceable for expressing and representing in this historic moment in our nation the need for a sincerely revolutionary movement."[3] Then the Socialist Congress at Ancona that spring expelled, at Mussolini's behest, all who would not sever their connections with the Masonic order. One could not serve two masters; besides, Masonry was inherently bourgeois. This Congress confirmed Mussolini's leadership, not only of the dominant revolutionary wing but of Italian socialism as a whole.

By the summer of 1914 Mussolini had made it clear that he found serious imperfections in Italian Socialism. Many in his party, certainly within the dominant revolutionary wing, agreed with him. In retrospect it is easy to see that Mussolini was heading for heresy, and to see also how deeply and how early its seeds had been planted within him. But this was obvious neither to Mussolini nor to his Socialist confrères at the time. Quite the opposite: they judged him, and rightly, to be a sincere, knowledgeable, and effective Socialist militant.[4]

After Mussolini's break with socialism it became fashionable in some circles, especially Marxist ones, to charge (without ever apparently realizing the implications for Italian socialism of these charges) that Mussolini had never been a "real" Socialist, that this man who at a very young age had risen to the highest ranks of his party had never been anything more than a self-serving rhetorician and poseur.

Whether or not Mussolini was "really" a true or a false Socialist, what is indisputable is that he was an *important* and an *influential* one. By the summer of 1914, the thirty-one year old son of a Romagnole blacksmith sat on the party's national directorate, edited the party's national organ and was, according to Denis Mack Smith, a most distinguished British historian of modern Italy, Italian socialism's "most outstanding personality." Yet within a few short months of his triumph at the Ancona Congress, Mussolini would resign his editorship and suffer excommunication by the party in which he had spent his entire life. What brought about Mussolini's rupture with socialism was not a dispute over office or doctrine or editorial policy or pride of place. It was in fact nothing less than a world war. Confronted with the guns of August, the Socialist party would mechanically erect a sterile neutralism into a party dogma. Mussolini would attempt to lead his comrades out of this politically impossible position, but this time they failed to follow him. The costs of their failure were to be enormous.

·IV·

A WORLD WAR

"Struggle is the origin of all things."

"Today the war. Tomorrow the revolution."

Benito Mussolini

RED WEEK

In June 1914, united Italy experienced the most serious insurrection in its history, the famous "Red Week." It began with an antidraft demonstration in Ancona, upon which the police opened fire. A general strike was proclaimed and the violence spread rapidly. Railroad tracks were torn up and telegraph wires were cut down. In several north central provinces insurgents disarmed or drove out the military police and regular army garrisons. In the Romagna the republic was proclaimed, and the red flag flew from the city hall in Bologna.

This was the supreme test of whether the fury of the masses could make a revolution. It failed. The proletariat could temporarily rock the established order, but could not pull it down. Fiery slogans, incendiary gestures, and unrestrained passions could not make up for indiscipline, cloudy thinking, and lack of coordination. Most crucial factor of all, the great bulk of the army remained loyal to the throne, and through this instrument order was gradually restored in all the disaffected areas. The young editor of *Avanti!*, who had been skeptical of this undisciplined revolt's prospects from the beginning, observed all these events and drew from them an important conclusion: an unleashed mob could not make the revolution so long as the state was supported by an intact and loyal army.

These upheavals had not yet subsided when the Austrian attack on Serbia produced the long-dreaded European war.

Archduke Franz Ferdinand was fifty-one years old in 1914. He was the grandnephew of the old Emperor Franz Joseph, whom in the normal course of events he would succeed as ruler of the Habsburg Empire. Franz Ferdinand held what were regarded in certain circles as enlightened ideas, ideas that offended and frightened powerful persons and groups within the Empire. He wanted to transform the Dual Monarchy (the partnership between the Austro-Germans on one hand and the Hungarians on the other) into a triple monarchy (admitting the large Slavic component to a real share of power). This angered the Empire's Germanic elements. It also gravely displeased the Serbian government; Serbia did not want Austria-Hungary to solve the problem of its dissatisfied Slavic elements, but to be destroyed by it. Franz Ferdinand was also in favor of universal suffrage, which outraged the Hungarian landowning aristocracy. Clearly, the coming to the throne of Franz Ferdinand would upset many plans and unleash unpredictable forces.

In June 1914, the Archduke traveled with his morganatic Czech wife on a goodwill tour of the newly annexed south Slav province of Bosnia (today part of Yugoslavia). There he and his wife, while riding in an open carriage in the streets of Sarajevo, were shot dead by a Serbian student. This savage act was the break in the dike separating Europe from a sea of blood. Within a few weeks Germany and Austria-Hungary were at war with France, Russia, and Great Britain.

The outbreak of the war came for many reasons. The Serbs had aspirations to unite all the southern Slavic peoples into a Greater Serbian state. Such a regroupment would require stripping Austria-Hungary of her large Slavic territories, that is, it would require the disintegration of the Habsburg Empire. (That is why the Serbs feared the accession to the throne of Franz Ferdinand, who sought to reconcile Vienna's Slavic subjects.) The Habsburg government had for many years been determined to put an end to this threat by humiliating and then swallowing insolent Serbia. The French, for their part, had long thirsted to reconquer Alsace-Lorraine, torn from them by Bismarck after the Franco-Prussian War of 1870. Germany's Kaiser Wilhelm expressed his irresponsibility and megalomania most dangerously in his jealous determination to build a navy equal to that of Great Britain; the British looked upon these oft-expressed plans as a mortal challenge to the very survival of their nation's independence. The Russians, as always, pressed greedily upon Constantinople and the Balkans.

Undergirding all these perilous desires was one fundamental condition: an international system based upon anarchy and the survival of the strongest. These circumstances drove all the major European powers into a search for security that expressed itself in a massive buildup of armaments, a keen competition for colonial territories in Asia and Africa, and the construction of rival alliance systems. In German eyes, the worst possible scenario would be simultaneous war with her neighbors France and Russia. Her search for security against this dreaded double confrontation drove Germany to build up her armed forces to the point where they would be adequate to deal with any contingency. This, of course, meant that Germany became far stronger than either France *alone* or Russia *alone*. Thus France and Russia, in self-defense, came together in an iron-clad alliance that brought about the very encirclement that Germany so feared. To break out of this mortal encirclement, the German general staff had for a generation been perfecting its plan—the famous Schlieffen Plan—to deliver one great knockout blow against France in the first days of the war.

Thus, when Austria attacked Serbia, Russia, self-appointed

protector of the Slavic peoples, moved to attack Austria. Germany was long committed to aiding Austria, while France dared not stand aside and see her Russian ally humiliated by Germany. That is why the murder of an Austrian Archduke in distant Bosnia meant that huge German armies must smash through little Belgium.

A watershed in Western development had been reached, the time had finally arrived to settle accounts for the failure of Napoleon to unify Europe, for a hundred years of balance-of-power politics. The lights were going out. The war would devour a whole generation of young men, undermine Western civilization's self-confidence forever, signal the end of Europe's world hegemony, stimulate the uprising of the colored peoples, establish the Bolsheviks in power, set the stage for Hitler, and begin the process that culminated in Russian and American domination of Europe itself.

This war would also open up the road for a march on Rome.

Italy was bound to Austria and Germany by the Triple Alliance. Yet the course of action of the Vienna government, neither informing her Italian ally of her plans against Serbia, nor offering her any compensation, violated the letter of the Alliance, and the spirit had long ceased to exist. Italy declared her neutrality.

For many years, influential opinion in Italy had been openly critical of the Triple Alliance. Italian statesmen had made it clear from the beginning that the treaty would never be permitted to entangle them in a war with Great Britain. Then, Italy had long been treated by Berlin and Vienna as less than an equal partner. Finally, although the Triple Alliance was explicitly defensive, Austria was clearly committing aggression against Serbia, as Germany was to do so much more shatteringly against Belgium. Hence Italy's declaration of neutrality was logical and expected; so was her declaration of war upon Austria the following May. In spite of all these considerations, in spite of Italy's entrance into war on the Allied side being clearly in her interest and theirs, it has long been the style to paint Italy's actions in those months between August 1914 and May 1915 as stemming entirely from Machiavellian calculation and cynical opportunism. In a similar manner (and perhaps for similar reasons), the profound metamorphosis in Mussolini's political thinking during those fateful and exciting months is often sweepingly dismissed as the acrobatics of a congenital opportunist. For some, no price is too high to pay in order to sustain the thesis that "Mussolini was always wrong"; nothing suggests this more than the conventional "explanations" of why Mussolini changed his views on the issue of neutrality-versus-intervention.

Like most other Italian Socialists, in the first days of the war Mussolini supported Italian neutrality, for an immediate entrance into the war would have, according to the terms of the Triple Alliance, placed Italy at the side of the Germanic powers, an outcome repugnant to perhaps every single Italian Socialist in 1914. Soon, however, Mussolini (again like many another in his party) began to feel very uneasy in this neutralist position. Rallying under the slogan of "Defense of the Nation," every major Socialist party in Europe was backing the war efforts of its own government (especially in Germany). To support Italian neutrality meant in effect to support German militarism and the survival of Austria-Hungary. To be neutral meant lining up on the same side not only with the Vatican, but also with the proper and parliamentary wing of the Socialist party that Mussolini so thoroughly disliked. It meant tacitly accepting the leadership of Giolitti, the unchallenged chieftain of bourgeois neutralists, and giving yet another new lease on life to his system of parliamentary deals and southern patronage. Mussolini could not resist the logic of the situation: "If the bourgeoisie is neutralist, then the socialist proletariat should be interventionist."[1] Italy, shoulder to shoulder with the democratic Western allies, should be fighting a "revolutionary war" against the combined forces of militarist reaction; after the war, the armed populace could demand vast concessions for their sacrifices and would get their demands or make revolution at home.

MUSSOLINI AND THE WAR

The interventionist forces were growing in strength every week. Their phalanx already contained the irredentists, who yearned to unite the "unredeemed" territories of Trent and Trieste to the motherland and so fulfill at long last the noble dream of the *risorgimento.* Most syndicalists and republicans, and a growing number of Socialists, also joined the chorus for entry into the war. They received the powerful support of the most prestigious of all establishment organs, Milan's daily *Corriere della sera* (*Evening Courier*), the proudest achievement of Italian journalism and the most influential newspaper in the country. Prime Minister Antonio Salandra and Foreign Minister Sydney Sonnino were both pro-British (indeed the latter was half-English), and were clearly maneuvering to take Italy into the war on the Allied side. When that happened, for the Socialist party to pursue a policy of "neither cooperation nor sabotage" would be disastrous. The party would isolate itself from the majority of the nation, and even from other "left-wing" forces, not only at home but in all of Europe. Mussolini analyzed the impossibility of the Socialist party's "revolutionary defeatism": either Italy would win the war, thus exposing the Socialist defeatists to severe reprisals from a triumphant regime; or the regime, beaten at the front, would be overturned by the defeatists. If that happened, then the revolutionaries placed in power would have to (a) make a Carthaginian peace with the victorious enemy at the gates, or (b) wage war themselves against the enemy, only now with a new, untrained, and unequipped revolutionary army. (In fact, a few years later the Bolsheviks found themselves forced to adopt *both* of these calamitous courses: first Brest-Litovsk, then defeat by the Polish army.)

It was not cold political logic alone that was carrying Mussolini along his fateful path. His earlier experience in Switzerland and the Trentino had left a bitter aftertaste of Teutonic disdain in his mouth, while the nationalist implications and premises of much of the syndicalist writing to which he was so attracted had been working subtle changes in his thinking. These elements came vigorously boiling to the surface in August 1914, when he wrote editorials for *Avanti!* severely critical of the German invasion of neutral Belgium. His intense inner struggle—loyalty to the Socialist party and considerations about his future career within it on one side, as against the inescapable logic of events and the residue of resentments on the other—approached a crisis point during the month of September. Finally, on October 18, 1914, Mussolini electrified the party and the whole nation. In a ringing editorial in *Avanti!* entitled "From Absolute Neutrality to Active Neutrality," Mussolini sought to lead his party away from dogmatism and closer to a realist assessment of events. Deftly combining standard Socialist analysis with traditional Italian national aspiration, Mussolini identified the Austro-Hungarian Empire as not only the oppressor of the Italian population of Trent but also as the true bulwark of reaction in Europe! He pointed out to his readers that the Belgian, French, and German Socialist parties had already accepted the necessity of acknowledging the reality of the Nation, and the proletariat's inextricable involvement with it. For the Italian proletariat to be indifferent to the fate of their country would be the zenith of folly for which the price would be extremely high. "Reality," he insisted, "is moving with an accelerated rhythm. We have the most singular privilege of living in the most tragic hour of the history of the world. Do we, as human beings and as Socialists, want to be inert spectators of this tremendous drama? Or do we want to be at least in some way the protagonists? Socialists of Italy, remember that sometimes the letter of the law can kill the spirit. Let us not save the letter of the party if that means killing the spirit of Socialism." It was the supreme gamble of Mussolini's life thus far, and it failed. Two days after Mussolini's editorial, the Directorate of the Socialist Party issued a manifesto rejecting "the war which the bourgeoisie in every country has prepared for by subtly corrupting public opinion, saturating it with threats from imaginary dangers." The Directorate went on to condemn the German and French Socialist parties for supporting the war efforts of their respective countries, and praising the Russian Bolsheviks for their antinational intransigence. Even though his position had won the support of men like Antonio Gramsci (who would later become the founder and patron saint of the Communist party of Italy) Mussolini had been publicly rebuked by the leadership of the party he had done so much to shape. Shortly thereafter he resigned the editorship of *Avanti!*, probably the most bitter renunciation he ever had to make in his entire life. But his pen would not be stilled. On November 15, 1914, there appeared the first edition of the brand new *Il popolo d'Italia*, Mussolini's own newspaper, with which he intended to further his views among the proletariat. In the turbulent history of Italian Socialism there were venerable precedents for this bold plan, designed to appeal to the party members over the heads of their leaders, but in that impassioned autumn of 1914 many Socialist leaders were completely outraged by Mussolini's tactics and were ready to accuse and convict him of treason against his party.

The new journal was subtitled "A Socialist Daily"; its masthead also carried two quotations, one from the revolutionary Louis Blanqui—"He who has steel has bread"—and another from Napoleon—"A revolution is an idea which has found bayonets." The paper did well, reaching a circulation of 80,000 (high for those days) in a few months. *Il popolo d'Italia* clearly benefited from subsidies from Italian interventionists, from the French and Belgian Socialist parties, and perhaps also from the French Embassy in Rome. This financial support has given rise to that most often-reiterated and tenaciously held accusation against Mussolini, that he was a sellout; that is, that he abandoned his lifelong membership and influential position in the party of his father in order to become the publisher of his own newspaper.

But the facts do not support this accusation. Mussolini was already boss of *Avanti!*, one of the country's principal newspapers, for which he worked very hard and the paper's circulation was steadily increasing. Only thirty-one, he was the coming man of Italian Socialism. Would Mussolini—*especially* if he were as coldly calculating as his enemies alleged—throw all this over just to start up a fledgling paper based on the uncertain support of a foreign government? As Ernst Nolte has observed, "To a socialist [and to a newspaperman like Mussolini] the editorship of *Avanti!* was worth more than the bourgeois prime ministership."[2] Besides, Mussolini lost his editorship of *Avanti!* and was expelled from the party only after being repeatedly warned to bridle his interventionist views. Surely all this is strange behavior for an opportunist of no principles! Undoubtedly Paris was worth a Mass, but would most people consider the combined hostility of Giovanni Giolitti, the Roman Catholic Church, the Socialist Party and the German Embassy to be outweighed by a printing press?

What about money? Was Mussolini bought by "French gold"? Certainly it is a strange tale to hear: a lifelong Socialist and son of a Socialist, indeed a leading figure in one of Europe's most revolutionary Socialist parties, accused of selling out for mere money, especially since Mussolini had all his life been notoriously careless about money, never seeming to have two lire in his pocket and hardly ever buying even a little present for his mistresses. In later years, his life-style as dictator would be simple, even austere. Once a businessman, seeking the hand of his daughter Edda, asked what her dowry would be. The dictator of fascism replied with ferocity: "No dowry! She has nothing and neither do I!" Gaudens Megaro, a severe critic of Mussolini, concluded that "after an extensive study of all the available evidence it seems clear to me that venality was not the motivating force in causing Mussolini's abandonment of the socialist cause."

Faced with these complexities, critics of Mussolini's move to interventionism have resorted to the theory that Mussolini had never actually been a "real" Socialist at all, as his expulsion from the party proved. Apparently no one who has once gazed upon the Marxian tabernacle could ever sincerely question the infallibility of the directorate of the Socialist party. By turning away from the Socialist path, Mussolini showed himself not merely wrong but *wicked*, and nothing a wicked man says can ever have any truth or value. That was the essential position of most of his Socialist critics then, and thus it remains to this day. (And if, indeed, as his detractors claim, Mussolini was nothing but a backsliding opportunist, a poseur, a false Marxist, a snake in the proletarian grass, what does this tell us about the political and psychological acumen of the Socialist party that elected him to high posts, expelled eminent leaders at his behest, and entrusted him with command of its national daily?)

Perhaps the true explanation of his course is the most obvious one. Mussolini had imposed his views on the party before, at the Reggio Congress of 1912; undoubtedly he thought he could do it again in 1914, especially since the explosion of events had already convinced Socialists all over Europe that neutralism and "revolutionary defeatism" were untenable. And it was the very best Marxism to expect a social revolution after the war. Having temporarily failed in his objective, in October 1914, to turn the Socialist party around, Mussolini was willing to take the consequences rather than swallow his beliefs. He even fought duels in those impassioned days with those who questioned his sincerity. We do not have to be more cynical than Mussolini was supposed to be. All recognize that the Great War changed an entire world; why could it not have changed the mind of one Romagnole politician?*

*This is the position of Herman Finer in his classic *Mussolini's Italy*.

Teutonic militarism." They endorsed no other action of the Italian monarchy that might seek to advance its own interests as opposed to those principles enunciated in the Declaration, nor would they support either throne or cabinet in any "base opportunism" or "underhanded and usurious" policies. Soon after the Declaration was issued, Italy did in fact declare war upon Austria-Hungary (May 1915). In August, the editor of *Il popolo d'Italia* was drafted and assigned to the eleventh Bersaglieri Regiment. This was to be his second period of service in the Italian army, in which he would spend the next seventeen months, six of them at the front.

Mussolini the soldier kept a diary. In it he recorded grim descriptions of life at the front and the sufferings endured by the men: the trenches eternally muddy from rain, the ground eternally slippery from stagnant pools of water and human blood; clothing always filthy and shoes always wet; food that was never on time and was usually cold or mixed with dirt when it finally arrived; the inescapable lice, the soul-shriveling cold; the ever-present danger of disease from improperly treated wounds and the general filth; the unexpected discovery of headless bodies; the nights made sleepless by enemy fire and a sky filled with eerie lights; the all-pervading, mind-numbing noise and stench of war.

But there was a lot more to Mussolini's war than this. The cold air, simple food, and tough regimen of the Italian Alpine army slowly turned the thin, feverish, and pale young newspaperman from Milan into a robust and self-confident figure with a broad chest, thick neck, and good muscles (which he would henceforth always be ready to exhibit).

As a soldier in the 11th Regiment of the Bersaglieri during World War I

And there was the sad, touching, almost boyish camaraderie of war. "I have spent," reads one entry in his diary, "an afternoon full of happiness and true brotherhood with young men from Calabria and Sicily who had never been away from their sunny lands before and now sit amid freezing water on the top of Europe." He joyfully records a sad, cold, and lonely Christmas night suddenly transformed and refulgent when a comrade unexpectedly popped into the gun position with a glorious roast chicken. Mussolini, the lonely boy of Predappio, reflected upon these experiences. "Great friendships are not perfected on school benches, nor in political assemblies. Only in front of the magnitude and suggestiveness of danger, only after having lived together in the anxieties and torments of war, can one weigh the soundness of a friendship or measure in advance how long it is destined to go on."

Mussolini had been, and clearly would be again, an important figure in Italian political life. His support of the war was notorious and indeed had cost him a great deal. Here surely was a man who for many reasons should have been made an officer. But he was not. The General Staff had decided that, war supporter or no, Mussolini's political antecedents—he had been, after all, the leading revolutionary Socialist in the country for years—disqualified him from being an officer. This decision carried the approval of Prime Minister Salandra himself. Nevertheless, Mussolini was a good soldier. He was promoted to corporal in February 1916 and eventually was made a sergeant. (He took care to have a romantic photograph of himself taken in his noncommissioned splendor.) Then in February 1917, the explosion of a howitzer killed several men in his vicinity and severely wounded Mussolini. He spent several weeks convalescing in a military hospital. The Italian nation was no longer just an abstraction to be appealed to, a slogan for mobilizing men to action; it was now literally something for which he had shed his own blood. One day the hospital received a visit from Victor Emmanuel. He came to Mussolini's bed and the two of them, the head of the ancient House of Savoy and the ex-revolutionary antimonarchist, exchanged wartime generalities. Mussolini's period of military service was now at an end and he would return to the equally bitter battle on the political front.

During Mussolini's months at the front, the Socialist party continued with its plodding adherence to a policy of defeatism, really no policy at all. While peasant conscripts froze and bled on the Alpine front, while patriots of all degrees alternately wept or exulted at the war bulletins, Italian Socialists stood sullenly aside. The isolation of the Socialists had never been greater, their morale lower, and their confusion higher. This was primarily the result of having cast out Mussolini. Within eight years of his expulsion by his Socialist comrades, Mussolini would triumphantly march into Rome. In contrast, by rejecting him and his plan for inserting the proletarian mass into the national mainstream, the Socialists had sealed their doom. They would never again have the chance to rule Italy.

In the early stages of the war, the all-out support rendered to the German militarists by the German Socialist party, Europe's wealthiest and best-organized ("We are threatened by the horror of enemy invasion," said a spokesman of the German Social Democratic party as their armies prepared to march into little Belgium), confirmed him in his new belief that Socialist internationalism had been little more than an instrument of German hegemony. It followed that the Socialists of Italy, in opposing the Italian war effort, were directly serving the interests of the Kaiser and his warloads. By 1917 he had serious accusations to bring against his former Socialist comrades in another country, the Bolsheviks, who had worked to undermine the morale of the Russian army and had seen their aims fulfilled when hundreds of thousands of Russian troops, seduced by the Leninist promise of "bread, peace, land," engaged in the most massive desertion in military history. The Bolsheviks thereby opened their country to the march of the German war machine and obliterated Russian influence from the councils of the nations.

"It would be hyperbole," Mussolini wrote in September

1917, "to credit the Bolshevik preaching with the total present state of affairs, but it is certain that the propaganda and activity of the Leninists have accelerated the process of disintegration begun under the old regime."[3] (Many, including the Italian commanders, would similarly blame the near-fatal disaster at Caporetto on Socialist agitation behind the lines.)

Mussolini began to view the Leninists as either in the pay of the Kaiser or at the very least "the betrayers of Russia." The treaty of Brest-Litovsk between the Germans and the new Bolshevik government, signed in March 1917, four months after Lenin's coup d'etat, confirmed Mussolini's opinion of the Russian Marxists. Agreed to at Lenin's insistence, against considerable opposition within the Bolshevik party, the treaty could only be termed calamitous for Russia. All the gains she had made since the days of Peter the Great were lost. By the treaty the Moscow government recognized the independence of the Ukraine. Georgia and Finland also became independent. Poland, along with the Baltic states, was ceded to Germany. Further territorial concessions were made to the Turks, and the Bolsheviks additionally agreed to pay a heavy indemnity. Russia thus gave away much of her prime agricultural land and most of her industrial base, so painfully built up under the Tsars. Of supreme importance from the viewpoint of their former Western allies, the Bolshevik government by its actions allowed Germany's leaders to shift their eastern-front armies toward a final assault on Paris. It was, for the West, the darkest hour of the war.

Lenin claimed to have made his disastrous peace with Germany at Brest-Litovsk in order "to save the revolution in Russia." But by handing such a victory to the German militarists, he was in reality betraying the revolution *in Germany*. Besides, if Germany, thanks to peace on its Eastern front, now went on to win the war in the West, how would the Russian revolution survive then? Clearly, any continuation of the war against Germany by Lenin would have had to be along the lines of Mussolini's "revolutionary war"—Socialists allied to other elements in the common defense of the nation. It would also have had to be a war in alliance with the pro-war Western Socialists. But Mussolini perceived that Lenin wanted to be supreme in Russia and supreme in a new revolutionary Socialist international, and was willing to sacrifice anything and everything to that end. Mussolini loathed Lenin for this: "The government of Lenin is German!"[4]

Mussolini's feelings of frustration and bitterness over socialism were close to all-embracing by 1918. The Socialists of Germany supported the Kaiser's war of conquest; the Socialists of Russia supported a disastrous anti-Western peace; the Socialists of Italy supported Lenin, promising to imitate his deeds. Mussolini had always been a man of profound faith, faith in the Socialist revolution. What was the former party firebrand to make of these catastrophic errors of socialism?

NEW VISIONS

As the distinguished student of Spanish fascism, Stanley Payne, has written, "the violent tensions of twentieth-century life have centered around two poles: strife between social classes and warfare between nations." Fascism was an effort to put these two conflicts in the right order of priority.

For classical Marxists, warfare between nations was merely a struggle among ruling classes for control over natural resources and markets; such fights were rich men's fights, and the poor, especially the urban working class, could have no interest in them. "The workingman has no country." The true, decisive struggle was the class war, a cosmic upheaval that took place not between but *within* nations. When the revolutionary proletariat finally rose and put an end to classes and the capitalist system, then nations, nationalism, and nationalist wars would recede into the barbarous past.

However disconcerting to those devoted to the classical theory, it had been apparent for some time that the proletariat was not really revolutionary at all, especially in those societies where it was large and well-organized, such as Britain, Germany, and the United States. However heroically one might resist this increasingly obtrusive fact of a nonrevolutionary proletariat capable of rising merely to a "trade-union consciousness," by the first decade of this century, as we have seen, much soul searching had occurred within the breasts of Socialist luminaries. In Germany, Eduard Bernstein offered one solution: since the proletariat is nonrevolutionary, socialism should take the path of parliamentary reformism. For those who yearned for revolution, this sort of heresy was worse than treason. For Lenin, if the proletariat was too obtuse to envision its destiny, it was clear what was to be done: organize a sect of professional revolutionaries totally dedicated to their sublime calling, men and women inured to all dangers, willing to sacrifice home, security, career, and love, an iron band who would make the revolution *for* the proletariat in place of the revolution *by* the proletariat. In a somewhat similar manner Mussolini, along with most syndicalists, had long ago discarded a belief in a spontaneous mass rising of the oppressed; masses of people, even the chosen working masses, were inert and passive. History was made by minorities who knew how to take advantage of a crisis (such as war) to mobilize large numbers by appealing to emotionally compelling symbols and myths. Mussolini the Socialist had openly and frequently declared his adherence to the concept of the Socialist revolution as the task of an elite minority.

European socialism was still debating the ominous implications of a nonrevolutionary proletariat when World War I broke out. From the Socialist point of view, the most extraordinary thing about this barbarous struggle among capitalist ruling classes for domination of the world market turned out to be the enthusiasm, indeed the zest, with which millions of Socialist workers in every country reacted to the appeal to defend their respective nations. National loyalty was everywhere triumphing over class solidarity, over internationalism; the workers, it turned out, had a country after all. Proletarian nationalism surprised all good Socialists, utterly scandalized Lenin and caused Mussolini to reflect deeply upon the meaning of that most un-Marxist phenomenon, the nonrevolutionary, nationalist working class.

Many syndicalists, of course, had long before concluded that much of Marx's teachings, focused on the inevitable proletarian revolution in an industrially mature society, were quite irrelevant to the situation of a backward Italy. This was especially true of Marxist internationalism. The Italian proletariat, in the view of these "national" syndicalists, were oppressed not by the power but by the weakness of the Italian bourgeoisie; the *proletarian* revolution remained impossible because the bourgeois revolution remained incomplete. Italy was backward and impoverished—the bourgeois revolution was incomplete—because the country lacked, among other things, natural resources. The remedy must be sought in the acquisition of an overseas empire. Clearly then, for national syndicalists, the ultimate liberation of the Italian proletariat required an Italy united and disciplined enough to compete for a place in the sun with more developed imperial powers.[5] Just as clearly, the hitherto unsuspected power of the Myth of the Nation might be made to do the work of the old Myth of Revolution: the proletariat under Socialist leadership could now, by supporting the national war effort, be integrated into the national system. The historic alienation of the masses from the Italian state would be overcome, the workers would help deal a mortal blow to the forces of European reactionary militarism as embodied in Wilhelmine Germany, industrialization would receive a powerful boost, and the more urgent needs of the proletariat would have to be recognized. On the other hand, if Italy tried to sit out this war or if the Socialist party opposed the national war effort, then all Italians, and especially the workers, would be exposed to grave dangers. Mussolini tried desperately to communicate these views to his comrades, but for the bulk of the Italian Socialists, if events contradicted doctrine, too bad for events. So Mussolini had been expelled.

He spent the next three passion-filled years as a leading interventionist politician, and as a soldier in the trenches. Then, in October 1917, when the veteran Mussolini was back at his editorial desk, came the Battle of Caporetto.

DISASTER INTO VICTORY

Although Italy had, unlike any of the other major belligerents, literally picked the time of her entrance into the war, from the beginning her military situation was full of grave disadvantages. Intervention in the conflict had been opposed with greater or lesser amounts of vigor by the Vatican, the Giolittians, and the Socialists. Millions of peasants viewed the war as remote, if not incomprehensible. Italian military supplies, diminished by the war in Libya and by the upheavals of Red Week, had not been completely replenished. Her Austrian enemies were entrenched in mountains dotted with natural caves, but the Italian General Staff had prepared no plans for an offensive campaign. Just as Italy entered the war, the Russians suffered serious reverses, thus allowing Austria to devote more attention to the Italian front. The Serbs were Italy's allies, on paper; but the Serbian government knew that Italy desired to receive the coast of Dalmatia (the other side of the Adriatic) as part of her postwar recompense, and the Serbs wanted Dalmatia for themselves. Hence they failed to coordinate their military operations with those of the Italians.

The Italian Commander, General Raffaele Cadorna, was the author of a standard military manual; unfortunately he had no experience leading armies in real warfare. In fact, he had never before held an active command. Cadorna's practical, on-the-job education in modern large-scale combat was expensive; he wore down his army in a dozen costly offensives against the entrenched Austrians along the line of the Isonzo River, offensives that proved largely fruitless. All of Giovanni Giolitti's warnings against Italy's entering the war now seemed justified. (Nevertheless, the Italians did manage to capture Gorizia in

1916, one of the very few Allied land successes in that entire grim year.) And after being subjected to enormous Allied pressure, Italy finally yielded and declared war against Germany in August 1916.

Many Italian units fought well enough, but few individual Italian soldiers seemed to feel any sense of personal involvement in the war. Socialist antiwar agitation behind the lines undoubtedly had its effects on at least some young conscripts, and the general state of Italian morale was not improved when on August 1, 1917, Pope Benedict XV issued his call for a "White Peace"—no annexations and no indemnities.

But by 1917 the Austrians were also suffering deeply from the war. And so in the last half of 1917 the Central Powers devised a scheme to bring the war to a victorious end. They would destroy the morale of the French by knocking Italy out of the war with one superpowerful blow. Austrian troops reinforced by picked German army units (including a twenty-six-year-old officer by the name of Erwin Rommel*) made their move in October 1917. Using brilliantly unorthodox tactics of deep penetration, the Germans and Austrians caught the Italians completely unaware. The weary Italians were forced into a retreat that very nearly became a disaster. Poor leadership, the perennial curse of Italian arms, took its bloody toll once again; General Cadorna, who quarreled with his officers and bullied his men, watched as hundreds of thousands of Italian troops fell back a hundred miles. Italy's defeat seemed about to turn into national disintegration. (Typically, this agony is the only aspect of Italy's experience in the war that is well-known to the English-speaking world, thanks to the immortalization of the retreat in Hemingway's *A Farewell to Arms.*)

With a mighty effort of will, the retreat of the Italian army was halted before it became irreversible, and a new front was

*Rommel won the *Pour le merite* at Caporetto—an unheard-of honor for such a young officer.

established on the Piave River. General Cadorna was replaced by General Armando Diaz; the invertebrate Prime Minister Boselli (seventy-nine years old during the battle of Caporetto) was replaced by Vittorio Emanuele Orlando (destined to be one of the Big Four of Versailles). Exactly one year after Caporetto, the Italian armies launched a counteroffensive that broke the Austrian lines and allowed them to enter Trent on November 3. This campaign finally shattered the will of the Empire, which sued for terms. The collapse of their Austrian allies broke the nerve of the German High Command and they too sought an armistice, which was proclaimed on November 11, 1918.

The time of Caporetto, the dark days between the realization that the Italian army was in serious, perhaps terminal, trouble and the turning of the tide, had been agonizing for Mussolini. Italy faced national humiliation, even national disintegration. Certainly those bleak October days were as decisive in the intellectual development of Mussolini as the outbreak of the war itself or his expulsion from the party of his inheritance. Reflection upon the utterly mortifying defeat of Caporetto would lead Mussolini to the firm conviction that Italy needed not only national unity—unity among the classes—but total modernization, to equip her to meet the fearsome challenges that had arisen with the industrial age. As Louis Blanqui had observed, "Who has steel has bread." Above all, what Italy needed was not, as the Socialists had traditionally viewed it, more equitable distribution, but greater productive power. This conviction would be doubly confirmed in the next few years as Mussolini watched the dogmas of collectivism, embodied in the supercollectivist "War Communism" of 1918–21, ravage the Russian economy.

It would require years for Mussolini to sort out and arrange all this: the implications of the interventionist struggle and the war, and the inability of his former socialist colleagues to adapt their thinking to new times. Mussolini had long rejected liberal democracy because for him it meant the freedom of particular groups to struggle for their selfish ends against the interests of society as a whole. (As applied to Italy after 1860, that interpretation was not far wrong.) Now he must also reject socialism because it stood for a patently false dogma of internationalism and a persistent belief that it was possible to pursue the interests of one single class at the expense of the defense of the nation. In sum, both liberalism and socialism, at least in their Italian manifestation, were fallacious and destructive because they preferred the part to the whole, weakening the nation in a brutal Darwinian world of international conflict. For years after 1914, Mussolini was struggling toward a fusion of old and new concepts. As an exponent of Marxism and a leader of socialism, Mussolini had preached the impossibility of real peace in a world of injustice. Total rejection of a radically unfair status quo, ceaseless combat with the enemy, and disciplined organization under a pugnacious elite that this combat demanded—these fundamental orientations he retained from his former socialist faith. But Mussolini's efforts to understand the meaning of World War I had worked some profound changes. At the center of his belief structure the class had been replaced by the nation; the international triumph of the proletarian revolution had given place to the survival of the Italian people in a pitiless world of great-power confrontation. Mussolini was intellectually wandering in almost wholly uncharted territory because, heretofore, most people (except for the national syndicalists, who were not numerous) had believed that nationalism and socialism were at opposite ends of the spectrum. By the end of the war, specifics of an integrated program, even certain fundamentals, had yet to be worked out completely. The enormous difficulties in trying to create a satisfactory synthesis of socialism, modernization, and nationalism account for the wavering positions on certain questions, especially economic ones, that Mussolini adopted between 1915 and 1922. Nevertheless, as Europe entered the postwar period, Mussolini was firmly committed to the principle of collaboration of all Italian classes under the leadership of a greatly strengthened executive, in the interest of national modernization through maximum production. These concepts—a world of struggle, a centralized leadership, a strong state, a united people, a powerful economy—would become, and would remain, the essence of Italian fascism.

V

THE MARCH ON ROME

"The central idea of our movement is the State."

Benito Mussolini

"Mussolini's creative idea was grand."

Oswald Spengler

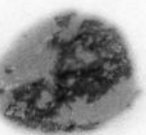

When revolutions or political upheavals occur, many observers like to identify deep-seated economic and social factors as fundamental to these events. Certainly, in post-1918 Italy, problems of postwar readjustment were very real, aggravated by a tremendous number of strikes. But to understand what happened in Italy during the four years between the end of World War I and the March on Rome, it is *political* variables that are important, even decisive: the weakness of governmental institutions, their low level of popular legitimacy, the politicians' ability and desire to form working coalitions, an almost complete absence of inspired and inspiring leadership. Fascism came to power—the March on Rome succeeded—because parliamentary government did not function properly.

To take one important example, there was the question of what Italy should get as a result of having been on the winning side in the war. Italy had in fact gained a great deal, perhaps more than any other European state: her hereditary enemy, the Habsburg Empire, had disappeared. Instead of sharing a border with a mighty Austrian Empire, Italy now had as her neighbor only the small Austrian Republic, with about six million inhabitants. In addition to this dramatic, incalculable improvement in her physical security, Italy had finally been able to annex those long-desired Austrian-held territories around Trent and Trieste. Italy was, as a result of the war, territorially complete and—as far as any country can be in a system of competitive nation-states—militarily secure. In contrast France, while also "victorious," still had to confront mighty Germany across her frontier, a Germany temporarily checkmated and in turmoil, but quite obviously capable of reopening the question of European hegemony at some not far distant date.

But in politics, as elsewhere, perceptions are often more important than reality. Many Italians perceived Italy as having been duped and swindled by her allies, and Italian sacrifices as having been in vain. The Treaty of London, by which Italy had entered the war in 1915, had promised her important colonial concessions. Instead, Britain and France had gobbled up Germany's African empire. Italy had been left empty handed and remained, despite her achievements in the war, despite her sacrifice of 600,000 dead, a relatively small, peninsular state with few natural resources and too many people.

FIUME

Frustrated in the colonial field, Italy sought territorial compensation in Europe, but she ran into the unpleasantly unfamiliar labyrinth of Wilsonian morality. Woodrow Wilson had arrived at the Paris Peace Conference proclaiming the sacred principle of national self-determination. This meant that every nation, every people, should be allowed to express its uniqueness through its own independent state, and every state should be homogeneous in population, inhabited by one, and only one, people. To elevate such a principle to the level of supreme political lodestar was very questionable; to put such a principle into practice proved absolutely impossible. Gross violations of the rule of self-determination were committed to satisfy the desires of Poland, Czechoslovakia, Yugoslavia, and Romania, mainly at the expense of the Hungarians. Wilson, therefore, felt he had to redeem his proclamation in some way, and he could be especially "moral" when dealing with the Italians. Wilson insisted that Italy should receive from the territories of the former Habsburg Empire no more than she was entitled to in justice. The Italians agreed completely; the problem lay in defining exactly what was meant by the phrase "justice for the Italians." The Italian government believed that their country's sacrifices in the war entitled it to a good measure of military security, while Wilson wanted them to be satisfied with noble abstractions. Wilson's lack of sympathy for Italy's claims was accompanied by tactlessness in dealing with her leaders. Italian anguish and resentment came to focus, almost by accident, on the essentially unimportant Adriatic port of Fiume. Dating from Roman times, ruled by Napoleon and then given to the Hungarians, Fiume was a largely Italian town with a Slavic hinterland. Yugoslavia desired the port as a vital commercial outlet, while Italy wanted it for both sentimental and strategic reasons. Wilson supported Yugoslavia. Fiume became an issue of symbolic gravity for the Italians, dividing them further from their erstwhile allies and mortally undermining the prestige of parliamentary government. A better example of the inability of the Italian parliamentary leader to control, influence, or at least run with events could hardly be imagined.

As the impasse over Fiume continued, Italian frustration grew. Finally, in September 1919, a group of adventurers, modern-day buccaneers, and mutinous Italian military personnel under the leadership of Gabriele D'Annunzio forcibly took control of the town of Fiume in defiance of the Rome government, the Allies, and the new Yugoslav state. This brazen move was intended to trigger a general army rebellion against the government, which did not in fact occur. It did succeed, nevertheless, in further diminishing the authority of the Italian state and reviving the "Garibaldian tradition" of direct action that Mussolini would soon be able to exploit.

Gabriele D'Annunzio was born in the Abruzzi in 1863. His poetry exerted enormous influence over the younger generation, and he was not without reason called the Nietzsche of Italian Youth. A supporter of the interventionist cause, D'Annunzio joined the Italian air corps. He became a dashing pilot, flying the rickety fighter aircraft of the day with incomparable morale-building and self-advertising panache, and winning many decorations from Italy and her allies. After the Armistice, D'Annunzio and his intimates (like so many who would join the Fascist cause) found it too painful to let go of the excitement and exaltation of the war. The turmoil over Fiume was a godsend to them. In the manner of Garibaldi's Sicilian expedition of 1860, D'Annunzio and his followers seized Fiume in September 1919.

The Fiume expedition, D'Annunzio proclaimed in terms that would shortly find their echo in Fascist oratory, "is the new crusade of all the poor and impoverished nations, the new crusade of all poor and free men, against the nations which usurp and amass all wealth, against the predatory races." He introduced the world's first "corporative" constitution, largely drawn up by the syndicalist Alceste De Ambris. He also clad his followers, as a symbol of soldier equality and a tribute to the heroic days of the war, in *la camicia nera*, the black shirt.

The Fiume affair triggered the first recorded mutiny in the history of the Italian army. Many officers and soldiers rushed to join D'Annunzio, often bringing tanks and trucks with them. The Italian government was completely paralyzed in the face of D'Annunzio's defiance, because many Italians of diverse parties, inside and outside the cabinet, secretly or openly rejoiced at the poet's bold gesture. And so Yugoslavia was warned by the Rome government not to attack Fiume, while D'Annunzio received visits from members of the Italian Royal House and a courtesy call from Admiral Enrico Millo, commander of Italian forces in Dalmatia.

The editor of *Il popolo d'Italia* observed these events, and the enormous popularity of D'Annunzio, with mixed emotions. He readily perceived the danger in the fact that D'Annunzio was much more a showman than a politician; as such, he might well make some serious blunder and perhaps trigger a popular reaction against nationalist "excesses." Furthermore, Mussolini was jealous of D'Annunzio's cult among patriotic youth. On the other hand, Mussolini simply could not afford to remain aloof from this outbreak of national passion, and so he flew to Fiume to take counsel with the poet-hero, whom he had met previously in Rome and with whom he had corresponded. Mussolini and D'Annunzio continued to write to each other about the possibility of provoking an army or a popular uprising inside Italy, but Mussolini gave no real support to such plans.

With D'Annunzio holding forth from his balcony in Fiume, with Allied and Yugoslavia pressures on the Italian cabinet mounting, with the hoped for rising against the Rome government even more remote, the sands of the corporative republic of Fiume ran out. In November 1920, Italy and Yugoslavia signed the Treaty of Rapallo that made Fiume a "free city." Giovanni Giolitti, back in office once more, sent the Italian navy to blockade D'Annunzio and his forces. On Christmas Day 1920, Italian warships in the harbor opened fire. D'Annunzio himself was wounded, and a few days later left Fiume. The glorious adventure had come to an inglorious conclusion.

The Fiume episode was to have profound effects on Italian politics. Fiume showed how deep and enduring were the passions aroused within the Italians by their "mutilated victory," the failure to obtain proper recompense for their contribution to Allied victory. It showed that the Italian state would tolerate much, even mutiny, in the name of patriotism. The general fragility of the state was underlined by the political unreliability of its armed forces. Much of the future Fascist political style, moreover, was invented in Fiume: balcony dialogues between a leader and his followers, black shirts, choreographed demonstrations. Most of all, there came together at Fiume that assembly of forces that, as Denis Mack Smith notes, "would soon carry Mussolini into power: an alliance of army veterans, nationalists, dissident socialists, idealists and adventurers."* D'Annunzio's followers—or most of them—in Fiume and in all Italy would soon join the growing ranks of fascism.

PARALYSIS IN PARLIAMENT

The grave problems faced by postwar Italy would have taxed the powers of any government, no matter how unshakably legitimate, widely popular, and politically clever it might have been. But, from the first moments of unity in 1860, the Italian government had never been any of those things, and the elections of 1919—the first in Italian history to be held with universal manhood suffrage—had produced a parliament that guaranteed the absence of effective, or even coherent, leadership. Almost all the problems within parliament during the period from 1919 to 1922 can be traced to two causes, one technical and one substantive. The technical cause of parliament's inability to provide effective government was the manner in which it was elected, a system called proportional representation. In an election with proportional representation, the number of seats that a party wins in the parliament is roughly proportional to its share of the popular vote; for instance, if 25 percent of the voters cast ballots for the Socialist party, the Socialist party winds up with 25 percent of the seats in parliament. On the face of it, this seems to be a very fair system. The difficulty is, actually, that the system is *too* fair.

Proportional representation guarantees that practically every party and every splinter group in a society will wind up with at least some seats, no matter how small the party's

*Last but by no means least, Fiume would provide Mussolini with his first important and popular victory in foreign affairs, when Yugoslavia admitted Italy's claim to Fiume in 1924.

support in the nation, how uncompromising its stance, or how unrealistic its program. Holding elections in this manner makes it inevitable that many different parties will come into existence and will compete for and win a share of power (that is, a share of seats in parliament). Now in a parliamentary system, the government (the cabinet) stays in office only as long as it enjoys the support of the majority of the members of parliament. Clearly, cabinet stability (and therefore the likelihood of pursuing long-range solutions to serious problems) is enhanced when such a majority is controlled by one single party. But proportional representation all but guarantees the impossibility of such a situation. Thus, in order to put and maintain a cabinet in office to deal with the country's business, it becomes necessary to construct a stable coalition between two or more different parties. This is not an easy task; political parties justify their existence on the basis of significant differences with other parties. Yet all this need present no insuperable obstacle to effective government, provided that the potential coalition partners share an area of agreement at least on fundamentals such as the legitimacy of the political order and the desire to avoid general economic collapse.

But here we come to the substantive cause of the inability of the Italian parliament to function properly. Proportional representation allowed the divisions within the Italian nation to be perfectly mirrored within the Italian parliament. The nature of the main political parties and the disputes among and within them rendered the formation of stable coalitions, and therefore stable cabinets, impossible.

The principal political parties in 1919 were the Liberals, the Popular (or Catholic) Party, and the Socialists.

The Liberals, in their half-century of power, had done quite a lot: they had erected a kingdom against much opposition, held it together through many trials, and guided it successfully through the stormy seas of World War I. Nevertheless, the Liberals had failed to provide the Italians with governmental institutions they could believe in at home, and vindication of their claims abroad. The Liberal party of 1919 was spiritually exhausted, intellectually unprepared to face the postwar world, and quite ill at ease in the new atmosphere of mass politics created by universal manhood suffrage and proportional representation.

The brand new Catholic party, the *Partito popolare*, was launched in the early days of 1919. The party found its base in the devout and populous rural areas of Northern Italy and in the network of Catholic banks, cooperatives, and labor unions that flourished in the region. Its program called for social reform, especially on the land, and (remarkably) ignored the Roman Question. The principal leader of the new party was the forty-eight-year-old Sicilian priest Don Luigi Sturzo. Father Sturzo was a professor of philosophy and a close student of Christian theories of government. To this broad intellectual formation he added a rich experience in practical affairs, having been a social worker, labor organizer, and deputy mayor of his home town of Caltagirone for many years (as a priest he was legally barred from holding the mayor's office itself). And because after the war the Trentino had become part of Italy, Sturzo was ably assisted in his direction of the Popular party by the young Alcide De Gasperi, the leader of Tridentine Catholicism who had confronted the young Mussolini many years before.* The *Partito popolare*, the first Catholic party in Italian history, received great assistance from Pope Benedict XV who, although officially aloof from electoral politics, removed the last impediments to voting by Catholics.** The Popular party issued a hopeful and provocative election manifesto and received 20 percent of the vote, a remarkably good

*De Gasperi would serve as prime minister of Italy from 1945 to 1953, longer than any other man since the overthrow of Mussolini.

**The ban on Catholics voting in Italy, originally known as the *non expedit*, dated from the days of Pio Nono. It had been modified by Pius X to allow Catholics to vote in contests where they could help defeat militantly anticlerical Socialist candidates. During the decade before the Great War there had been tacit but increasingly in-

showing for an infant party, especially since its votes were overwhelmingly concentrated in the north where elections were much freer and more honestly conducted than in the machine-dominated south. Yet in actuality, the Popular party made a far less noteworthy contribution to Italian parliamentary politics than its members or its leadership would have suggested. The Catholic party was not oriented toward *power* but only toward *influence*. Most of its membership and middle leadership consisted of provincial conservatives less concerned with governing and healing the nation than with preserving or extending the prerogatives of the Church.

The Socialists had done very well in the 1919 elections, receiving over 34 percent of the total vote, as compared with 23 percent in the last elections, those of 1913. But the Socialists were, as always, deeply divided on the important issues of the day. Many of them had totally misread the meaning of the years 1915–1918, and continued to misread the portent of 1919–1920, vowing to reproduce in Italy the Petrograd revolution of 1917.

The elections of 1921, called early to "clarify" the parliamentary situation, left parliament generally in the same fractured condition, only now there was the addition of an important contingent from the Fascist party, openly committed to a radical revamping of parliamentary democracy itself. And, for the first time in Italian history, a number of representatives of the Italian Communist party were elected to parliament.

The PCI (*Partito comunista italiano*) had been founded only in January 1921, after the latest of the innumerable schisms within the Socialist party ranks. In their first electoral cam-

---

timate and effective cooperation between the Giolitti machine and the Church leadership through the electoral brokerage agency called the Catholic Electoral Union. The Catholics provided votes for Giolittian candidates; in return they received guarantees on divorce, Catholic schools, and invaluable experience in electoral politics, on which they would build after the First and (with resounding success) Second World Wars.

paign they succeeded in placing fifteen men in the Chamber of Deputies. Their leader was the thirty-year-old Sardinian Antonio Gramsci, a graduate of the prestigious University of Turin. Gramsci has become something of a cult object in our own day, and there is no denying that he was an intellectually gifted and personally sympathetic figure. But the facts are that under Gramsci's leadership the Communist party contributed in no negligible way to the triumph of fascism. One recalls that Gramsci had been an admirer of Mussolini the Socialist firebrand in the prewar days, and had even been sympathetic to Mussolini's efforts to appeal to the rank and file of socialism over the heads of their leaders on the issue of intervention in the war. By 1921, Antonio Gramsci was much more interested in taunting his former fellow Socialists than in effectively analyzing fascism or in helping to generate a coalition against its growing strength. Or rather, for Gramsci's Communists "everything was fascism: the state, the bourgeoisie, democracy, socialism." The disarray on the Left could hardly have been more complete, and Lenin and Trotsky were beside themselves at "this folly and incompetence." The Communists (not to speak, of course, of the Socialists) could never grasp what fascism was, they had no plans to stop its march to power, and after fascism had arrived in power they remained confused, divided, and passive. In 1926 Mussolini ordered the arrest of the whole PCI leadership, which was accomplished with no trouble at all. Thus, through one of the many ironies of Italian politics, Gramsci was kept alive for many years under the eyes of Fascist guards, while he recorded for an admiring posterity his thoughts on the Italian past and the Communist future, instead of ending up, as so many European Communist leaders of that era did, tortured to death in the cellar of one of Stalin's prisons, or buried in an unmarked grave on some island of the Gulag Archipelago.

Thus the Italian parliamentary system between 1918 and 1922 produced cabinets that were neither *to be* effective nor *to seem* effective. Powerful minorities, moreover, would not have been happy even if the system *had* worked effectively. Most Fascists viewed parliamentary politics as a source of weakness, the symbol of a second-class Italy much in need of rejuvenating discipline and faith. Many Catholics viewed the troubled parliamentary system as merely the latest in a long line of adversaries with which the eternal Church had to deal. Most Socialists and all Communists viewed it as a worm-eaten structure to be torn down in the erection of the proletarian utopia. And as cabinet succeeded cabinet and wasted year succeeded wasted year, the forces of fascism waxed stronger and stronger.

Yet even as late as the end of 1921, there was a sure and simple maneuver that could have prevented the Fascists from coming to power, and this was a coalition between the Socialists and the Catholics. This course, however, was viewed as impossible by major elements within both parties. The Socialists refused to accept cabinet responsibility because they did not want to "save the bourgeoisie" from the "just consequences" of all the latter's "errors." Nor would the Socialists accept the populist credentials of the Catholic party as authentic; how, they asked, could one possibly be a good Catholic and a real progressive? The Popular party, for its part, could hardly be said to have had clearer vision. The *popolari* wanted to extract concessions from the Liberal State, not to rule over it. Besides, Pius XI and numerous bishops detested the Socialist party and all its works and pomps; the notion that the Italian Socialists, with their ferocious anticlericalism, might rise to power in Italy in alliance with a professedly Catholic party raised the blood pressure of the entire clerical establishment to an unsuitably high level.

The simple, absolutely essential truth to grasp here is this: all the non-Fascist and so-called anti-Fascist elements in the country—the Liberals, the *Popolari*, the Socialists, the Communists—preferred the pursuit of mutual recriminations and vendettas to the erection of an effective barrier, and thus an effective alliance, against the Fascists. And not for the last time, as will be seen.

All this explains why, three and a half years after the national elections of 1919, when the Socialists and *popolari* together won a clear majority of the votes and not a single Fascist was elected to the Chamber of Deputies (Mussolini himself being ignominiously defeated in his stronghold of Milan)—all this explains why the Fascists were able to gather into their ranks a large and vigorous following and march on Rome with absolutely no opposition from anybody!

THE BIRTH OF FASCISM

Because certain events are familiar to us, they begin to seem inevitable. This is a trick the mind plays on itself, and should be guarded against in evaluating the coming to power of Mussolini. It is really quite extraordinary that it was Mussolini who eventually ended the postwar crisis in Italy and took over the direction of affairs. Consider that Mussolini and his followers had been highly visible and vociferous in their support of Italy's intervention in the Great War, an intervention that had been a matter of policy and not of strict necessity (Italy was not about to be invaded, as Belgium, France, and Russia had been). Consider further that the war had lasted much longer than expected and had been unbelievably expensive in blood and money, while Italy emerged from the war not with a colonial empire, as envisioned in the Treaty of London, but with only relatively small border adjustments in Europe, adjustments that might have been easily obtained through diplomatic negotiations with Austria in 1915. Finally, consider that Mussolini and his Fascists continued not only to defend the intervention and the war but to glorify them as the greatest and most important achievements of Italians since the fall of Rome. How did the Fascists not only escape being drowned in the flood of postwar disillusionment, but actually manage to rise from the position of little more than a heretical Socialist sect to that of the paramount political force in the country in only a few short years?

Of the many factors that came together to make possible the triumph of fascism, one stands out above all the others: the incompetence of its opponents. Crudely put, the failure of the Socialists caused the victory of the Fascists. It would be a grave error to conceive of fascism as nothing more than a reaction against revolutionary Marxism; Mussolini was a product of that tradition himself, and he retained certain of its characteristics until the day he died. It is often rightly remarked that Mussolini had many points of view and modes of thought in common with the intellectual patron saint of Italian Communism, Antonio Gramsci. Fascism, as one author puts it, was not a counterrevolution but *another* revolution.[1] Nevertheless, the Fascist revolution would have been quite impossible had it not been for Socialist confusion and misperception, in short the insistence to the bitter end by most Socialists that the Leninist model be applied in Italy.

Mussolini had acutely diagnosed the fundamental errors of the Socialists. First, they wanted to carry out a Petrograd-style revolution (it had been a coup, really) in a country whose situation was in no way analogous to Lenin's Russia. The Bolshevik model involved the destruction of the technical-managerial class, which had been replaced with a bureaucracy more authoritarian and less efficient (a catastrophe from which Mussolini would draw many lessons). Second, the Socialists were rejecting, indeed ferociously assaulting, the former interventionists and the returning veterans, many of whom would have been glad to join with the Socialists in forging a new Italy worthy of her victorious soldiers. Mussolini would devote the years 1918 and 1919 to an attempt to win the Socialists away from the Lenin obsession, arguing (in the canonically correct Marxist mode) that in Italy the duty of the proletariat was to help complete the bourgeois revolution.

As the year 1919 opened, Mussolini was thirty-five years old. The authorities had been keeping an eye on him for many years, as they did with all potentially troublesome persons. A secret police report[2] of the period describes him as enjoying very good health, which permitted him to work all the time. It was his habit to sleep until very late in the morning and leave for the office of *Il popolo d'Italia* around noon; he would come home around three o'clock the following morning. All day, every day, was consumed with politics and newspaper work. (Perhaps not entirely; there was still time for amusements; Mussolini continued to be sexually active and had several affairs during this period, sometimes simultaneously.) The police report describes Mussolini as having a lot of friends; he was emotional and sentimental, forming intimate relationships with some and developing inplacable hostility to those who crossed or opposed him. He was generous with that little money he had, especially among his comrades for whom he would often make real sacrifices. (Money meant little to Mussolini, but he knew how much it meant to others.) The police judged him to be very intelligent, with the ability to penetrate men's true desires. Armed with these valuable insights, he was bold and made decisions quickly. The report considered Mussolini's change of position on the war during 1914-1915, from Socialist neutralism to active interventionism, and pronounced his conversion as having been sincere. Mussolini was "a man of thought and action, an effective and incisive writer, a lively and persuasive speaker." He was ambitious for the first rank, "convinced that he represents an important force in the destiny of Italy." Decades later, after Mussolini's death, what was left of the Socialist party would be led by Pietro Nenni, with whom Mussolini had once shared a prison cell in the Romagna days; in 1919, however, Nenni helped organize a local branch, a *fascio*, of the Fascist party in Bologna. Nenni described Mussolini, whom he knew intimately, as having "the eloquence of a Marat." A little later Georges Sorel would write of Mussolini that "nobody knows it yet but he is the only man of energy who can repeal the weaknesses of the government." All this testimony from diverse sources paints a portrait of the postwar

Mussolini as a man of energy, ability, and passion; one clearly marked out, not only by himself, to play a major role in the affairs of his nation.

To this end, Mussolini organized the first *Fascio di combattimento* at a meeting in Milan's Piazza San Sepolcro in March 1919. The name of the new movement embodied many ideas with which Mussolini wished to be identified. This was to be preeminently a movement of veterans in defense of veterans, while the fasces—bundles of rods bound together with an ax in the middle—were the ancient symbol of Roman authority. Many groups in Italian history had adopted the name "fascist" to denote their unbreakable unity; the most recent use of the term, before the meeting in San Sepolcro, had been by a group of members of parliament who insisted on a more vigorous prosecution of the war. The new organization was supposed to be the vehicle by which the working classes would be moved away from their old and ineffective leaders, an instrument for the conversion of the proletariat from revolutionary internationalism to revolutionary nationalism (the path Mussolini himself had traversed between 1914 and 1918). This fundamental aim, along with Mussolini's still strongly socialist habits of thought and expression, accounted for the decidedly "leftist" tone of the first Fascist electoral platform (a republic; abolition of the Senate; votes for women; land reform in favor of veterans; heavy taxes on war profits). It was not a document that would ever have to be put into effect by any cabinet, but a banner to attract the workers away from the hallucinations of their leaders. These first efforts suffered total defeat; Mussolini himself was badly beaten for parliament in Milan in 1919. The failure of the Socialists, or even of a major segment of their party, to respond to Mussolini's efforts to convert them to a reforming nationalism eventually sealed their fate.

The Italian Socialist party had always contained some of the finest intellects and most generous spirits in the country, but by 1919 its political tactics had degenerated into a wholely disastrous sectarianism. The Communist Giorgio Amendola wrote that the Socialists made a fatal error in not realizing how important it was that Italy had—for the first time in her history—been victorious in a war, and this the greatest of all wars. Despairing of Socialist confusion and incompetence, one wing of the party broke away to form the Italian Communist party, under the leadership of the brilliant Antonio Gramsci. But the Communists were even more hypnotized (if possible) by the Leninist mirage than their former comrades. Leninism presupposes a beaten country and a disintegrated army, while Italy was a victorious country with her army intact. That is why Mussolini rose to the premiership and Gramsci went to prison.

Politics in northern and central Italy soon began to resemble a small-scale civil war, with the Fascists on one side and the Socialists and the Communists on the other. Fascist "squads," often composed of or led by ex-officers, became very important during 1920. They were originally organized to protect the premises of Mussolini's newspaper, *Il popolo d'Italia*, from the Socialists, but the tactic of using punitive squads soon became common in rural areas. The effectiveness of the squads in physically dismantling the structures of socialism won much sympathy and many recruits for the Fascists, who seemed to be the only ones who knew how to counter the intimidation so long practiced by the Socialist agrarian unions.

While the Fascists introduced elements of military precision and organization into political violence, Italian politics had unfortunately been characterized by violence since the foundation of the kingdom. One recalls Garibaldi's expeditions of "volunteers"; the rigging of plebiscites; the vigorous use of troops against strikers, Sicilian peasants, and southern "brigands"; the "management" of national elections; official toleration of D'Annunzio and his freebooters; not to mention the government's deliberate intervention in the war, in defiance of large strata of public opinion.

Then, there were the Socialists, with their incessant demonstrations, strikes, uprisings, and "Red Weeks." Marxist socialism in general, with its emphasis on class war and proletarian dictatorship is, to say the least, ambiguous about the democratic process. Marxian logic could certainly be used (and has been) to justify the conclusion that if a democratic majority votes against socialism and cannot be educated out of this unprogressive attitude, then if possible that majority's will must be set aside. In Italy after 1918, the Socialists gave any number of instances of their willingness, even eagerness, to coerce the nation. The number of strikers, for example, rose from less than two thousand in 1918 to one and a half million in 1919 and over two-and-a-half million in 1920.[3] Then there were the editorials in *Avanti!* in December 1920, calling for the wives and daughters of policemen to be treated "like whores," or the frequently repeated promise that the Italian Socialists were going to do what their confreres had done in Russia, with presumably similar consequences for the royal family, officers, churchmen, and smallholders. In January 1919 *Avanti!* promised that after the Socialist revolution, "within a short time all parties will be eliminated."[4] Railway workers would halt trains and force soldiers or even priests to get off, with similar humiliations inflicted on the educated, including physicians and professors. The militant "reds" of northern Italy were so intoxicated by revolutionary rhetoric that even "the little down-at-heel undernourished clerk was scowled at in the trams and in the streets because he was a "pen-pusher" and thus not a "worker."[5]

Socialist violence in the countryside was worse. Rural Italy had been for generations the scene of a real class war, and the living standards of the landless laborers were shocking. Socialist rural unions could have been the answer to this situation, but their tactics were eventually disastrous for their own cause. Socialists were atheists, so landless laborers who had their children baptized were beaten up; Socialists were revolutionaries, so lone policemen were beaten up; Socialists believed in collectivization, so laborers who entered into sharecropping or leaseholding agreements were beaten up. Finally, Socialists were against war, so many veterans, even peasants who had been drafted, could not be admitted to the party. All this is why, years later, Communist leader Palmiro Togliatti called Socialist policies "a vain exercise in bullying."

Above all things, it is in the Socialist attitude toward the demobilized soldiers that the key to the ultimate ruin of their party is to be found. In the words of the professional anti-Fascist Gaetano Salvemini, the reds "in 1920 redoubled their efforts in a stupid and malicious campaign of hatred and contempt against those who had been decorated in the war."[6] Disabled veterans were mocked in the streets of their own villages, even spat upon, for being the dupes of the establishment. Officers in uniform were hooted at and attacked in the streets of the great cities. These veterans, certainly in their own eyes, had risked their lives to defend the stay-at-homes, many of whom were militant Socialists exempted from the draft because they worked in strategic industries. And after all the soldiers' sufferings, neither the Allied Powers nor the Italian Socialists would give them their due. Fascist violence, then, was in large measure the response of men who had seen their sacrifices derided and their comrades of wartime literally spat upon, men who further had been threatened with punishment when the revolution should finally arrive. Thus, again to quote anti-Fascist Salvemini, "the main appeal of the 'Anti-Bolshevik' offensive lay precisely in the vindication of the rights the dignity of the disabled soldiers and those decorated in the war."[7]

We have to keep in mind, moreover, in discussing Fascist violence against the Socialists in 1920 and 1921, that the latter could at almost any time have put a stop to it by joining—or merely *supporting*—a coalition cabinet pledged to a restoration of law and order. This the Socialists repeatedly refused to do. They wanted revolution not coalition. Thus they were caught between dialectical delusions about the "inevitable collapse of bourgeois society" on one side and the rising tide of Fascist vengeance on the other.

To reiterate an important point: it was the catastrophically mistaken policies of the Socialists after 1914, and again after 1918, that permitted the rise of fascism from a small sect to the most vital force in the country. Unwilling to form a cabinet (though they were the largest party in the Chamber), unable to make a revolution (though quite capable of frightening large segments of the public with their ferocious rhetoric), the Socialists succeeded only in preventing anybody else from dealing with Italy's problems. Having rejected the nation, opposed the war effort, baited the bourgeoisie, threatened the Church, exhausted the workers, and humiliated the veterans, the Socialist party would soon reap what it had sowed. "Fascism," in the words of the Communist Giorgio Amendola, "conquered on the basis of a genuine consensus."

It was against this militant and inept socialism that fascism launched its punitive expeditions, that began as street brawls in Milan in 1919 and reached the proportions of small military expeditions in the farming regions of Emilia by 1921. In contrast to that of the Socialists, the Fascists viewed their own violence as directed by patriots against traitors, and hence as justifiable, a form of national self-defense. "We challenge the right of our opponents to complain about our violence," roared Mussolini at Udine on September 20, 1922, "because compared to what was going on in those unhappy years of 1919 and 1920, and compared to that of the Bolsheviks in Russia, where two millions were executed and another two millions imprisoned, our violence has been child's play."

Nevertheless, Mussolini had experienced growing distaste for the intensity of this combat. In many areas it was coming to resemble that class war that he had learned to abhor, with the rural Fascist squads objectively, in some instances, defending the class interests of some of the most selfish and retrograde elements in Italian society. Besides, certain sectors of the middle class were beginning to fear Fascist disorder almost as much as they had formerly feared Socialist disorder. Most importantly, this strife among Fascists, Socialists, and sometimes *Popolari* was dividing those most opposed to the stale corruption of the Liberal state. Mussolini had long realized that a real renovation of Italy would eventually require a grand coalition among the Socialists (representing the urban workers), the *Popolari* (the northern peasantry) and the Fascists (the northern-middle and lower-middle strata). Shortly after the 1921 electoral success, in which he and three dozen other Fascists had been elected to parliament, Mussolini took a step toward this historical and decisive realignment by signing the so-called Pact of Pacification with the Socialists, calling for a suspension of hostilities. The Pact, and Mussolini's leadership along with it, were immediately challenged by locally powerful Fascists. They had borne the brunt of a bitter struggle against socialism in the provinces for too long to suddenly submit to a peace dictated from above. Moreover, in some areas, they had established the ascendancy of Fascist agricultural unions over those of the Socialists and were unwilling to risk those gains in any truce with their defeated rivals. Most of these rural Fascist leaders could not grasp, even if they had been interested in doing so, Mussolini's vast designs. A real schism within fascism appeared likely. Mussolini hesitated, going so far as to resign from the Fascist national executive committee; but in the end he could not face the prospect of leaving or breaking up the Fascist movement that he had created and built up. He could not face the prospect of starting all over, of going back to 1914. The situation became more clarified when, in October 1921, the Socialist Party Congress proclaimed its revolutionary and Leninist plans and repudiated pacification or collaboration with anybody. Shortly thereafter Mussolini capitulated to the Fascist hard-liners. A compromise formula restored him to leadership but effectively killed the Pact of Pacification—for the time being.

Mussolini had been resoundingly thwarted in his scheme to bring together all the anti-status quo forces in the nation. He would try again another day. In the meantime, if the Socialist masses could not be won over, Mussolini would have to seek allies elsewhere. He began to abandon his old anticlericalism—not a difficult thing for the son of the pious Rosa Maltoni and the brother of the devout Arnaldo to do, really, since it had been for him mainly a symbol of his socialist commitment. Besides, Mussolini the nationalist appreciated the status Italy gained by possessing the capital and providing the central bureaucracy of the Roman Catholic church; he was deeply gratified by the "400 millions in all countries who look to Rome." Also, that antique Romagnole republicanism would have to be jettisoned, a small price to pay for the sympathy of the army, already very friendly to fascism but deeply loyal too to the House of Savoy.

Some authors speak authoritatively about the social composition of fascism, that it was a middle-class or lower-middle-class movement, as least "essentially," or "predominantly." In fact, we do not have much hard data on this question. What we do know indicates that active Fascists generally came from the same strata from which all parties recruited their activists, and that fascism had leaders and adherents from all segments of Italian society, including the proletariat. Fascism was primarily a movement of *resentments*: resentment of Italy's low status in the international order, resentment of Socialist bullying, resentment of incompetent politicians, resentment against the anonymous power of big business and high finance.

Important from the very beginning were those labor elements, the "syndicalists," who wanted a thorough renovation of Italian society but were, for various reasons, hostile to the Socialist party and susceptible to nationalist appeals. "The revolutionary syndicalists, together with the Socialists who had left the party with Mussolini, formed the hard professional core of the new movement in 1919."[8] Soon added to these foundations were students, large numbers of the "intellectual proletariat" (many of whom came to fascism via the bizarre

"Futurist" movement), and above all, veterans, especially former officers, volunteers, and commandoes (from whose romantic ranks Mussolini derived the idea of the black shirt as the Fascist party uniform).

During 1921 fascism became a mass movement in the countryside. It was these rural elements (which often had an urban base, as in Bologna or Ferrara) that would so vehemently oppose the Pact of Pacification. Fascism from the first hour had been a mixed bag of elements, but this influx of "agrarians" altered its nature profoundly; many of these newer Fascists were less interested in the rejuvenation of Italy than in the physical dismantling of socialism in the countryside. These elements changed the internal balance of fascism and circumscribed the authority of Mussolini to a degree; some writers go as far as to speak of the urban fascism of 1919 being "swamped" by rural fascism of 1921, the "fascism of the intervention" being inundated by the "fascism of interest." But this is a somewhat schematic and artificial view. All growing movements attract supporters for diverse reasons (including selfish ones) and it would be impossible to separate into neat segments those who became Fascists primarily from patriotism, youthful exuberance, admiration of Mussolini, a belief in the teachings of syndicalism, a longing for the lost comradeship of the trenches, detestation of the Socialists, some private need for combat, the crudest class interest, or from some other motive or combination of motives.

That fascism was definitely not a movement of the privileged classes is illustrated by its relationship with the Italian Nationalist Association (ANI). These Nationalists were driven by a sense of the unfulfilled greatness of Italy. Preoccupied with questions of foreign policy, their domestic formula espoused a centralized state directing rapid economic development. The ideology of the ANI was an attempt to adapt traditional conservatism to the industrial age. The Nationalists had excellent connections at court and in army circles, but they were unable (and perhaps unwilling) to appeal to a mass base, remaining confined to fairly small groups of upper-class origins. This was what "differentiated the *fasci* from the Nationalist or the various minor anti-Bolshevik leagues." Fascism had the elements of a real mass base, and thus was the only possible instrument that could "channel the revolutionary forces into a national camp."[9] It was this Fascist combination—a nationalist orientation plus popular appeal—that led some industrialists to support even the openly radical fascism of 1919. Although they were rivals in some parts of the country, although the social backgrounds of many Nationalist leaders could not have differed more glaringly from those of Mussolini, the similarity of many of their basic aims helped draw fascism and the ANI together. Mussolini eventually abandoned his demand for a republic, mainly to please the monarchist officer corps, but in part also to satisfy the Nationalists. (Indeed, in October 1922 the Nationalist militants—the Blue Shirts—were prepared to fight the Fascists in the streets if the latter's March on Rome should assume an anti-monarchistic direction). That fascism was a synthesizing movement par excellence would be demonstrated by the amalgamation of the Fascist party with the ANI organization in 1923. Such leading Nationalists as Alfredo Rocco and Luigi Federzoni accepted seats in Mussolini's first cabinet, and were to provide fascism with a more establishmentarian tone, protection in the mortal crisis of 1924, and a tendency to play down the party itself in favor of the centralizing state. The continuing influence of the Nationalists on Mussolini is another reason why Italian fascism never developed along the more totalitarian lines of its imitator to the north. But the contribution of the Nationalist Association to the triumph and the ideology of fascism should not be overblown. Without Mussolini, the ideas of the ANI would have remained those of a small if influential sect. Nor did Mussolini, armed with the insight of the national syndicalists, need the ANI to teach him the importance of an appeal to national sentiment.

IDEALS AND AIMS

A generation ago it was fashionable to affect the view that Mussolini had no firm ideas, that fascism had no real aims or program except the seizure and retention of power. Mussolini was often contrasted (much to his disadvantage) to Lenin, who supposedly possessed an integrated and world-embracing philosophy indicating the correct strategy and tactics for all time, or at least for *his* time. Mussolini's own words, apparently placing small importance on elaborate social theories and specific programs, are often used to bolster this line of argument, the thrust of which is that here is another reason why fascism need not be taken seriously or studied thoroughly.

But this is very misleading. Mussolini's "command of contemporary philosophy and political literature was at least as great as that of any other contemporary European political leader."[10] And in the heat of the post-1918 crisis, when Mussolini expressed his impatience with spinning ever more elaborate theories and demanded action instead of verbiage, he was thinking in a most Marxian manner; after all, as the founder of Marxism had pointed out, the task was not to explain the world but to change it. And yet the theoretical preoccupation of the Marxists (not only in Italy) seeking to impose the Leninist model on their own country where it did not apply, ended in their complete defeat and the destruction of all their plans. There should be no confusion on this point: the size of the Communist party in today's Italy owes a great deal less to the power of its philosophical categories than to the power of the Anglo-American armies in 1944.

The comparison of the "theoretical" Lenin with the "opportunistic" Mussolini may be satisfying from a polemical viewpoint, but it is poor analysis. True enough, fascism attracted a wide diversity of supporters, and emphasis on loyalty to the personality of Mussolini was in part an attempt to substitute for a highly elaborate program that might encourage centrifugal tendencies within the ranks of the Fascists and commit the regime *a priori* to positions whose advisability was unclear. But it is not necessary to exaggerate this pragmatic tendency within fascism, nor should one exaggerate the ideological consistency of Lenin's policies. Consider the following points. First, in August 1917, Lenin published one of his most influential works, *State and Revolution.* In it he declared the purpose of revolution was to "shatter" the state. In a society in which the proletariat had triumphed, "the state will begin to wither away immediately after its victory." Lenin further renounced "every organized and systematic use of violence" because after the revolution "people will grow accustomed to observing elementary rules without force or subjection." Now this went right into the trashcan the day after the Petrograd coup. (Indeed, the very seizure of power in Petrograd was much more in keeping with the teachings of Louis Blanqui than of Karl Marx.) In 1921, when bolshevism had reduced Russia to the verge of starvation, Lenin introduced the New Economic Policy (NEP). In its replacement of grain requisitions by taxes in kind, the abolition of compulsory labor service, and the restoration of small businesses to private ownership, the New Economic Policy of Lenin bore remarkable resemblances to the Old Economic Policy of capitalism. Now if these breathtaking reversals are not fundamental repudiations of long-held Marxist beliefs, if they were instead merely "tactical adjustments" to reality, cannot such a description apply also to alterations in Mussolini's policies during his many years in power?

By 1922, from his experiences as a Socialist firebrand, Fascist founder, corporal in the trenches and party chief in parliament, from his reflections on the writings of Marx and Sorel, Bergson and James, Pareto and Le Bon, Mussolini had hammered out certain basic tenets that became the hallmark of fascism for friend and foe alike, that had important implications for both policy and style. The chief of these doctrinal elements were nationalism and elitism. *Nationalism* meant that the nation was not just an abstraction or a word, but a real and tangible thing, the highest human reality, great, eternal, and completely worthy of service and sacrifice. In serving the nation, in living for and if necessary dying for the nation, each man and each woman, no matter how humble or obscure, could transcend the limitations, the pettiness of everyday life, and participate directly in the most profound drama of human existence. Perpetually threatened as it was in a world of Darwinian competition, the nation needed everyone's dedication. The Great War had been the latest and greatest but certainly not the last of its dire perils.

Other imperatives flowed from the principle of nationalism. In order to be certain that the sinews of defense would be abundantly available, the nation needed to be built up economically; hence the Fascist emphasis on *production*. Increased production demanded the *repudiation of class warfare*, which could only weaken the nation by disturbing the production cycle. The living example of revolutionary Russia—writhing in chaos and starvation, robbed of her richest provinces, put out from the councils of Europe—profoundly affected Mussolini and other former Socialist revolutionaries. The Italian proletariat could expect no real improvement in its lot as long as the country as a whole remained impoverished and backward. Italy's long-stalled industrial revolution must be completed. Class warfare must be replaced by class cooperation, with regularized structures embodying the concept of society as a living organism: these imperatives provided the basis of *corporatism*.

> *By the end of the First World War, Mussolini was prepared to articulate the conviction that Italy, as an integral unity including all classes and all persons, was as disadvantaged as the proletarian class ever conceived itself to be. Italy was, in fact, a "proletarian nation." The entire nation, faced by the impostures and imperialisms of the "bourgeois" or "plutocratic" nations found itself denied sustenance and place.*[11]

So within Mussolini, the Socialist of Forlí merged with the nationalist of Milan.

To the Fascists, one of their main tasks was to install a sense of nationhood and national pride in a people for whom these sentiments were still largely absent after sixty years of nominal unity. As regional loyalties and religious wars had kept Italians divided and weak for centuries, so in post-1918 politics the great enemies of national feeling were, in Mussolini's eyes, class conflict and those who exploited it. "We declare war against socialism," he proclaimed at the founding meeting in San Sepolcro, "not because it is socialism but because it has opposed nationalism." Socialist internationalism was not a sentiment of the masses but of the schoolmasters and professional officeholders who ran the Socialist party. "We deny your internationalism," cried Mussolini in his first parliamentary speech in June 1921, "because it is a luxury only the upper classes can afford. The common people are desperately attached to their native soil."

The Marxists viewed Italy and all modern countries as rigidly divided, like ancient Sparta, into a class of rulers and a class of slaves. But Mussolini countered: "We deny that there are only two classes; there are many. We deny that you can explain all of human history by economic determinism." Events were to suggest the relative merit of these opposed viewpoints.

For the old belief in class, Mussolini offered a belief in the nation. "We have created our myth," he said at the Fascist Congress of Naples in October 1922, a few days before the March on Rome. "Our myth is the Nation, our myth is the greatness of the Nation." The Nation "is not merely the sum of individuals, nor the instrument for parties to attain their goals. Rather it is an organism made up of endless series of generations. . . ."[12]

In his first speech in the Chamber of Deputies, Mussolini questioned Prime Minister Giolitti about the safety of the northern frontiers. This nationalist chord, constantly played, won Mussolini the sympathy of powerful segments of the army. Of course many officers and troops were already favorably disposed to the Fascists and their leader because they viewed them as the interventionists who supported the army during the war and defended the veterans afterward. Mussolini was well aware of the crucial value of this army support, which would play such a decisive role at the hour of the March on Rome.

The feelings expressed by Mussolini and his followers have been described as "reactive nationalism," which is "generally the consequence of a history of humiliation. Industrial development and military capability thus tend to mark the occasion for the redress of old grievances."[13] Productivity—economic development—thus became a watchword of the Fascists, who "declare their support for whatever system guarantees maximum production and maximum prosperity, whether it be individualist, collectivist, or something else." But collectivism, at least as practiced in Leninist Russia, was clearly not working. On the contrary, declared the Fascist agricultural program of 1921, "Communism is the father of famine." (With the Soviets of the 1980s, after sixty years of "bad weather," still unable to feed their people and forced to turn again and again to the West for foodstuffs, the Fascist evaluation of Communist agricultural policy seems to have been a perceptive one.)

The Fascist slogan "Rome or Moscow" began to take on a complex meaning: national regeneration, rejection of Lenin's regime and its would-be imitators at home, and (implicitly) a reconciliation between the Italian State and the Roman Church. The secret of Mussolini's ultimate conquest of power lies partly in the ineptness of his opponents, partly in the attractiveness of a program of radical reform grounded in nationalist sentiment.

As nationalism comprised one pillar of Fascist ideology, elitism comprised another. Mussolini's elitism was rooted in his hereditary Marxism, a fundamental tenet of that faith being the forcible seizure of supreme power by a specific class of persons, a segment of the community endowed with a "historical mission." Elitism also flowed logically from a rejection of liberalism, with its exhaltation of quantity, safety, and mediocrity bitterly condemned by men like Sorel and Pareto, with whose works Mussolini was very familiar.

Theoretical objections aside for the moment, the empirical record of liberalism as it actually functioned in Italy between 1860 and 1920 was not very inspiring, especially from a nationalist point of view. Of course elitism—the belief that power must be placed in the hands of those who have manifested an ability to wield it effectively—implies *authoritarianism*: once the best citizens are in control at last, what is needed is to extend, rather than to hobble, their ability to serve and protect the nation. Elitism also suggests *statism*, the celebration of the state as the expression of the nation and the instrument through which the elite exercise their authoritarian leadership. Through unity, discipline, and sacrifice, Italy would attain to the *moral strength* necessary to compensate for her *material weakness*. The passion of Sorel would transcend the determinism of Marx.

The Italy of 1922 was, in terms of Machievellian theory, a "corrupt state"; to avert the denigration of Italy in Europe, to avenge the denigration of the ex-soldiers within Italy, a new leadership class was essential. Such a new elite, whose credentials were the stigmata of sacrifice, passion, and vigor, was fortunately near at hand: the veterans. The "generation of the trenches" must be organized under the banners of fascism. The Fascists' title to legitimacy as rejuvenators of the nation depended not on votes but on the historical correctness of their actions. "The right to the political succession belongs to us," Mussolini declared, "because we were the ones who pushed the country into the war and led it to victory." The squabblings and dealings of politicians, the endless debates of theoreticians, had too long been a curse in Italy. "It is not programs that are lacking but rather men and willpower," proclaimed Mussolini in September 1922. "Our program is simple: we want to govern Italy." That is, in return for political power, "we propose to give discipline to the nation."

The unchanging goals of fascism included a quasi-monopoly

of power by a Fascist elite in order to pursue national regeneration through increased productivity at home and self-assertion abroad. These ends would be attained through the elimination of strikes, suppression of anti-national activities, improvement of the economic infrastructure, and propaganda directed toward an increased national pride and belief in the national mission (the new "Roman Empire"). The essence of the Fascist world view, of their set of political ends and means, has been concisely summarized in terms of "two programmatic themes that were equally recurrent and insistent in Fascist ideology: (1) the collaboration of all 'productive' classes in the defense of the 'proletarian' fatherland in the service of (2) the maximum development of the nation's productive capacities."[14]

By the fall of 1922, Mussolini had developed an attractive set of symbols and prescriptions that, combined with his political acumen and polemical abilities, had won him a large, devout, and growing following. Made up mainly of smallholders, students, and veterans, they were drawn together by common grievances, enraged at a common enemy, highly mobilizable, truculent, and avid for power. The time of crisis was now at hand.

POWER AT LAST

The outline of the situation in which the March on Rome unfolded was this: In August 1922, the Socialists called yet another general strike, again enflaming middle-class resentments and fears, again allowing the Fascists to assume the role of defenders of the nation and of order. Poorly planned and poorly supported, the strike was an utter disaster, totally demoralizing the working class.[15] Mussolini knew that any forcible takeover of power on his part would receive no effective opposition from that quarter. In the weeks that followed, many of the most important Liberal leaders sought to enter into negotiations with Mussolini, hoping to add him to a coalition that would support their respective ambitions to become prime minister. Most important of all, the army was largely neutralized by the sympathy many officers had for the Fascists, and the presence within the Fascist inner leadership of several former generals.

The elections of 1921 had seen the Fascists enter parliament for the first time, with thirty-five seats. This unimpressive number did not begin to reveal the true strength of the movement; by October 1922 the Fascist party, having enrolled about one million members including tens of thousands of ex-officers, could field a party militia two hundred thousand strong. Nothing like this had been seen before in Italy, or Europe.

By the fall of 1922 Fascist morale and membership were at a peak; after the failure of the general strike, expectations within the party were high. It could be fatal to disappoint these expectations; fascism must obtain at least a share of power, and soon, or its ranks would grow confused and factious like the Socialists. Since no group in parliament was willing to satisfy the Fascist demand for substantial representation in a new cabinet, the decision to stage a demonstration of power—a march on the capital—was taken on October 16. Particular urgency was added to the decision because everybody knew that Giolitti was preparing a comeback as prime minister. He had once ordered the navy to bombard the followers of D'Annunzio; he would doubtless have few scruples over ordering the army to fire on the followers of Mussolini. Besides, many within the party had been urging a march for a long time, especially the old syndicalist Michele Bianchi, who kept up Mussolini's resolve when the latter appeared to waver at the last moment. As Vilfredo Pareto wrote to Mussolini: "It's now or never."[16]

Giovanni Giolitti wanted to be premier one last time and return to power at the head of a very broad coalition that included the Fascists, thus fulfilling the role of political miracle man. Mussolini knew of these plans and kept Giolitti dangling. At the same time he entered into negotiations with Antonio

Salandra and Luigi Facta, each of whom also wished to head "national" coalitions. While Mussolini negotiated with the politicians, he organized the march.

The success of the March on Rome would depend above all on two things: retaining the benevolence of the army, and avoiding anything that would shock the Rome government into precipitate action. Mussolini knew that a struggle with the army must be avoided at all costs. Ideologically, Fascists were nationalists above all, and a clash between a nationalist party and the national army would have been a nightmare. Sentimentally, most of the Fascist leaders were veterans of the Great War, or veterans of the interventionist campaign, or (like Mussolini) veterans of both. Strategically, a successful rising against the army was impossible, as the bloody fiasco of Red Week had shown in 1914. The Fascists were aware that they enjoyed widespread sympathy especially among the officer corps, and Mussolini had received further reassurance on this vital point when, at the time of the Naples congress, a prominent general had told him that the Fascists were very popular with the southern garrisons. The queen mother delivered the same sort of information to a group of Fascist leaders whom she entertained at about the same time.

It was in order to avoid frightening the administration in Rome, especially the king, that the March on Rome took the form of a slow maneuver instead of a sudden rush to the capital. The strategy was for the marchers to converge on Rome from several directions, taking over railway and telegraph stations, city halls and administrative buildings, thus producing in the capital a growing sense of isolation and helplessness.

The actual direction of the March was in the hands of four men, the *Quadrumviri.* Principal among this quadrumvirate was the labor agitator Michele Bianchi. He was, like Mussolini, a journalist by profession, and the two men were of the same age. Bianchi was the Secretary-General of the Fascist party, a post he had achieved after a career as turbulent in its way as that of Mussolini. Before the war Bianchi, a syndicalist, had been active in agriculture strikes in various provinces. During 1914–1915 he played a prominent role in the effort to kindle support for the interventionist cause among workingmen. He volunteered for the army, and later served on the staff of *Il popolo d'Italia.* One of the founders of fascism at the San Sepolcro meeting, he later became very much committed to the idea of a March on Rome, more than once putting pressure on an unconvinced Mussolini. Indeed, later Mussolini would identify Bianchi as the real "brains" behind the undertaking that put the Fascists in power.

General Emilio De Bono sported a great white patriarchal beard, although he was only fifty-eight years old at the time of the March. He held several high army posts during the war. He joined the Fascist party while still in the army, but he was not disciplined for this breach of conduct—an unmistakable sign of the high favor in which the officer corps held the Fascist movement. A monarchist, experienced with techniques of organization, well versed in military tactics, De Bono brought to the Fascist party practical experience in the organization of the March and invaluable contacts with the highest army circles.

The third member of the quadrumvirate was Captain Cesare De Vecchi, one year younger than Mussolini. An attorney, he came from a Piedmontese landowning family, and had many valuable friends at the royal court. He served gallantly in the war and was decorated and promoted many times. He was the principal organizer of the Fascist party in the populous Piedmont, the historic nucleus of united Italy.

The last of the directors of the March on Rome was the twenty-six-year-old Italo Balbo. He had gone off to fight in the war when he was eighteen, and had been completely molded by his experiences in that grim struggle. As a youth, Balbo had proclaimed leftist sympathies, and at the time of the March he still retained marked republican tendencies. But he had been deeply affronted by Socialist insults experienced during and after the war, insults directed at him and other veterans on the streets of countless Italian cities and villages. And so he joined the Fascist party, becoming the leader of fascism in the turbulent province of Ferrara. He joined Bianchi in insisting to Mussolini that the March had to take place sooner rather than later. The youngest and most dashing of the major party leaders, he was perhaps the most personally attractive member of the entire Fascist party elite and was certainly a great favorite of Mussolini's in those early years.*

The Fascists began their mobilization on October 27. The response of the government was better than one could have dreamed: Prime Minister Facta resigned. The king then tried to appoint former wartime leader Antonio Salandra, but Mussolini firmly refused an invitation to serve in his cabinet. During the night of October 27–28, as news poured in of the occupation of one town after another on the roads to Rome, the king pondered the consequence of ordering the Rome garrison to defend the city from the approaching Fascists. A bloody confrontation between the royal army and the Fascist party would ultimately benefit the Socialists and the Communists. Besides, there was no guarantee that the garrison could in fact keep the Fascists from taking over the city; for that matter, there was no guarantee that the troops, or most of them, would obey an order to fire on the Fascist columns. The mutinies of army units in Dalmatia in support of D'Annunzio might well be repeated in Rome in favor of Mussolini. Was it worth running such risks to defend "Liberal Italy," to defend that old calculating machine Giolitti and his retinue of disloyal bootlickers or to defend that scheming little Sicilian priest Sturzo and his gaggle of aged altar boys? Most of all, to defend those

*Balbo later led record-setting mass flights of aircraft from Rome to Rio and from Rome to Chicago. Mussolini eventually promoted Balbo to the rank of marshal and sent him off in 1933 to govern dreary Libya, where he did a great deal to encourage Italian immigration. Balbo was shot down over Africa in 1940 by Italian military aircraft.

The March on Rome

repulsive Socialists? No, it was not worth it. The King told Facta he would not sign an order placing Rome under martial law, and the crisis was over. Mussolini must be sent for; the lonely little boy from the Faenza school must be invited to come down from Milan to the city of popes and kings and take command of the destinies of his countrymen.

Somewhat anticlimactically, about 14,000 rainsoaked and famished Fascists paraded through the streets of Rome on October 30, not to compel Mussolini's appointment to power but to celebrate it. This event represented, in a sense, the final victory of the interventionists of 1915 over the neutralists.

After so many crises, strikes, fights and failures, "the March on Rome came almost as a relief" to most Italians.[17] Appointed Prime Minister, Mussolini also took the portfolios of Foreign Affairs and Interior, a sign of his determination "to get the country moving again." Important leaders of the Nationalist Association received key posts: Luigi Federzoni became Minister of Colonies, and Alfredo Rocco was made Undersecretary of the Treasury. To gather together as much parliamentary support as possible for his new government, Mussolini handed out the rest of the cabinet posts to representatives of all leading parties except the Socialists: this Mussolini cabinet was a true Grand Coalition, including assorted Liberals, leading *Popolari* and others, with the Fascists themselves in the minority.

Mussolini was thirty-nine years old in October 1922, the youngest prime minister in his country's history. Only a few years before, he had been expelled from his hereditary party, was without family connections, without money, and without military fame. That one could manage to rise from such a low estate to the commanding heights of power was against all odds, against all sense, and little short of a political miracle. In effect, his enemies—Liberals, Catholics, Socialists—put him in power because they refused to do what was necessary and obvious to keep him out of it.

Having achieved power, what would Mussolini do with it?

·VI·

THE DICTATOR

"The art of those who govern consists above all in the science of employing words."

Gustave Le Bon

In October 1922, no one, including Mussolini, could have dreamed that he was going to remain in power for twenty years and impose a totally new politico-economic system on the country. The rise of fascism had involved a great deal of violence and counterviolence, but what Mussolini most probably had in mind in October 1922 was several years of authoritarian rule tempered by an outward deference to constitution and parliament. Italy had experienced that kind of rule before.

Francesco Crispi, for example, had been prime minister from 1887 to 1891, and again from 1893 to 1896. He traded for votes in the Chamber of Deputies with bridges, railways, and aqueducts. He engaged heavily in electoral manipulation as well; even as late as 1900 the average Italian parliamentary district counted only 4,500 voters, so it was not too difficult for a cabinet to see to it that enough districts returned favorable deputies. Crispi used to enter into deals with criminal elements, including the Mafia, to make sure that the Chamber of Deputies contained the proper proportion of pro-Crispi members. When General Luigi Pelloux was prime minister (1898-1900), he announced his decision to rule not through parliamentary majorities but through royal decree. Troublesome opposition deputies might find themselves arrested, and Pelloux even closed parliament down altogether for a three-month stretch. As Gaetano Salvemini wrote: "There is nothing new about Mussolini's 'dictatorship'; the Italian parliament has produced nothing but dictators for as long as I can remember. Crispi was a dictator, Giolitti was a dictator, Salandra, Orlando, etc." In any event, it would be a "grave error." according to Communist party godfather Palmiro Togliatti, "to think that fascism took off in 1920, or even during the March on Rome, with a predetermined plan for a dictatorial regime such as it was to become."[1] Many, including some Socialists, believed that Mussolini (who before he became prime minister had never set foot inside a government ministry building) would be tamed by the responsibilities of office.

These hopeful expectations seemed well-founded. The first twenty months of Mussolini's rule are conspicuous for their constitutional and consensual aspects. Mussolini had been legally appointed to office by the king; he presented to parliament a cabinet that was a broad coalition. Neither strikes nor protest demonstrations greeted his investiture. He was receiving very cautious advice from Vilfredo Pareto[2] and he assured everyone from D'Annunzio to Gentile that he would be "intelligent enough not to abuse our victory," and that civil liberties would be respected.[3]

FIRST DAYS OF POWER

Within a few days of the March on Rome, the new administration seemed to be well-launched. Sir Ronald Graham, who would represent the British Government in Rome from 1922 to 1934, had an interview with Mussolini and sent a favorable report back to his superiors. Then came Mussolini's first official address to parliament on November 16. Considering all the circumstances, the speech can not unfairly be termed generally conciliatory. Mussolini began on a menacing note: "I

The newly appointed Prime Minister and his First Council of Ministers

could have turned this lifeless grey hall into a bivouac... I could have closed parliament and made an exclusively Fascist government. I could have, but chose not to, at least for the present," because, he went on reassuringly, "I do not wish to govern against parliament." Then came announcements that could only soothe the parliamentary breast. Budget deficits had to be reduced. "Internal policy can be summarized as economies, work, discipline. The law will be respected at any cost." Fascist foreign policy would be one of "peace, dignity, and firmness" while "peace treaties, good or bad, once signed and ratified, should be carried out." In his peroration the new prime minister exhorted his parliamentary audience to "work with pure hearts and alert minds to ensure the prosperity and grandeur of the fatherland."[4] The speech received the approbation of many parliamentary leaders, including Giolitti and De Gasperi. Giolitti remarked that since parliament had been unable to provide strong government, the country had found it for itself. These were all good omens. Shortly after this successful address, the Fascists merged with the eminently establishmentarian Nationalist party, giving further cause to believe that fascism was being "transformed."

"In the first year and a half of Mussolini's government, there actually was a great deal which lived up to the expectations of the liberals and the conservatives."[5] Many felt that a corner had definitely been turned. On his way to attend the Lausanne Conference in November 1922, called to settle the Turkish question, Mussolini was enthusiastically greeted along the route by great crowds. He became the first prime minister ever to visit Sardinia. In May 1923, King George V visited Rome. He was favorably impressed with Mussolini and awarded him the Order of the Bath. The British monarch remained well-disposed toward the Italian prime minister for many years thereafter. Luigi Albertini, publisher of Italy's most prestigious newspaper, the *Corriere della Sera* of Milan, would one day bitterly oppose Benito Mussolini in the Senate; but in 1923 he wrote: "Mussolini has given the government freshness, youth and vigor, and has won favor at home and abroad."[6] The London *Times* said on October 31, 1923, that "it is incontestable that Italy has never been so united as she is today."[7] Fascism had come to power at a time of worldwide economic upbeat; painful postwar readjustments had been partly completed. Economic life increased in tempo. Most notably, work days lost through strikes declined from seven and a half milion during the year before the March on Rome to less than a quarter million during the following year.[8]

In foreign affairs, Mussolini was able to obtain the symbolically vital city of Fiume for Italy in a peaceable manner. On the pretext of restoring order to the troubled city, Mussolini had ordered the Italian army to take over the administration of Fiume in September 1923. The Yugoslavian government wanted to reach a general settlement with Italy to lessen her dependence on the so-called little Entente, the Czech-Romanian-Yugoslav alliance which the Belgrade government saw as increasingly dominated by Czechoslovakia. Besides, King Alexander I of Yugoslavia admired Mussolini and so by the Pact of Rome, signed in January 1924, Fiume at last came into the legal possession of the Italian people. For this triumph Mussolini was awarded the Collar of the Annunziata, the highest royal decoration, entitling him to be addressed as "Cousin of the King."

New trade vistas were opened up when Italy recognized the Bolshevik regime. Italian fascism, of course, publicly prided itself on having stopped a Bolshevik revolution. The Vatican, moreover, was not at all receptive to the idea of formal diplomatic relations between Italy and the Soviets. And the official Bolshevik view of the March on Rome had been hostile: fascism equalled capitalist reaction. Yet the unofficial representative of the Russian government in Rome advised the Russian Foreign Ministry that "obviously it is simpler for a revolutionary government like Mussolini's, a government answerable to no one, to come to terms with the Soviet government." The Russians yearned for recognition by the Western powers; true,

Germany had established relations with her in 1922, but Germany was, like Russia, something of an international outcast. And Mussolini hoped that formal diplomatic relations with the Bolshevik regime would undercut any serious opposition to Mussolini from the Italian Communist party. (And indeed, this would turn out to be the case during the Matteotti Affair, just about to burst upon the scene.) So Mussolini's government announced its intention to recognize the Russian government in February 1924, becoming the first of the Allied states to establish formal diplomatic relations with the Soviets.

In light of all these events and trends, "no one disputed [Mussolini's] proud assurance at the beginning of 1924: 'the whole rhythm of Italian life has been accelerated.'"[9]

MUSSOLINI AND THE CONSERVATIVES

Much of Mussolini's program between 1922 and 1924—to strengthen the executive branch, build a firm parliamentary majority, bring an end to social strife and especially to the constant strikes, pursue the country's industrial development, and give Italy a respected and influential voice in international politics—was endorsed by many Italians who were by no means Fascists. These aims, plus his long-term goal of reconciling the working class to the nation, would indeed constitute a revolution for Italy. But Mussolini wanted this revolution to be based on consensus: every major group in Italian life must endorse, or at least acquiesce in, his program. If this were not the case, either there would be no revolution (for powerful interests would emasculate it), or it would have to be bloody and destructive (as in Communist Russia). Between liberalism and bolshevism—between sterile inertia and bloody unheaval—Mussolini sought a *via terza*, and the search for this "third way" provided the underpinning for many changes in policy during the succeeding years. Thus, "from the March on Rome . . . to June 1924, Mussolini believed that the basic political problem of fascism was to develop ways of achieving national reconciliation in order to broaden the consensus behind the regime."[10] Mussolini's consensus politics would involve (1) reassurance to non-Fascist conservatives, (2) stabilization of his position in parliament, and (3) an attempted rapprochment with the Socialists.

The most important conservative force in the country was, of course, the army. It was willing to support Mussolini for at least two reasons. First, most officers reacted positively to the Fascists' emphasis on order, patriotism, preparedness, and defense of veterans' rights; at a minimum, almost all officers undoubtedly preferred Mussolini to the only perceived alternative, the hated, veteran-baiting "reds." Second, with its tradition of loyalty to the House of Savoy and with its best officers trained in the crack royal military school at Turin, the officer corps was intensely monarchist and understood that to move against Mussolini would be to humiliate the king. Victor Emmanuel, rightly or wrongly, had evaluated the situation in October 1922 as a choice between Mussolini and civil war. Having chosen the former, he committed the throne—and thereby the army—to a Fascist experiment. Right before the March on Rome, Mussolini had told the Naples Congress of the Fascist party that Italian unity rested upon the House of Savoy. After he had been appointed prime minister, Mussolini deferred to the king in public and thus reassured the army. Although Mussolini grumbled about the king from time to time for many years thereafter, in the words of his biographer Ivone Kirkpatrick, "if there was one man to whom he was consistently loyal during his life [after 1922] it was the king."

To further appease the army and conservative opinion, in July 1923, the violent "squads" of Fascist militants were turned into a state militia called the Voluntary Militia for National Security (MVSN). The Militia was to be tax-supported, open to non-Fascists, under oath to the king, and under the control of the prime minister. General De Bono was appointed first commander of the organization. The creation of the Militia greatly displeased the radicals in Mussolini's party because they saw it (correctly) as a move to restrain them. Mussolini went ahead with the plan, however, for exactly that reason: the new Militia was seen as yet another sign of the increased legalitarian attitude of the Fascist party.[11] The purpose of the Militia was stated to be the internal political defense of the regime, not the external defense of the nation; this was to calm fears and jealousies among army officers. Trouble was inevitable between the regular armed forces and the Militia, however, especially since Militia officers were granted equal status to officers of the royal army. Heavy-armed units of the MVSN would in later years see action in both Ethiopia and Spain, and the costly maintenance and equipment of the Militia ultimately weakened the overall position of the army. In 1923, however, it all seemed well worth it.

However small the chances really were in 1922 for a "Bolshevik" success in Italy, many businessmen found Marxist political rhetoric frightening and Marxist economic prescriptions unsound. Although relations between big business and the Mussolini government always remained stiff at best,[12] financiers and industrialists were greatly pleased by the labor policies of the regime as expressed in the agreements of Palazzo Chigi (December 1923) and Palazzo Vidoni (October 1925). Through these pacts, Fascist unions became the sole bargaining agents for labor, and the Confederation of Industry *(Confindustria)* agents for management. Negotiations were to be supervised by the state, with strikes and lockouts forbidden. The endless, raucous, wasteful disputes of the postwar period seemed to be over.

Perhaps Mussolini's most important domestic policy was the reconciliation of Church and State, culminating in the Lateran Accords, by which "Mussolini won more instant popularity . . . than anything else he ever accomplished."[13] The Accords were not signed until early 1929 and will be discussed in another chapter, but Mussolini began moving toward a conciliation with the Vatican right away. In his first address to parliament he declared his intention to protect the Catholic religion, and asked God's aid for his undertaking. Soon crucifixes reappeared in the classrooms, religious instruction was made compulsory in state schools, chaplains were appointed to the armed forces, members of religious orders were exempted from the draft, the Bank of Rome was saved from disaster, and (not least) government stipends to bishops and pastors were increased. Mussolini the former Socialist atheist even had his children baptized (April 1923). The Vatican did not reply churlishly to these overtures: Pius XI began slowly but unmistakably to withdraw his protection from the Catholic (Popular) party.* This would open up vast fields for Fascist cultivation: the Catholic masses, mainly peasants of the north, disdained the Liberals only slightly less than they feared the Socialists; henceforth deprived of their own party, they had no real alternative to accommodation with the patronage-dispensing, law-wielding and crucifix-hanging Fascists.

THE ELECTION OF 1924

Stabilization of parliament—that is, creation of a reliable, long-term pro-Mussolini majority—would require new elections under a new electoral law. Proportional representation, it was widely agreed, favored a multiplicity of parties and thus prevented the emergence of a cabinet firmly supported by a compact majority. If a stable government was desired, proportional representation would have to be scrapped. Giacomo Acerbo, a thirty-three year-old undersecretary of state and a former secretary of the Fascist party, introduced a proposal for

*Father Luigi Stuzo resigned as head of the Popular party in June 1923, most likely as the result of Fascist pressure on the Vatican. After the development of the Matteotti Affair, Cardinal Gasparri, Papal Secretary of State, urged him to go abroad in order to avoid reprisals. Sturzo left Italy for London in October 1924, on a Vatican passport. He returned to Italy and played an active role in politics after World War II.

an electoral system that would practically guarantee a functioning majority in the Chamber. The Acerbo bill provided that any party or coalition of parties that won a plurality of the votes in the country at large (provided that plurality equaled at least 25 percent of the total vote cast) would be awarded 65 percent of the seats in parliament. (This system was not so very different from the way in which presidents of the United States are chosen: in 1968, Richard Nixon received less than 44 percent of the popular vote but 56 percent of the electoral votes; in 1912 Woodrow Wilson received 42 percent of the popular vote and 82 percent of the electoral votes; in 1860 Abraham Lincoln received less than 40 percent of the popular vote, 59 percent of the electoral votes.) Mussolini's enormous efforts to have parliament pass the Acerbo bill indicate that he intended, as he had often declared, to rule through parliament. After all, any Italian cabinet worth its salt could easily scrape together 25 percent of the vote (Crispi and Giolitti had shown there was really nothing to it), and the opposition vote would be, as usual, fragmented *ad infinitum.* In pleading for the passage of this bill, Mussolini made the "most parliamentary" speech of his entire career.[14] Fully aware that the Acerbo bill would in effect guarantee Mussolini a constitutional parliamentary majority for the next five years (at least), the Chamber of Deputies, although it contained only three dozen Fascist members, nevertheless passed the bill in November 1923, by a vote of 223 to 123. The majority who voted for the bill was made up of diverse elements: (1) staunch Mussolini supporters, plus (2) those who trusted that Mussolini would be tamed by responsibility and become the center of a great conservative coalition, (3) those who feared Fascist reaction if the bill were defeated, and (4) those who, however much devoted to parliamentary principles, believed that drastic reforms were called for in every aspect of national life, including a long-term cabinet supported by a stable majority—even a Fascist majority.[15]

The fact that Mussolini wished to win a real victory in the subsequent (1924) elections—not only seats but in popular votes—is "beyond dispute."[16] A new, pro-Mussolini Chamber of Deputies would free him from dependence upon the king and upon the radical wing of his own party. To attract as many voters as possible to the Fascist electoral list, Mussolini saw to it that many compromises were made with non-Fascist elements; a "star-studded" list was constructed (including former Prime Ministers Salandra and Orlando), completely pro-Mussolini but only partly pro-Fascist.

In this crucial hour, when fascism had arrived in power but had not yet entrenched itself, Mussolini's opponents, preferring their mutual vendettas to an anti-Fascist coalition, displayed the same disunity that had admitted Mussolini to power in the first place. In addition to the Fascist "Big List" (which included many Liberals, *Popolari*, and ex-Socialists), there were the Catholic list, seven Liberal lists, and at least three Marxist lists, including the Communists who had absolutely no chance of winning and could only further fragment the anti-Fascist vote.* The Fascist campaign stressed the moderation of the cabinet's policies, protection of the rights of the Church, and an appeal to patriotism (underlined by the annexation of Fiume). Coercion and intimidation played their traditional role in the election, although Mussolini had made it clear to the prefects that he wanted none of the embarrassment overseas that blatant electoral violence would cost him;[17] as a matter of fact the Fascists did best in those areas of the country where pre-election violence was least. Other factors, ranging from admiration down to grudging support were much more important in explaining Mussolini's great victory ("in the north and center of Italy, bourgeois and middle-class opinion was undoubtedly in the great majority behind the government"[18]). Praise from the Vatican, the southern habit of automatically

*The leadership of the Communist party had expended some effort in trying to get the various opposition parties to field a united anti-fascist list, but the other parties would not go along with the idea.

voting for the government of the day, and the scandalous (or ludicrous) divisions among the anti-Mussolini forces all contributed to the outcome. In any event, on election day, April 6, 1924, the Fascist list received four and a half million votes, against two and a half million for all the others combined (although the total opposition vote in the northern regions of Piedmont-Lombardy-Venezia was slightly larger than that of the Fascists). The pro-government Big List received 355 seats in the Chamber; the largest opposition group was the *Popolari*, with 40 seats (the Communists won only 19). Such authorities as Denis Mack Smith, Edward R. Tannenbaum, Herbert W. Schneider, and Ivone Kirkpatrick accept Mussolini's victory as "incontestable" and "valid."[19] Luigi Sturzo, erstwhile head of the Catholic party, who of all Italian politicians probably lost the most by Mussolini's triumph, questioned the *meaning*, not the *reality*, of the Fascist electoral victory.[20]

THE MATTEOTTI AFFAIR

With the election safely out of the way, Mussolini was now ready to try the greatest act of *trasformismo* in Italian history: the separation of the Socialist politicians from the Socialist masses and the incorporation of the latter into his coalition. Mussolini had already tried to have some Socialist labor leaders join his cabinet in October 1922, but had been unsuccessful.[21] Now it was time to try again. Addressing the new parliament on June 7, 1924, a conciliatory Mussolini spoke of the "educational" value of opposition.[22] Feelers were put out to Socialist union leaders.[23]

Then came the disappearance under suspicious circumstances of Socialist Deputy Giacomo Matteotti, a few days after he had made a violently anti-Mussolini speech to the Chamber. This event, completely upsetting Mussolini's agenda, was destined to have a fateful effect on the course of history.

Giacomo Matteotti had been born in 1885, the scion of a well-to-do family of Po Valley landowners of Tridentine origins. The well-educated Matteotti joined the Socialist party at an early age, and had attended the Reggio Emilia party conference in 1912, the scene of Mussolini's first great triumph. Matteotti was elected to parliament in 1919, and reelected in 1921 and 1924. He was also made secretary general of the Socialist party.

Dark and ascetic, thin-voiced and quick-tongued, Matteotti enjoyed vitriolic debate in the Chamber. Soon after the elections of April, Matteotti had risen to challenge the validity of the outcome in many northern districts. On June 4, he and Mussolini had engaged in a heated exchange on the floor of the Chamber. But things cooled down, and three days later Mussolini delivered his conciliatory speech in which he in effect urged the Socialists to join with him in the renewal of Italy. On June 11, Matteotti failed to return home.

A tremendous outcry inside and outside Italy over Matteotti's disappearance rocked the Mussolini government to its foundations. Signora Matteotti visited the prime minister and expressed her anxieties. Mussolini told her he hoped nothing serious had happened, and assured her that his government would leave nothing undone in the effort to locate her husband. It was during these days that Mussolini began to develop those stomach ulcers that were to plague him for the rest of his life and, as Ernst Nolte writes, "there is no reason to doubt the sincerity of his lamentation: 'only an enemy who had spent long nights thinking up some diabolical thing could have perpetrated this crime, this bestiality.'" (Other commentators also subscribe to the view that Matteotti was killed in order to embarrass Mussolini with the Socialists.)[24]

In a dramatic move many opposition deputies, mainly the Socialists, withdrew from parliament. The members of this so-called Aventine Secession* vowed not to return until the

*In the 2d century B.C., Gaius Gracchus and a mob of Roman plebs set up their banners of rebellion on the Aventine Hill. This was a most injudicious historical analogy for the opposition leaders to choose; the Aventine plebs were massacred and Gracchus himself committed suicide.

king had dismissed Mussolini and appointed an opposition leader (i.e., a Socialist, a leader of the party that had just been overwhelmingly repudiated by the electorate) in his place. The Matteotti Affair, as a matter of fact, was only the pretext for the Aventine Secession, not its cause. "What is important to note is that the idea of such a secession was already current in the first week of June 1924, before the murder."[25] That is to say, the opposition was ready to walk out of parliament because of its disastrous defeat at the polls. After a generation and more of overheating the political scene with their revolutionary rhetoric and revolutionary acts, the Italian Socialists were now demanding that, as a consequence of an act of violence committed against a member of the Chamber of Deputies, an institution they claimed to despise, they should now be appointed, by a king they had vowed to overthrow, to political power in a state they had declared to be illegitimate. It is not clear how many in the Italy of those days were able to appreciate so much irony. In any event, by withdrawing from parliament "the political opposition ran away from the scene of battle," committing "the most stupid action imaginable."[26] Mussolini was the object of hostile demonstrations organized by the opposition parties, and blistering press attacks against him increased when the corpse of Matteotti was finally discovered several weeks after his disappearance. (All this uproar at least proved that in the summer of 1924 Italy was no dictatorship as that term is understood today.) Not all opposition deputies joined the Aventine walkout, while the Communists, upon discovering that the Aventine leaders intended to do nothing but declaim, soon returned to their seats in the Chamber. Nevertheless, the Aventine was to prove a momentous event in Italy's political development for it "condemned to failure the idea of an assimilationist, outwardly legal, constitutionally conservative form of fascism,"[27] toward which Mussolini had been working.

Everything about the Matteotti Affair makes it impossible to believe that Mussolini ordered the crime, or even knew about it beforehand. Mussolini had a large majority in parliament behind him, as well as the support of the king, the army, and the Church, and he was on the verge of splitting the Socialist opposition. Matteotti presented no threat to him or his power whatsoever. Besides, the details of the murder suggest that the intention of Matteotti's abductors had been merely to give him a beating. To kill Matteotti, a well-known figure in Rome, it was not necessary to kidnap him; gunfire or a hand grenade would have been much safer. Then, there were no gunshot or knife wounds on the body, indicating that the victim died of a heart attack. Most important of all, the body was found only a short drive from Rome's center, in a hole so shallow that it could not properly be described as a grave. Such a botched affair could have been premeditated only if the intention had been to ruin Mussolini's reputation and bring down his government.

By the fall of 1924 over a thousand Fascists were in jail on charges of violence, and Mussolini had removed General De Bono as head of the police. Eventually, several low-level Fascists would be convicted and sentenced for the killing of Matteotti. There was no evidence that would stand up in court linking Mussolini to the crime. Two decades later, after the fall of fascism and the killing and discrediting of Mussolini, the trial was reopened. Once again attempts to implicate Mussolini in the murder were unavailing (and more testimony was offered to the effect that the crime had been the result of the determination of many that Mussolini and the Socialists should not make a reconciliation). Nevertheless, at the height of the crisis in the summer and fall of 1924, Senator Albertini and others were holding Mussolini "personally responsible" for the Matteotti killing. His resignation as premier would undoubtedly be followed by his indictment for murder.[28] Mussolini must have pondered the judicial treatment he could expect under the circumstances: the Aventine Secession, loudly proclaiming Mussolini's guilt, had occurred before there was even a *corpus delicti*; the Aventine leaders simply *assumed* that Matteotti had indeed been killed, that Mussolini was personally culpable, and that this culpability would be established (one way or another) in court.* The murder of a Fascist deputy in September in "retaliation" for Matteotti provided Mussolini with more food for thought. In any event, Mussolini did not resign, and the king, following the advice of Giolitti, Salandra, and Orlando, would not dismiss Mussolini until and unless parliament passed a motion of no confidence. (Many years later Victor Emmanuel's son Umberto would write that the king, his father, had not acted against Mussolini because he had "exact knowledge" that Mussolini had had no direct involvement in the crime.[29])

To bring about the removal of Mussolini, therefore, would have required a parliamentary coalition between the opposition, on one hand, and the non-Fascist elements and Fascist waverers within the parliamentary majority, on the other. The creation of such a coalition would have needed a great deal of tact and sagacity on the part of the opposition leaders. Instead (predictably), the Aventine leaders demanded of the majority not only the removal of Mussolini, but also that his erstwhile supporters in parliament offer a plea of guilty to all the "crimes" of recent years and submit to appropriate penalties to be determined by a new, mainly Socialist cabinet. Not suprisingly, few members of the majority rushed to accept these terms.

Meanwhile, the aging Liberal lion Giolitti criticized the secessionists, telling them their duty was to remain in the Chamber. But how could they comprehend his words, when most of them did not believe in parliaments and elections but

*It is sometimes stated that, even though Mussolini had no direct role in or knowledge of the Matteotti murder, he was still guilty of it because he had created the "climate of violence" in which such an event became inevitable; as if this "climate of violence" owed nothing to years of Socialist strikes, "Red Weeks," riots, demonstrations, boycotts, assaults on veterans in the streets, promises to introduce Bolshevik terror in Italy, the whole theory and practice of class war.

instead advocated revolution and the dictatorship of the proletariat? At the same time, tentative feelers from the Catholic party toward the Socialists were brought to a frustrating standstill by both the opposition of the Vatican to any alliance that would bring the Socialists to power, and by the fragmentation and rivalries within the Socialist camp itself. Symbolic of all the confusion and mixed emotions of those days was the content of a newspaper interview with the Liberal Senator Benedetto Croce, in July 1924, the very apogee of crisis. In the interview, Italy's supereminent philosopher-historian observed that "the heart of fascism is love for Italy"; further, "one cannot expect or desire that fascism would fall all of a sudden" because "it has answered serious needs and has done a lot of good, as any honest man must recognize."[30] (Senator Croce had previously come to the conclusion that the *Popolari* were unfit to govern Italy because, being both democratic and papal, they must also be illogical and insincere.) Meanwhile, Giovanni Giolitti continued to attend sessions of the Chamber of Deputies, and was on occasion seen to applaud the speeches of the prime minister. Well-known personalities like Guglielmo Marconi, now a Senator, and former Prime Minister Boselli expressed public support for the regime, and in November 1924, the Senate passed a motion of confidence in the Mussolini cabinet by a vote of 208 to 54.

Thus the opposition had both issued a mortal challenge to Mussolini and given unmistakable evidence of its own impotence—a combination of moves aptly called by one commentator: "The egregious tactics of the inept sectarian groups."[31] Once again cherishing rhetoric and recrimination over anti-Fascist cooperation, the opposition parties preserved Mussolini in power; they played into the hands of those intransigent and revolutionary Fascists who began to demand that Mussolini show the opposition a strong hand, to say the least. These Fascist radicals pointed out the essence of the situation, already well understood by Mussolini: the opposition parties were anti-nationalist, they could rally nothing approaching a plurality of the voters to their respective or collective standards, yet they were clearly determined to prevent Mussolini from governing, even though he had come to power by the rules and had shown great appeal at the polls. Having failed to prevent the March on Rome, having been thoroughly beaten at the ballot box, the Socialists still intended to recoup all, to annul the electoral verdict of 1924, and to hoist themselves into power by draping the corpse of Matteotti around the shoulders of Mussolini (rather a far cry from the "inevitable" proletarian revolution). Mussolini found himself confronted by an opposition that was not only "disloyal" but implacable.

THE DICTATORSHIP BEGINS

The opposition had frittered away most of a year in fruitless negotiations, abortive plots, rootless gestures, and café rhetoric. Mussolini at last picked up the gauntlet. On January 3, 1925, he delivered to the Chamber a fateful speech. "I declare in the sight of this assembly and before all the Italian people that I assume, I alone, full responsibility, political, moral, and historical, for all that has happened. . . . Gentlemen, Italy wants peace, it wants tranquility, it wants calm in which to work. We will give it to her with love if possible or with force if necessary." He thus challenged his opponents, but received no further adverse reactions. After all those months of tension, there had been no parliamentary censure, no move from the king, no coup by the army, no raising of barricades, no gunplay at Palazzo Venezia, and now—not even a good fistfight in the Chamber. Thus the Matteotti Affair ended, not with a revolution of the masses but with a scowl from the prime minister. The "I am responsible" speech of January 3, 1925, may be taken as the real end of Liberal Italy, the first milestone on the road to the Fascist dictatorship.

About one hundred arrests followed immediately upon the conclusion of the speech; over the next two years Mussolini erected the edifice of a completely authoritarian regime. The prime minister was given power to issue decree laws (this really did not change much; the Fascists still had their majority in parliament and they would pass anything Mussolini wanted into law). Elected mayors were removed and new ones appointed. As a newspaperman, Mussolini naturally devoted a great deal of attention to controlling the press; the Press Law of March 1925 forbade newspapers to stir class hatred, advocate crime, hamper foreign policy, disturb the national credit at home or abroad, disparage the nation, the Pope, the king, the royal family, national institutions, or friendly states. The Public Safety Act of November 1926 stated that after two written warnings, a political offender could be sent into internal exile (like the writer Carlo Levi, who recorded his period of internal exile in *Christ Stopped at Eboli*). All these new laws were to be enforced by the secret police organization called OVRA (the letters didn't stand for anything; Mussolini made up the name to frighten the impressionable).

But the emergence of a full-scale Fascist dictatorship did not mean a Holocaust or a Gulag Archipelago. What mainly changed after January 3, 1925, were *attitudes*; everybody knew that fascism was in power to stay. Mussolini did not require the destruction of his enemies, only their submission. Luigi Sturzo, former head of the Catholic party, wrote: "Anti-fascism must go to Canossa, after which the ex-adversaries may live in silence, and abjection."[32] (Except that at Canossa, it had been the politician who submitted to the priest.*) According to a Paris newspaper published by exiled Italian Socialists, political prisoners of the Mussolini regime were almost never subjected to torture.[33] Many who were arrested for political crimes were later found to be innocent and released, "a procedure," notes Hannah Arendt, "quite inconceivable under conditions of Nazi and Bolshevik terror."[34] Some anti-Fascists fled

*The village of Canossa and its castle are located in the Apennines, not far from the Romagna. There in the year 1077 Emperor Henry IV stood barefoot in the snow for three days before being pardoned for a political offense by Pope Gregory VII.

abroad during 1925, and even later. But most of them stayed in Italy all through the Mussolini regime and, according to Denis Mack Smith, "were left unmolested as long as they abjured politics." In Stalin's Russia, it has been estimated that in 1937 there were six million persons in slave-labor camps; and earlier the "collectivization drive and liquidation of the Kulaks" took "about ten million lives."[35] The number of persons condemned to death for political crimes in Fascist Italy between 1925 and 1943 was around twenty-five.[36]

Mussolini assumed office in 1922 according to constitutional forms, amid the acclaim, acquiesence, or apathy of most groups in Italian life. He pursued coalition tactics based on appeals to patriotism, class collaboration, and increased productivity. The atheist Mussolini ardently wooed the Church; the revolutionary Mussolini secured the election of a friendly parliament. Then the ex-Socialist Mussolini turned to transforming the Socialist opposition. It was to prevent this last development that Matteotti rose on the floor of parliament and delivered an address designed to provoke the Fascists to violence. The overzealous attempt of some stupid Fascists to "teach Matteotti a lesson" completely destroyed Mussolini's careful plans and eventually drove him to vigorous repressive measures. The most suffocating irony of this situation lies in the fact that Matteotti's deliberate provocation brought about the dictatorship that he did not want—and that Mussolini did not intend. It is not to say that Mussolini was some sort of democrat in the rough; he could hardly be that, trained as he was in the pugnacious schools of Marx and Sorel. It is rather that, backed by so many strong groups and for so many different reasons, Mussolini did not *need* to become a dictator, or at least no more of a dictator than Francesco Crispi had been. But the Socialists, who had first raised Mussolini to national prominence and later helped him into power through their confusion of Italy with Russia, finally confirmed him in power with their indecisiveness and sectarianism. In short, "the Socialists," as Stuart Hughes wrote, "bear the primary responsibility" for the "collapse of Italian democracy," a stern judgment with which many distinguished observers, both European and American, concur.[37] The Matteotti Affair destroyed forever any chance of a real reconciliation between the Mussolini government and the bulk of the Italian working class; the much schemed-about grand coalition of Fascists, Socialists, and Catholics was finished. "One of Mussolini's possibilities was gone forever, and among all the possibilities it was precisely that one which had been based least on his *fede* and temperament and most on his insights: that of being the head, not the dictator, of a social democracy."[38] Thus, the death of Matteotti and its melancholy sequence represented a sort of final, twisted victory of the Socialist party over the former editor of *Avanti!*

VII
THE CONCILIATION

"By being on good terms
with the Pope, one can
dominate the conscience
of a hundred million men."

Napoleon

"The Church won in the end.
It always does."

Luigi Barzini

Ever since 1870, when Pius IX declared himself the "Prisoner of the Vatican," refused to appear outside St. Peter's, and excommunicated the House of Savoy, Italian politics had been preoccupied with the seemingly insoluble Roman Question. Francesco Crispi had written that whoever settled the Roman Question would become the greatest of all Italians. Benedetto Croce justified Italy's joining the Triple Alliance because it provided protection for the country against papal claims—twenty years after Cavour's death! And as late as 1915 the Salandra cabinet had insisted that the Pope be excluded from any peace conference after the war.

Most Fascists were instinctively and clamorously anti-Christian; turning the other cheek was definitely not their mode. There was not a single important Fascist figure known to be a devout Catholic. Many inside the party shared the attitude of leading heroes of the *risorgimento*, that the Church was an obstacle to Italy's political and moral regeneration. Some feared that any reconciliation with the Vatican would diminish the power of the State, a possibility absolutely abhorrent to any good Fascist. Nevertheless, fascism and Catholicism had some common enemies in Italy, and both Pius XI (elected in 1922) and Mussolini realized that they could give each other important things. Mussolini wanted the positive backing of the Church in his struggle against the Socialists; he also wanted the withdrawal of Church patronage from the Popular party, which he feared and detested. Thus, as early as 1921, Mussolini had begun making unmistakable signs that a future government headed by him would be interested in negotiating an amicable end to the Roman Question. "I affirm," he declared, "that the Latin and imperial tradition of Rome is today represented by Catholicism" (in his lexicon this was a handsome compliment). Let the Vatican give up its temporal claims; then, Mussolini believed, its charitable and educational mission would receive from the Italian government all those essential aids that the modern state can provide.

On the other side of the Tiber, in the Vatican, ever since 1870, the traditional policy toward the Kingdom of Italy had been one of aloof immobility. The Italian kingdom was impious, its occupation of Papal Rome was immoral and inadmissible. Under this cold and daunting surface, however, a number of subtle but important changes had been working themselves out for many years before Mussolini ascended to the premiership.

EVOLUTION OF VATICAN POLICY

The first man to be elected pope in the twentieth century was Giuseppe Sarto (1835-1914), who took the name of Pius X. At the time of his election Cardinal Sarto had been Patriarch of Venice, an office that can only be termed an incubator for modern Popes: besides Sarto in 1903, Venice sent Cardinal Roncalli to the Chair of Peter in 1958 as John XXIII, and Cardinal Luciani in 1978 as John Paul I. The Conclave of 1903 (which occurred when Mussolini was twenty years old) was an unusually dramatic one. The death of the long-lived Leo XIII had left his secretary of state, the Sicilian Cardinal Mariano Rampolla, the leading contender. Rampolla, who was sixty at the time of the Conclave, had been Leo's secretary of state (the equivalent of prime minister) for sixteen years. His election would therefore provide valuable continuity to Church policy in those troubled times. But the arguments against him were very weighty. He was viewed by many as much too pro-French; and he was, like the late Leo, a nobleman. A change of tone and direction in the Papacy seemed to be a wise move, in terms of both tradition and psychology. But the most telling argument of all was that wielded by Emperor Francis Joseph, who pronounced his veto against Rampolla through the mouth of the Cardinal Archbishop of Cracow (unlike the Conclave which elected Pius IX, this time the Habsburg veto was on time). And so the Cardinal electors turned to Sarto of Venice. (Rampolla had his belated victory nevertheless; the next Conclave would select his protégé to be Benedict XV.)

The new pope, sixty-eight years old in 1903, was much less aristocratic and much more Italian than his distinguished predecessor. Indeed Giuseppe Sarto had never been outside Italy in his entire life. His family, of the province of Treviso, had been financially unable to educate him for the priesthood, and so his seminary expenses were defrayed by the charity of others. His character was one of simplicity and kindliness. Unlike Leo, Pius X made people sit down in his presence, sometimes even offering his own chair. Throughout his reign he used a simple nickel watch of no value whatever. He would become the first pope of modern times to be canonized. He would be raised to the dignity of sainthood, however, for his personal virtues, not for his political acumen. Shortly after Pius X ascended the papal throne, the ferocious anticlerical reaction to the Dreyfus Affair broke over France. The complete collapse of Vatican policies toward France helped induce Pius to adopt a more accommodationist stance toward the

Italian kingdom. His basic idea of politics was that Catholics in Italy—indeed Catholics all over the world—should take instructions from their bishops on how to vote. In Italy, this policy caused great confusion. Different bishops had different perceptions of where the Church's political interests really lay. Sometimes an electoral district would overlap two or more dioceses, and the bishops concerned would wind up supporting opposing candidates. To avoid any more of this dangerous and ridiculous chaos, Church leaders created the Catholic Electoral Union, headed by laymen, to coordinate election strategies throughout Italy.

Pius X died in 1914 just as the war was bursting over Europe. He was succeeded by the sixty-year-old Cardinal Archbishop of Bologna, Giacomo Della Chiesa, who took the name of Benedict XV. Benedict was the son of a noble Genoese family. His father, a marchese and very devout, nonetheless insisted that his son have a secular education before preparing for the priesthood; thus the young man entered the seminary with a law degree from a state university. In 1870, when Italian troops took possession of Rome, Giacomo was seventeen. The event made a deep and lasting impression on him. Fifty years later, to celebrate the anniversary of the occupation of Rome, the Italian railway offered half fares for travelers to the Eternal City. Three priests from Pope Benedict's former diocese of Bologna took advantage of the reduced fares to come down to Rome and visit him; the pope refused to receive them. Any observance of the taking of Rome was an insult to the pope, and the fact that priests—priests from his very own Bologna!—would participate, however indirectly and unthinkingly, in the impious celebration left the Holy Father speechless.

Giacomo Della Chiesa had made his career in the Papal diplomatic corps, as the protégé of Cardinal Rampolla, Leo's Secretary of State. Della Chiesa served in Spain and then as a functionary in the secretariat. Rampolla was not reappointed by Pius X; instead the secretariat of state fell to Rampolla's bitter rival, the half-English, half-Spanish Cardinal Merry Del Val (1865-1930), who saw to it that Della Chiesa was eventually removed from the secretariat and "demoted" to the archbishopric of Bologna. Della Chiesa was denied—for seven years—the cardinal's hat which had invariably graced the see of Bologna; indeed the red hat was not bestowed until Rampolla died, making it crystal clear that the denigration of Della Chiesa was really part of a vendetta against his great patron. As it happened, Archbishop Della Chiesa was created cardinal just two months before the Conclave of 1914 that made him Benedict XV. After the election, Cardinal Merry Del Val was given exactly forty-eight hours to vacate his offices at the Secretariat of State.

Benedict was pope during the holocaust of World War I. The demands upon the papal charity reached unprecedented heights. Benedict, in answer to the innumerable and pitious appeals that came to him, first spent his private fortune, then the Vatican treasury—when his successor came to the throne in 1922 he found the Vatican exchequer practically empty.

One of those stories that Romans love to tell concerns the legendary generosity of the aristocratic Pope Benedict. Once a seamstress of the city of Rome made a wager with her friends that she could wangle money from the pope. She wrote Benedict a letter recounting a sad history of her family and requesting 50 lire. In reply, the pope sent her 20,000 lire. Stung with shame, the seamstress again wrote to the pope, confessing her deceit. She received an answer to the effect that pontifical charity could not be taken back, and that she should distribute the money to the poor of her acquaintance.

In the bloody depths of the war, Benedict issued a letter in which he referred to the struggle as "useless carnage." This observation was in a profound sense true, but the Allied government viewed it as undermining morale, and they made bitter and menacing protests to the Vatican. The German government clumsily tried to aggravate the rift between the

Vatican and the Italian kingdom by publicly favoring the creation of an independent Papal State. And Article V of the Treaty of London, whereby Italy had entered the war on the Allied side, had stipulated, at the insistence of the Italian government, that the Holy See was to be permitted absolutely no part in the postwar settlement. Clearly, the time to resolve the longstanding disputes between Roman Church and Italian State was drawing near. It was mainly with this consideration in mind that Benedict warmly (but, of course, unofficially) welcomed and encouraged the new Italian Popular party in 1919.

THE ADVENT OF PIUS XI

The Conclave that assembled in 1922 to choose a successor to Benedict was a long one. The man who eventually emerged to rule the Church of Rome under the name of Pius XI was a compromise choice, sixty-five-year-old archbishop of Milan, Achille Ratti. Ratti, the son of a petit bourgeois family, spent his boyhood amidst the Lombard scenes of Alessandro Manzoni's *I Promessi sposi*. The Lombards were sometimes called the Scotchmen of Italy, a reference to their supposed hardheadness and lack of sentimentality, characteristics that Achille Ratti was to display both before and after his election as Pope.

Pius XI was unique among modern Popes in that he was neither a pastor nor a diplomat. At the time of his election in early 1922, he had been a cardinal for less than a year, and he had headed the Archdiocese of Milan for only five months. True, he had served Benedict XV for a time as Nuncio to Poland—a phoenix-like country, newly emerged from the poisoned ashes of World War I. His embassy to Poland, moreover, while relatively brief and coming late in his life, was nevertheless to help shape his pontificate in important ways. While in Poland, Ratti faced a two-fold problem: how to persuade the Polish hierarchy to divest itself of medieval privileges and attitudes, and how to deal effectively with the country's "gentleman dictator," Marshal Józef Pilsudski. From his Polish vantage point Ratti was able to form a clear and frightening idea of how the Bolsheviks were dismantling the once-splendid edifice of the Russian Orthodox Church, and he was one of the very few foreigners to remain in Warsaw while it was besieged in 1920 by the Red army. His diplomatic experiences in the East would in the not far distant future have profound consequences for Italy and for fascism.

But these adventures notwithstanding, the new Pope Pius XI was, in his formation and his habits, a librarian. He had spent the greater part of his professional life laboring in the great Ambrosian library of Milan. There, in the intellectual capital of Italy, Ratti became well acquainted with the dominant political and cultural trends of Europe; he also traveled widely. For recreation, the bibliophile priest devoted himself to mountain climbing. The methodical librarian and the adventurous mountaineer met in the complex personality of Pius XI, providing rich intellectual and spiritual resources for the man who would exchange thunderbolts with Mussolini, Hitler, and Stalin, all at the same time.

Pius XI requested Cardinal Gasparri, who had served Benedict XV as secretary of state, to continue in office. This reappointment of Gasparri (who had been more than once a major contender for the papacy in his own right) indicated the continued ascendancy of the Leonine party in the leadership of the Church. But before that, the new pope signaled that he was prepared for sweeping new departures in the field of the Church's relation with the Kingdom of Italy. Within a few minutes of his election (in early 1922, several months before the March on Rome), the new pope broke a precedent of fifty years by appearing on the balcony of St. Peter's to bestow the ancient blessing *urbi et orbi*, to the city and to the world. This dramatic and totally unexpected gesture was widely and correctly interpreted as a sign that the new ruler of the Roman Church was prepared to deal finally and at last with that thorny perennial, the Roman Question.

The capture of power by Mussolini's legions a few months later served to increase the level of interest within the Vatican concerning relations with the state. Fascism had shown its willingness to employ violence not only against the Socialists but also against the social infrastructure of the Church. Clearly the apparently long-term Fascist regime would attempt more and more to force the Church into its framework. Thus Pius felt that he was faced with the following alternatives: either a defiant attitude toward the educational and philosophical claims of fascism, leading almost certainly to large-scale violence and the physical curtailment of the Church's activities and presence; or a written agreement with the regime that would clearly spell out the relations between Church and State, thus providing legal standing, political security, and financial stability to the Italian Church and regularizing the relations of the pope (the Bishop of Rome) with the nation.

These weighty considerations were supplemented by others. The war had demonstrated that the Italian State was a permanent entity. The question uppermost in the mind of Pius thus became: who would control it? It must not be the Communists, whom the Pope had come to fear and loath while on his diplomatic mission in East Europe. Democracy—especially the less edifying Italian version—was too frail a reed to protect the Italian Church from such a danger. Parliamentary institutions could not be relied upon to deal firmly with the Bolshevik danger, nor protect the Church's prerogatives, nor even to guarantee public order. An important consequence of these papal views on the shortcomings of parliamentary government was this: in contrast to his predecessor Benedict XV, Pius XI did not view the *Partito Popolare* as an instrument the Church could use or an organization it should support. Pius was not unwilling, therefore, to take the Fascists at their own evaluation as a sure bulwark against a Red Italy. Further, being of a classic nineteenth century European clerical mentality, he was preoccupied with the juridical aspects of the Church's presence in the world, and firmly believed that the mission of the true Church could be strengthened if its spiritual glory were shown forth in close association with earthly political power.

Finally, the sixty-five year old diplomat-pope hoped that Mussolini would become the architect of an alliance of Catholic states stretching from Lisbon to Budapest with its center at Rome, an alliance that would "shut out Communism, contain German expansion, and constitute a new force of balance and social order in Europe." In a word, Pius had big plans for this Mussolini.

Thus, during 1923 and 1924, the pope deftly but unmistakably withdrew his protection from the Popular party, a course of action Mussolini found highly significant and deeply gratifying.

To be sure, some elements high within the Church were not at all certain that a settlement, no matter how superficially favorable to the Holy See, could be truly in the best interests of the Church. The longstanding political and legal disagreements between Church and State in Italy—indeed the refusal of the pope even to recognize the existence of the Kingdom of Italy—at the very least verified the Church's claim to political independence, a consideration of no small importance to an organization with membership and establishments in every land. [1] But Pius XI wanted an agreement.

On the other side, Mussolini not only had to face widespread opposition to any apparent concessions to the Church among many of his most loyal Fascist supporters, but also the notorious anticlericalism of Victor Emmanuel III. Like the pope, however, Mussolini wanted an agreement, and he posited only one unalterable condition for negotiations: the agreement, when completed, must include a repudiation by the Holy See of any further territorial claims upon Italy.

THE PACTS

It took, as a matter of fact, six years of hard bargaining to produce the documents that became known as the Lateran Pacts (after the pope's Lateran Palace). Both Mussolini and Pius XI exercised close supervision over the details, and were aided by their most distinguished and reliable counselors. Especially prominent in the latter stages of the negotiations for the government side was Alfredo Rocco, a former professor of law at the University of Padua. Born in 1875, Rocco had begun his political life as a Socialist but soon abandoned that party to join the Nationalists, among whom he rose to leadership. He served Mussolini as minister of justice from 1925 to 1932, exercising enormous influence on the theory and practice of the ever-developing Fascist state. His prominent role in the Lateran negotiations was a guarantee that the rights of the Italian state would, to say the least, receive due consideration.

The interests of the Vatican were ably represented by two distinguished churchmen who betwen them linked the past and the future. Pietro Gasparri, son of poor Umbrian peasants, had been born in 1852. A brilliant seminary student, he was sent at the age of twenty-three to teach Canon Law at the Institute Catholique in Paris, the world center of Roman Catholic intellectual life. Later he served as apostolic delegate in Latin America. Pius X had set him in charge of the codification of Canon Law and for the completion of this monumental task he was granted the red hat in 1907. Upon the outbreak of World War I, Benedict XV had made him secretary of state. Gasparri was a leading candidate in the 1922 conclave and, in an unusual move, the new Pope Pius XI requested Gasparri to continue as secretary of state. The other principal Vatican negotiator was Eugenio Pacelli. Monsignore Pacelli came of a noble Roman family; his grandfather had helped found the Vatican's semiofficial newspaper *L'Osservatore Romano*, and his brother Francesco, a distinguished attorney, also played a vital part in the Lateran negotiations. Ascetic and aristocratic, grave and hardworking, friendly and gracious, Monsignore Pacelli had been sent by Benedict XV to Munich as Papal Nuncio, in which post he negotiated concordats with the governments of Bavaria and Prussia. Everybody agreed that Pacelli had a bright future.*

Negotiations were completed early in 1929, and the actual signing of the agreements took place at the Lateran Palace on February 11, the anniversary of the coronation of Pius XI. Cardinal Gasparri acted as host to the prime minister and afterward presented Mussolini with a gold pen, a gift from the Pope, with which the secretary of state had signed the documents. The long-sought conciliation was a fact.

The Lateran Pacts consisted of three parts: a treaty between Italy and the Holy See, a concordat regulating the position of the Italian Church, and a financial settlement. Although disagreements became evident even before the ratification, including grave ones concerning the interpretation of certain clauses, most key questions were definitely settled. The Kingdom of Italy recognized papal sovereignty over the State of Vatican City. The papal territory was certainly minuscule: 109 acres around St. Peter's Basilica, along with certain other churches and palaces in the city of Rome, and Castel Gandolfo. But Vatican City enjoyed all the attributes and badges of an independent state; it had a flag, an army, courts of law, a police force (and a jail), a mint and a post office, a newspaper and a

*Pacelli was made cardinal in 1929, and secretary of state the next year, succeeding his old teacher, Gasparri. Pius XI always made it discreetly but completely clear that he wanted Pacelli to be his successor. He sent Cardinal Pacelli everywhere, to Budapest, to Buenos Aires, to Lourdes, even to the United States. When Pius XI died in 1939, the clouded international scene dominated, even more than was usual, the conclave to choose the next pope. The Cardinal Electors overcame the tradition against a secretary of state mounting the throne of Peter, choosing Cardinal Pacelli on the very first day of the balloting. Pacelli took the name of his predecessor, the first pope in a very long time to do so, giving further indication of the Church's determination to maintain continuity in those days of peril. Pius XII was also the first Roman-born pontiff in more than two and a half centuries, and would be the first as well to avail himself of the political potential which germinated in *Azione cattolica.*

Mussolini and high church and state officials at the Lateran Palace after the signing of the Lateran Pacts in 1929.

radio station, even an elementary school. Religious marriages were granted legal status. The Catholic religion ("foundation and capstone of education") was to be taught in both primary and secondary schools.* In addition, the educational and charitable mission of the Church was greatly benefited by the substantial sums, both in cash and securities, that Italy handed over to the Holy See as indemnity for renouncing its claims to the former Papal States. (Under the 1871 Law of Guarantees, the Kingdom of Italy had appropriated a large annual sum to the Vatican to help make up for its lost tax revenues from its former territories, but these monies had never been accepted.) With characteristic hyperbole, but not without a certain justification, Pius XI declared that the pacts had "given God back to Italy and Italy back to God." (Mussolini remembered how at Faenza the priests had given him bread with ants in it; now he gave them billions of lire. They had found him unworthy to remain at their school; now they told their flocks that he was a man sent from God.) It is interesting to note that, although clearly a victory for Catholicism in the temporal sense, the Lateran Pacts nevertheless received the favorable vote of all the Jewish members of the Italian Senate.[2]

Mussolini, fascism, and Italy all derived clear benefits from the settlement. The Vatican extended full recognition to the Kingdom of Italy with its capital in Rome. Henceforth, there need be no conflict, however slight, within the consciences of

*This provision marked a major defeat for Giovanni Gentile, among others. A Sicilian, Gentile had been a collaborator of the great Benedetto Croce, and had taught philosophy at several universities. Gentile belonged to the Liberal party and had few Fascist contacts until he became Minister of Education under Mussolini in 1922. He carried out educational reforms which lessened the traditional Italian emphasis on memorization and stressed understanding and expression. Gentile directed the production of the monumental *Enciclopedia italiana*, became head of the Fascist Institute of Culture, and was called the philosopher of fascism. His Hegelian principles, however, led him to oppose the Lateran Pacts, thus his influence on Mussolini declined. All Gentile's works were put on the Church's Index of Forbidden Books in 1932. In 1944, at the age of sixty-nine, Gentile was gunned down on his own doorstep by Communist partisans.

those who wished to be both devout Catholics and patriotic Italians. Nor could any foreign state now threaten Italy with dismemberment in the name of "liberating the Prisoner of the Vatican." Like Napoleon and his Concordat of 1801, Mussolini found his government immensely strengthened at home and abroad. The Lateran Pacts won Mussolini the sympathy of Catholic prelates, parties, and newspapers all over the world. At home, relations between the State and clergy were almost always friendly after 1929, especially so in the Romagna, Mussolini's home.

With his keen political instincts still unimpaired, Mussolini seized the opportunity to call a national election to ask approval for his regime. The results of the March 1929 plebiscite were overwhelmingly favorable, and "constituted an undoubted triumph for fascism."[3] 8,500,000 votes were cast for the Mussolini list of candidates, and less than 140,000 against. (Yet Mussolini expressed his disappointment to Austen Chamberlain that 23,000 of those negative votes were from his adopted hometown of Milan.) Many factors contributed to Mussolini's victory. There was the general approval of his "forward" foreign policy. There was the usual disarray among the opposition: most anti-fascist elements inside and outside Italy campaigned vociferously for abstention from the polls, although the Communists urged people to go to the polls and vote "no." But preeminent among all the factors accounting for the overwhelming vote of approval was the goodwill among Catholics generated by the Conciliation; thirty thousand parish priests, vigorously seconded by the Jesuits, advised the faithful to look upon Mussolini as (in the phrase of Pope Pius XI himself) "a man sent to us by God." And so, "with the Conciliation and the election of 1929," writes his biographer Ivone Kirkpatrick, "Mussolini reached the high plateau of his career."

Subsequent relations between Mussolini and Pius XI (as between Napoleon and Pius VII) were far from totally tranquil. Mussolini fully realized that by making peace with the Church he had strengthened, not weakened, the Italian State and Italian Nation, and his own reputation as the greatest Italian politician since (at least) Crispi. "We have not resurrected the Temporal Power," he told Fascist party delegates, "we have buried it." Indeed, he always considered the Conciliation to be the major success of his entire career.

Yet Mussolini remained, as he had been, deeply ambivalent toward the Church of Rome and its leaders. He rejected the Church's internationalism, and resented it as an obstacle to his complete control over the Italians. More importantly, Mussolini's admiration for the Church, which was great, was not in terms of theology but of authority and power. Mussolini respected the Church's worldwide influence, her generally very high-quality leadership, her *permanence*. He had for years pondered how these qualities which so attracted him could be harnessed to the purpose of Italy and of fascism. (In 1921 he had remarked that "Catholicism can be used for Italy's national expansion.") Mussolini believed that he had been very generous to the Church in the Lateran Settlement, and understood that Vatican interests required a strong, stable, and united Italy, which he was in the process of erecting. Indeed, Mussolini publicly proclaimed, Christianity had been able to rise from a provincial sect to global power only because its center had moved from Palestine to Rome. And finally, in the face of what many Fascists believed to be the enormous concessions made to the Church, Mussolini the former Socialist firebrand and Romagnole "priest-eater" had to show that he had not become an altar boy. This was clearly a set-up for trouble, even if on the other side of the Tiber they had been willing to avoid all near occasions of conflict with the regime.

For their part, Pius XI and his advisers could not possibly have avoided some sort of collision with the government. This was owing in part to the indefatigable personality of the pontiff, but more importantly to certain peculiarities of Roman Catholic political philosophy. In this philosophy, Church and State are separate and quite distinct entities, or at least should be. The Church is supreme in purely religious matters, the State is supreme in purely secular affairs. But in those questions having implications both spirtual and temporal, questions pertaining to both God and Caesar (called by Catholic philosophers "mixed questions"), the State must accept "guidance" from the Church. And it is, of course, *the Church that defines* which matters or questions are "mixed." Among areas so defined are education and the family, broad fields indeed; how few and how inconsequential must be those policies of the State that have no effect upon either education or family life. The function of the State in matters relating to education and the family is, putting the point baldly, to carry out the teachings of the Church. Anyone who could expect Mussolini and his Fascists to accommodate themselves to this grandiose clericalism would probably expect a panther to play dominoes.

The inevitable clash occurred primarily over the organization called *Azione cattolica*, Catholic Action. Pius XI deeply cherished Catholic Action, envisioning it as a unified army of dedicated laymen under the direction of specially trained clerics, defending and propagating the values of the Church in the modern world. In the eyes of the pontiff, political parties divided Catholics, but Catholic Action would emphasize those things which united them, like fundamental ethical principles. The Fascists, however, could not tolerate the existence of a national organization independent of any control by the State or the party, and it was with the greatest reluctance that the Mussolini regime recognized the lawful existence of *Azione cattolica* in Article 43 of the Concordat.

To Pius XI, Catholic Action was outside and above politics, and hence outside the jurisdiction of the State. But for Mussolini, there was "nothing above the State, nothing outside the State." The Church claimed the role of supreme guide of moral and ethical questions, but had not Mussolini declared: "Let no one think of denying the moral character of the Fascist State. . . . The State, as conceived and realized by fascism, is a spiritual and ethical unit for the organization of the Nation. . . ."

But there was much more than a philosophical dispute involved here. The Fascists saw in Catholic Action the skeleton of a future anti-Fascist (or at least non-Fascist) political party, and with very good reason. Most of the leadership group of the former Popular party were now busy within Catholic Action. Under their tutelage, thousands of young men and women were learning the valuable skills of public speaking, fund raising, and leadership identification, skills that were now employed to advance Roman Catholic piety but which obviously could be turned overnight into the basis of a political party, with branches and activists in every town between the Alps and Sicily. The ink was hardly dry upon the Lateran Accords when elements of the Fascist press began to heap invective upon the unpatriotic and potentially dangerous character of *Azione cattolica*. (It is interesting to note that Mussolini himself kept strictly aloof from these attacks.) Soon violent clashes between Catholic Actionists and Fascists became disconcertingly common. Finally, on June 29, 1931 (feast of Sts. Peter and Paul) Pius XI issued his fiery encyclical *Non abbiamo bisogno* ("We have no need"), a polemical masterpiece unlike anything ever issued before or since by a modern pope. In the letter, Pius completely rejected charges that Catholic Action was either a threat to the regime or an alternative to patriotism, and eloquently protested the persecution to which great numbers of peaceful and loyal Catholic citizens, including priests, were brutally subjected. (The Pope also declared that the Fascist party oath as it stood was unlawful for Catholics to take, but since all men must eat, and a Fascist party card was becoming a prerequisite for more and more categories of jobs, Catholics were advised to take the oath with mental reservations.)

The publication of *Non abbiamo bisogno* was followed by a dramatic increase in physical assaults on the premises and membership of Catholic Action. But in response to the encyclical, foreign criticism of Mussolini also began to mount alarmingly. It seemed that all the immense good will that Mussolini had won for himself and for Italy through the Conciliation might disappear forever. (Besides, the controversy over Catholic Action was taking world attention away from another encyclical Pius had issued a month earlier entitled *Quadragesimo anno* ("In the Fortieth Year"). That document had rejected both communism and laissez-faire liberalism, and advocated certain central themes of corporatist theory, especially class harmony and cooperation under state tutelage. *Quadragesimo anno*, in the eyes of many, came very close to a papal endorsement of at least certain fundamental ideas that were supposed to constitute the basis of Mussolini's economic and social thinking.) Arnaldo Mussolini, loyal Fascist and devout Catholic, warned his brother that this state of affairs—domestic and foreign indignation—could not go on. At the same time, Pius sought to remove what were in Fascist eyes the most offensive characteristics of *Azione cattolica* by reorganizing it along a diocesan rather than a national level, and replacing election of officers by episcopal appointment. And so, in August 1931, verbal and physical Fascist attacks on Catholic Action suddenly ceased. Six months later, Mussolini and Pius met on the third anniversary of the pacts, and the Catholic Action dispute that once seemed likely to pit Church and State against one another in a desperate and unpredictable confrontation, simply withered away. Mussolini would grumble from time to time, even making hair-raising threats against the Pope or the Church in the presence of his intimates. But he was much too intelligent (and too cynical) to try to take on—in Italy—the Roman Catholic Church in a battle that could leave his cherished national unity in shreds even if he won it.

Relations at the very highest levels between Church and State would deteriorate again, especially with the growth of governmental anti-Semitism in 1938 and 1939. Nevertheless, at lower levels Catholicism and fascism coexisted comfortably right up to World War II. No doubt the Vatican of Pius XI preferred Mussolini (if not all Fascists) to the previous system. And critics of Vatican policy within the Church did not hesitate to point out the embarrassing fact that the Roman Question had begun with a government of Catholics and ended with a government of agnostics. It would be a vulgar error, however, to adopt the conclusion that Pius XI was "pro-Fascist." The Holy See was inhibited from an open or sustained confrontation with, or even a cold aloofness from, the Fascist regime for many reasons. One was fear of Fascist reprisals against Catholic organizations and personnel. For another, the Lateran Pacts had seemed to most of the world's Catholics (especially after Pius's effusive rhetoric) to settle any serious problem once and for all. Continued disputes between the Holy See and the Italian State might come to be viewed by less well-informed Catholics around the world as esoteric and, eventually, boring. Nor could the Vatican ignore the fact that most Italian Catholics either viewed the Mussolini government as by far the lesser of evils, or supported it outright. Even in the darkest days of World War II, many of the parish clergy would still preserve sentiments of gratitude to the *Duce*, this support being especially valuable to the regime in rural areas. Besides, in the same year as the Lateran Pacts (which required six years of hard-nosed bargaining), the Holy See signed a concordat with the Socialist government of Prussia; and it was under Pius XI that the excesses of author and future collaborationist Charles Maurras and the *Action française* were condemned. Nor did the Vatican ever try to make a secret of its profound disapproval of Fascist "statolatry," or its official anti-Semitism, or Mussolini's growing entanglement with Hitler's Germany after 1936. Indeed, in March 1937, Pius went so far as to issue the encyclical *Mit brennender Sorge* ("With Burning Heart"), a scathing, root-and-branch condemnation of the Nazi doctrine of blood worship and race hatred. (This letter caused Mussolini much embarrassment; Hitler might well be unhinged on the Jewish issue, but the papal action called into question Mussolini's mastery in his own house.) But in practice Church and State got on well enough in the 1930s. Napoleon feuded bitterly with the Pope after his concordat, even having the frail old Pius VII tossed into prison. Mussolini's pact was much more successful. Vatican and regime correctly evaluated one another; they were not mortal enemies, only troublesome competitors. Most importantly, they had common foes, inside and outside of Italy. Nothing illustrated the situation better than Vatican reaction to the Spanish civil war that erupted in 1936. Many have professed to be surprised and scandalized that the Vatican, indeed almost the entire Catholic world, would support Francisco Franco in that dark and bloody conflict. But in the eyes of almost all Church leaders of the time, the civil war appeared (and not without reason) preeminently a struggle between those who would protect and those who would exterminate religion. In his encyclical *Divini Redemptoris*, issued early in 1937, Pius described the situation in Republican Spain as one of relentless war upon the Church and its members. "Every vestige of the Christian religion," he wrote, "has been eradicated, even though intimately linked with the rarest monuments of arts and science." He deplored the "slaughter of bishops and of thousands of priests and religious of both sexes" and many "laymen of all conditions and classes. And this fearful destruction has been carried out with a hatred and a savage barbarity one could not have believed possible in our age." Mussolini's government became increasingly heavily committed in Spain on the side that the Vatican could only hope and pray would win. Mussolini's reasons for supporting Franco had little, of course, to do with the defense of religion. But the Spanish civil war was yet another important instance where Pius XI could only agree that the interests of the Catholic Church and the policies of the Fascist regime were complimentary. (Even so, the Vatican did not grant diplomatic recognition to the Franco government until 1938, when it was in *de facto* control of most of Spain.) Nobody knows, of course, what would have happened if the Vatican had had to deal with a Fascist regime whose head was no longer Mussolini. Yet a number of devout Catholics held important government posts, especially in the judiciary, and many Fascist leaders could well appreciate the value of an informal and operational alliance with the Church. While there were no devout Catholics among them, Fascist leaders almost always took care to observe the outward forms of religion so important to the ecclesiastical mentality of the old school. In summary, Pius XI had his faults, and he certainly was by nobody's definition, least of all his own, a liberal or a democrat. But that did not make him a Fascist, or a bad man, or even a bad statesman.

To the dyarchy of king and *Duce*, the conciliation added a dyarchy of Church and State. "The Church was one of the few institutions in Italy that fascism never penetrated; in the existence of this 'island' lies one of the fundamental differences between the Fascist regime and the other more truly 'monolithic' dictatorships of our time."[4] But the mutual support of Church and State after 1929 was not a retreat from Fascist aims but a logical extension of them. The essence of Mussolini's domestic program consisted in stopping all the strikes and all the arguing and getting his people to be more productive, more disciplined, more like the Romans of the textbooks. He was content to rely largely on propaganda and example, and to be satisified with incremental change. The benevolence of the Church would be invaluable in his attempt to "raise the consciousness" of Italians, while on the other hand a war of extermination against the Church would utterly destroy plans for national reunification and rejuvenation, and probably the regime as well. For the same sort of reasons, Mussolini valued the monarchy as a symbol of national unity, and he remained loyal to his king, after his fashion, right up to the moment when the king betrayed him. Thus, while Mussolini liked to talk a lot about Fascist "totalitarianism," in reality there was perhaps no group in Italy (except the Mafia) with whom Musolini was not willing to try to make some kind of accommodation, provided such a deal could be viewed as contributing to national development. Hence the cataracts of human blood which Lenin, Stalin, Hitler, and Franco willingly shed in their efforts to purify their nations of the politically or racially unredeemable, were absent in Mussolini's Italy.

VIII

LEADER, PARTY, AND PEOPLE

"The first task of a revolution is to destroy the old aristocracy; the second is to create a new one."

Gustave Le Bon

A PERSONAL PROFILE

Mussolini was the first prime minister of Italy to come from the working class. Ever aware of his humble origins and his lack of those social graces so prized in European diplomatic circles, he employed career members of the foreign office to teach him proper deportment. He learned quickly, and his tutors were further gratified by the fluency of his French. His German and English were only passable, but his command of these languages improved as time went on.

Both before and after he became prime minister, a remarkably large number of women claimed to have had liaisons with him, and Mussolini never denied any of these claims. The real wonder of it all is this: given his opportunities, his proclivities, and the fascination he exercised over certain types of women, how was he ever able to do anything *but* indulge his sexual appetite? His detractors would claim, many years later, that his visible physical deterioration was due to syphilis contracted in his youthful sojourns in Switzerland and Austria. (Would not the anxieties of leading an obviously losing war undermine the health of any man in his sixties?) Mussolini's heredity was also against him. His father died at the age of fifty-seven, his mother at forty-seven, and his brother Arnaldo at forty-six. Whether or not as a young man Mussolini had ever contracted venereal disease is a much disputed and perhaps unresolvable point; what is not disputed is that no physician who ever examined or treated him in his maturity claimed to have found any evidence of syphilis. On the contrary, such a condition was explicitly denied by medical professionals over many years, both before and after his death. Many of Mussolini's contemporaries, including Hitler, Kemal Ataturk, and F.D. Roosevelt, were rumored by their enemies to have syphilis. Apparently the only sure way to avoid syphilis is total abstention from politics. At any rate, the numerous amours of his salad days were eventually replaced by a stable relationship with the green-eyed, Junoesque divorcée Clara Petacci, daughter of a physician. Mussolini first met her in 1933 when she was engaged to be married. A couple of years later he made her his mistress when she left her husband. Clara was to become one of the few really long-lasting people in Mussolini's life, and she seemed content with her existence on the sidelines of the glory of her beloved "Ben." Indeed, one day she would literally lay down her own life in a futile effort to save the man she loved.

Tales of Mussolini the great lover—domineering lord of many a tender heart, a demanding and brutal Casanova—contrasted sharply with the official public image of the prime minister as model family man. Photographs of the *Duce* surrounded by his wife Rachele and their children abounded in the press, and such displays of simple domestic virtue on the part of the leader must have been especially gratifying to the clergy.

Before 1929, Mussolini stayed at the prime minister's residence in Rome, while his family continued to live in Milan. There were numerous vists, Mussolini telephoned Rachele almost daily, and the family was reunited from time to time in trips to the Romagna. Nevertheless, this was an arrangement less than seemly for the soon-to-be conciliator of the Church, the Man of Providence, and the exemplar of Roman *gravitas.* So eventually the whole Mussolini family ensconced itself in the Villa Torlonia on the Via Nomentana. The villa had been placed at the prime minister's disposal by Prince Giovanni Torlonia of the Roman banking family. The large, neoclassical estate had plenty of room for the Mussolini family, which now included five children—three boys and two girls. (Among these, Edda, probably Mussolini's favorite, would soon be wed to Count Galeazzo Ciano. A son, Bruno, would die in an air accident in 1941.) The grounds were ample enough for Mussolini to have a brief horseback ride every day before going to work. Outside, *carabinieri* in magnificent uniform and dour plainclothesmen kept watch.

Rachele Mussolini took advantage of all the space at the villa to raise chickens. At one time her husband kept a pet lioness, and there were also ponies for the children along with assorted dogs and cats. In December 1931, Mahatma Gandhi, escorted by a goat on a leash, stopped for a visit at the villa on his way to the London conference where he would refer to Mussolini as the savior of Italy.

Fashionable Roman society quivered with the expectation that the simple countrywoman Rachele would make all sorts of ludicrous gaffes at state dinners and receptions. She disappointed them by staying away from such functions most of the time, and devoting herself to the management of her household and her family. She often helped the maids of the villa with the household chores and enjoyed working in the gardens. But she also liked to avail herself of a chauffeur-driven limousine to take long rides with her children. While Rachele stayed assiduously out of the limelight in Rome, it was a different story in the Romagna, where she enjoyed playing the role of bountiful benefactress to her relatives and former neighbors. As the years went by, Rachele wanted to have more to say in certain areas of policy. On more than one occasion she advised her husband to retire, especially after the conquest of Ethiopia. She also warned him against those she suspected of being false to him.

Mussolini ignored all her advice, to his ultimate fatal disadvantage.

As for Mussolini himself, while the boy from humble Predappio did not let power go completely to his head (at least not right away), the prime minister did enjoy his little luxuries. He loved clean sheets on his bed. The staff at Villa Torlonia routinely changed the bed linen twice a week. Once Mussolini remarked to Rachele: "Ah, but just imagine if you could have clean sheets *every day. That* would be true luxury!" (It never occurred to him that a prime minister could order his sheets changed whenever he wished.) He liked a morning rubdown with cologne, enjoyed playing the violin, and took his exercise on horseback. He especially liked to see a film in the evening at the villa (among his favorites were Laurel and Hardy). He loved libraries, but hardly ever went to art galleries except on official occasions, because he hated Italy' s image as a sort of gigantic living museum. (This preference for libraries over galleries would baffle and annoy Hitler.)

In general, the prime minister lived simply and worked hard. He rose at six, went to his office at eight, returned home at nine in the evening, and was usually in bed by half-past-ten. His social life was restricted; he had no real friends except his brother Arnaldo. Because of a tendency to develop ulcers, a problem that had its genesis in the days of the Matteotti crisis, he never smoked or drank liquor, limiting himself to mineral water, milk, and an occasional glass of wine. He usually ate only pasta, with vegetables and great quantities of fruit; he fasted one day a week. He was, in short, "modest in his personal tastes as well as being a man who put in ten-hour working days and could not be reproached with making much of the spoils of office."[1] Nor could the members of his family; his brother Arnaldo died in 1931 in very modest financial circumstances. One might have expected that, in light of the poverty of his youth, Mussolini would have used his high office to accumulate money. Even his enemies, however, are agreed on the absence of venality in Mussolini's character. It was not money he wanted, for his interior wound was not caused by lack of material possessions. Mussolini's quarrel with the world lay in his feelings of disparagement, as a lonely schoolboy, as a member of the proletariat, as a son of the Italian nation. To salve this wound he sought acclaim and power for himself, his followers, and his country. To paraphrase Henry Kissinger, happy men do not become great men.

Mussolini, the former editor, remained an avid reader of newspapers from several countries, even during the hectic days of the war. He would clip, annotate, mark in colored pencils, and carefully preserve all kinds of articles, even those critical of himself. He had "an exceptional ability to grasp the substance of situations and what was essential,"[2] but he hated detailed work. This tended to encourage disobedience in those around and under him, since all could be fairly sure that Mussolini would never check up too closely to see if his orders were being followed to the letter, or if the information given to him was exact. "I am," he would exclaim from time to time, "the most disobeyed man in Italy!" Nevertheless, he hated arguments, personal confrontation, and face-to-face unpleasantness of any kind. This duality of Mussolini's—the philandering family man, the dictator who avoided unpleasant scenes with subordinates—was reflected in his attitude toward and relations with the Fascist party.

MUSSOLINI AND HIS PARTY

Before 1922, as a man outside the establishment, with neither the military laurels of a Caesar nor the overflowing coffers of a Crassus, Mussolini needed a party to make his influence felt. To need is not necessarily to get, but Mussolini not only got himself a party but built it into the first of its kind in the world, turning it into an instrument that within a few short years would help him ascend to the seat of power.

Mussolini owed this truly phenomenal success to the unsettled conditions of the postwar period, the inadequacies of his rivals, and his personal gifts of oratory, tenacity, and tactical ability. But underneath these obvious explanations there was Mussolini's early recognition of a profound truth: the Great War had created a new "mass," the men of the trenches, and this mass would not simply dissolve upon demobilization, but remain as the newest and potentially most important element in Italian politics. These were the men Mussolini would organize. The model for the new party, and for the national moral renewal the party would symbolize, "was provided by the men of the trenches, the assault troops—men who had faced the supreme test of will, dedication, and sacrifice. Their right to lead the nation as a vanguard elite was purchased with blood. They were to provide the military models for the new, revolutionary civic consciousness."[3] As Giuseppe Prezzolini wrote, "in this lay the novelty of fascism, in the military organization of a political party."[4]

Once Mussolini was in office, however, the movement was slowly allowed to atrophy. Hence Mussolini's power came to rest solely on his successful direction of the state; if that direction should ever cease to be successful, Mussolini would fall. The process by which the Fascist party stopped being the embryo of a new nation and turned instead into a hollow shell is a complex one. This is especially so since, along with the castor oil administered to unfortunate opponents, along with the braggarts and bullies and social flotsam so characteristic of certain Fascist circles, the party also consisted of some of the most idealistic and self-sacrificing elements in the population, especially those youths who were dedicated to the search for a renewed society of justice and dignity. (Many of these staunch younger Fascists, disappointed with the failures of the Mussolinian revolution would, after 1943, find their way into the ranks of the Communists.)

The increasing debility of the Fascist party after 1922 is sometimes attributed to the fact that fascism had been too successful too early. Lenin had had many years to train and weed his Bolshevik apparatus before the 1917 Petrograd coup;

Hitler had had well over a decade to drill his National Socialists. But on the day of the March on Rome, Italian fascism was less than four years old (less than two as a major national movement) and Mussolini was still in his thirties. The shortage of trained cadres, the absence of real traditions, and the looseness of party discipline rendered the Fascists totally unable to deal with the vast influx of new members right before and right after the taking of power.[5]

The original elites of fascism had been "born in the interventionist agitation of 1914–1915";[6] early fascism was urban, young, and radical. But that party had undergone two big changes in the years immediately before and after the March on Rome. First, a large and aggressive northern rural element had entered, determined to destroy the power of the Socialists in the countryside at any cost. These agrarians had made fascism a powerful national force, but had also caused Mussolini's Pact of Pacification to be aborted, and they still opposed his cherished dream of a grand coalition (Fascists, Catholics, Socialists). As time went on it became clearer to Mussolini that these numerous agrarian elements of the party, too consumed with local problems and too ready to resort to violence, could never be turned into a new ruling class.

The second big change came after 1922. Fascism had come to power not by carrying out a bloody revolution but by effecting a series of explicit or implicit compromises with powerful institutions in Italian society. In dramatic contrast to Bolshevik Russia and Nazi Germany, these institutions—throne, army, big business, bureaucracy, Church—retained during the dictatorship a notable degree of influence and even independence. "As far as possible, the old ruling class was to be absorbed, not destroyed."[7] That was the lesson Mussolini had learned from the chaos of Leninist Russia. One consequence of this was that right after Mussolini's installation as prime minister, hordes of the old order's adherents, especially officeholders, rushed to join the triumphant Fascist party, seriously blurring its image and diluting its fervor. There were real revolutionaries within the Fascist party, men like Roberto Farinacci (1892-1945), party boss of Cremona province and national Party Secretary in 1925. Farinacci and those like him, who were, as Togliatti recognized, in many ways close to being Communists, found themselves yoked together with conservative neomercantilists like Alfredo Rocco. The Fascist leaven was submerged in the lump of southern landowners and Roman bureaucrats, and many fervent first-hour Fascists left the party in despair.

Subtly but effectively helping to undermine the party's position and integrity was its own ideology. Fascism was committed to the concept of statism. "The central idea of our movement is the state," Mussolini had proclaimed; "this is our formula: everything within the State, nothing above the State, nothing against the State."[8] The passing years witnessed the development of this doctrine. In his 1932 article on fascism for the *Enciclopedia italiana*, Mussolini repeated that "the foundation of Fascist doctrine is the conception of the State: its nature, its duty and its aims. Fascism conceives the State as absolute, in comparison to which all individuals and groups are relative, only to be conceived of in their relation to the State." The Nation does not create the State; rather the State creates the Nation, which is "not a race or a geographical region, but a people, historically perpetuating itself, a multitude united by an idea and imbued with the will to live, the will to power, self-consciousness and personality." Fascism "reasserts the rights of the State as expressing the true reality of the individual." The State alone "truly transcends the contrasting interests of individuals and groups, ordering them to a higher end." Consequently, "human or spiritual values cannot exist outside the State, much less have any value. In this sense is fascism totalitarian. . . ." The State was the guide and the refuge of the people of Italy "who are rising again after many centuries of abasement and servitude to foreigners."

These exalted notions of the State left little room for a truly independent and self-regenerating party, especially since the party—any party—was by definition only a *part* of the nation. The petrification of the party began to be noticeable after 1925, when neither an external nor an internal enemy existed against whom the party elites might be rallied or needed. Later, the cult of the *Duce* was superimposed on the cult of the State, equally damaging to the party and to chances for an orderly succession of power, the safeguarding of which should have been the main concern and mission of the party. But how do you prepare for the orderly succession to an incomparable and irreplaceable leader?

For Mussolini's part, he detested certain of the party leaders, especially the agrarians. More importantly, his attitude toward the purpose of the party was purely instrumental: having served to carry him to power, it was henceforth very low on his list of priorities. Consequently, the party became more and more staffed by inadequate and even corrupt types. Here again is that dualism that confronts one at every turn. One side of Mussolini wished passionately to revivify those old Roman virtues of political probity and self-sacrifice for the common cause; the party would be the school for the training of a new, Roman generation. But another side of him was profoundly skeptical of the nature of man, especially of his own countrymen. "In modern society," he had written, "men act only out of self-interest or coercion." Hence Mussolini, who always had a hard time finding men who could give him loyal and competent service, was often unable to appreciate them when he did find them. Further, while he was aware of the spreading financial corruption* in many sectors of the party, he could not believe that even rigorous and sustained efforts to root it out would be really successful. As a result, sincere Fascists lost heart; that cynicism toward public life, which Mussolini had identified as

*Among the sources of this corruption was the family of Clara Petacci, Mussolini's mistress. Some of her relatives learned how to make good use of her relationship with the *Duce*, and in 1940 her brother was involved in an illicit gold traffic ring along with the minister of the interior.

a sickness sapping the strength of the Italian nation, was provided with yet another stimulus.

All these elements—too rapid growth, an essentially anti-party ideology, neglect by the leader—account to a large degree for the slow decomposition of the Fascist party after 1922 (the full extent of which would become all too apparent in 1943). But on a deeper level, fascism succumbed to a malady common to parties in all dictatorships. "Once the leader and his party are securely in power, their interests begin to diverge. The leader wishes to maximize his own power, which means that he must avoid becoming the prisoner of any particular institution or group. Unlike the president or premier in a constitutional system, he does not have any institutional basis of authority. He may hold many offices or none at all, but his power is clearly personal, not institutional. He thus necessarily opposes the development of institutions that could restrain his power. He tries to reduce the authority of the party, and to balance it off against the army, the bureaucracy, the police, mass organizations, and other groups. The leader comes to see the party more and more as a challenge to his personal authority as a leader."[9]

In short, an all-powerful leader cannot coexist with a "real" party, one not totally dependent upon him, however devoted to him it may be. Thus the Nazi party was slowly gutted of any real personality or existence.* Mao's "Cultural Revolution" destroyed the existing structure of the Chinese Communist party and subjected many cadres to humiliation and persecution. Stalin of course drowned the all-conquering Bolshevik party in its own blood, sparing neither those who had struggled

*Alan Bullock offers this grim picture of the Nazis in power: "The boasted totalitarian organization of the National Socialist State was in practice riddled with corruption and inefficiency under the patronage of the Nazi bosses, from men like Göring and Himmler down to the Gauleiters and petty local racketeers of every town in Germany. At every level there were . . . the familiar accompaniments of gangster rule: 'protection,' graft, and the 'rake-off.'"

side by side with Lenin nor the drabbest party hack laboring in remote obscurity.

Nothing like that occurred under Mussolini, whose regime was notable, perhaps more than anything else, for its relative lack of bloodshed. Lenin was actually more vigorous in persecuting opponents *inside* his party than Mussolini was with opponents *outside* his party. Mussolini came to envision the role of the Fascist party as primarily in local administration and in the trade unions; these and other secondary sectors would be a "training ground for the new governing class."[10] Mussolini had no intention, especially after 1925, of granting the party either independent participation in the life of the nation or greater control over its own internal affairs.[11] In one scholar's judgment, which may be considered only slightly overdramatic, by the late 1920s "Mussolini had accomplished the dismemberment of the revolutionary organization that had brought him to power."[12]

Despite these handicaps, elements within the party struggled to live and serve, especially under its most effective and certainly its most selfless secretary general, Augusto Turati (not to be confused with Socialist Party leader Filippo Turati), who ran the party from 1926 to 1930. In Turati's view, the party could best serve the regime by concerning itself with three tasks: the education of the youth; the winning over to the regime of a still largely aloof and suspicious working class; and the ensuring of an orderly Fascist succession to Mussolini when the time came. The most effective and popular work of the party was among the poor, especially poor youth, and war veterans, during the Depression. Fascist youth work was theoretically supposed to inculcate militarism. Actually most party workers stressed physical education, exhorting their charges to avoid alcohol and tobacco, to keep clean, to be courteous, and so on. Yet with all the well-meaning efforts of Augusto Turati, and all the enthusiasm of thousands of obscure party members who really were striving to make a contribution toward a new Rome, the party continued to decline from substance to shadow. The mummification of the once vital organization continued as the regime inexorably approached the time of its greatest testing.

ROME AND FLORENCE

Mussolini was always thinking about refashioning the Italians into a "serious" people. His model, of course, was the Romans. Restoration of Roman virtues, Roman *gravitas*, was a theme running throughout the propaganda and the daydreaming of the regime. "We dream of a Roman Italy," proclaimed the *Duce*, "wise and strong, disciplined and imperial." The New Rome would be built upon a Fascist ethic. "The Fascist virtues," Mussolini wrote, "are tenacity at work; the extreme parsimony of gesture and word; physical and moral courage; absolute loyalty in personal relations; firmness in decisions; affection for comrades; hatred for enemies of the Revolution and the Fatherland; unlimited faithfulness to an oath that has been taken; respect for tradition and at the same time the desire of accomplishment for the morrow."

In his *Enciclopedia italiana* article on fascism, Mussolini wrote that fascism wanted its members to be active mentally and physically. Life was a struggle, and men must make for themselves a worthy place; this required preparation of body, mind and spirit. "Life as conceived of by the Fascist is serious, austere, and religious." In short, "the Fascist disdains the easy life." In 1933 Mussolini set down a code of conduct for officeholders. According to this document, those who held posts of leadership in the new Italy should not frequent restaurants and

A New Rome built upon the fascist ethic was one of* Il Duce*'s fondest dreams—and a recurrent theme in propaganda.

SPQ

theaters; they should never wear top hats; they should, whenever possible, walk rather than ride; if riding was necessary, a simple automobile was desirable, a motorcycle preferable; they should mix with young people, keep office hours faithfully, and listen to the needs of as many persons as possible.

The Roman hopes of the regime were inevitably riveted on the next generation. It must be trained in an austere school of strenuous physical exercise and spiritual dedication to the *patria.* "If," said the *Duce*, "the world were not the world of ferocious wolves that we know, we would renounce our education, which we name, since hypocrisy is hateful to us, a warlike education." Ubiquitous slogans reminded youngsters that life was serious, that the world was Darwinian: *Credere, Obbedire, Combattere* ("Believe, Obey, Fight"); *Libro e moschetto, Fascista perfetto* (literally, "Book and rifle, perfect Fascist"). The new generation must be not only vigorous but numerous. Italians, therefore, must reverse the demographic trends of Western Europe and be fruitful, thus resoundingly refuting Spengler's chilling prophecy of a dried-up Europe whose hour had passed.

The facts were that the Italian birthrate had been declining, along with those of most other Western European countries, a situation that in the 1920s alarmed many, including Mussolini. All theories of international relations and military power place high value on the factor of numbers. The numbers of the Western Europeans were declining in relation to those of the Slavs (perhaps the harbinger of a new barbarian pressure on Rome). The Americans and the Japanese were also increasing at a disturbing rate.

But much more than military considerations entered into the calculations of those who found the decline in the Italian birthrate unacceptable. Many syndicalists viewed this trend as the result of hedonism, egotism, and a general decline in patriotism and confidence in the future. The theorist of nationalism Alfredo Rocco, the political philosopher Robert Michels, the demographer Corrado Gini all agreed, from their varying perspectives, that population decline was an unmitigated national calamity, that it was the unmistakable herald of moral and physical decay.

Thus, if Italy was not to abandon forever her aspirations to great-power status, if the Roman ideals of austerity of life and sacrifice for the State were not to remain a hollow pretense, the birthrate must be reversed. Besides, an expanding population would add further justification to Italy's demands for recognition of her colonial claims: a vigorous, growing people would need not only space for her children but also natural resources for the modernization of the economy to support the increasing population, which only colonies could provide. And so, in 1929, Prime Minister Mussolini announced that the Fascist State would massively intervene in the demographic question to prevent "national suicide."

The great cities were correctly identified as areas of unfruitfulness, the countryside as the source of future generations; hence the regime placed increasing emphasis on improving health and general living conditions in rural areas. Taxes on bachelorhood, subsidies to newlyweds, special wages for fathers of large families, public honors to prolific mothers, all the power and panoply of the State was marshaled in this "Battle of Births." Over a long term, however, the results were disappointing; while the government programs probably slowed the decline in births, they failed to arrest the overall trend. Clearly the re-Romanization of the Italians was going to take a very long time.

Along with his vision of a new Rome, there was Mussolini's fascination with Machiavelli. His often-professed admiration for the Florentine philosopher and politician has sometimes been used as a weapon against the leader of fascism, because everybody knows that "Machiavellian" means "wicked." The fact is that Niccolò Machiavelli has been the victim of a bad press. True enough, Machiavelli seems to deny the absolute quality of a moral law: "how we live is so far removed from how we ought to live, that he who abandons what is done for what ought to be done will bring about not his preservation but his ruin." And there is also that notorious dictum that "the end justifies the means." Aside from the fact that the latter observation may be understood to mean "nothing succeeds like success," one has to put Machiavelli's "immoral" teachings into context. A fundament of Machiavelli's thinking was the division of society into elite and mass, a ruling class and a ruled class. Machiavelli's advice is not for everybody, it is for rulers, those in whose hands the safety and liberty of society rests. *The Prince* is certainly not a handbook for regulating behavior in convents or bridge clubs. Machiavelli is taking the perfectly defensible position that by accepting high office, one is no longer subject to private considerations and the norms of private life; rather, one becomes the agent for the well-being of others. One is not free to do for or with others what one may choose to do for or with oneself. I may choose to sacrifice my own convenience, liberty, or life; I am not free to make that choice for others. Remember also that Machiavelli's advice to princes was penned in very difficult, even brutal, times; the politics of Renaissance Italy (Machiavelli lived from 1469 to 1527) was full of war, betrayal, and destruction. Machiavelli's keen observations of political life in those times and his own disappointing experiences produced in him a pessimistic turn of mind, especially on the subject of human nature. *The Prince* is permeated with the belief that many human problems have no real solution, that the task of the statesman is to choose among dangers and evils. "Let no state believe that it can always follow a safe policy, rather let it think that all are doubtful."

Machiavelli has been called the father of modern political science, of political analysis based on observable facts—what people actually do—and not on philosophical speculation or copybook maxims. This very empiricism, this respect for verifiable facts, led Machiavelli to give his prince much advice that the most fervent anti-Machiavellian would have to consider sound and even enlightened. Machiavelli warned, for example, against the destabilizing effects on society of too great a disparity of wealth between classes. Victorious princes should whenever possible seek to conciliate vanquished opponents. Above all, the wise prince, avoiding rapacity or arrogance, will respect both the dignity and the property of his subjects. Machiavelli was one of the first advocates of the maxim that good government is good politics. Beyond this, he was a convinced republican and a devout Italian patriot; *The Prince* can in fact best be understood as a manual for whoever would seek to free the Italian nation from the oppression of foreigners and give Italy order, dignity, and prosperity (and Mussolini would not have had any trouble imagining himself to be just that man).

Mussolini knew his Machiavelli. Father Alessandro would sometimes read from the works of the Florentine to young Benito after supper. Years later, Margherita Sarfatti observed that Mussolini often mentioned or quoted Machiavelli in conversation. For Mussolini, Machiavelli was "the teacher of all teachers of politics"; indeed *The Prince* ought to be "the *vade mecum* of statesmen" because "Machiavelli indulges in no illusions."[13] Mussolini liked to write about Machiavelli, and to draw conclusions from him to justify his actions and his regime. In 1924, the University of Bologna wished to honor the prime minister by conferring a doctoral degree upon him. Mussolini insisted that he first submit a thesis to an examining board; the title of the thesis was *Preludio al Machiavelli.* In this paper Mussolini warmly approved the teaching of his master that "government by consent," especially in delicate matters of foreign affairs, was neither possible nor desirable. "The doctrine of Machiavelli," wrote the prime minister, "is more alive today than it was four centuries ago." Another of Mussolini's favorite Machiavellian teachings was that armed prophets succeeded and unarmed prophets failed, an observation that influenced, among other things, the organization of the Fascist movement as a militarized party. Most of all, Mussolini derived from Machiavelli his somber views on the weaknesses of human nature and the tentativeness of human enterprise.

It was in part these two dimensions of Mussolini's intellectual equipment, the matter-of-fact Roman and the superpragmatic Machiavellian, that differentiated Mussolini from Lenin, Stalin, and Hitler. The latter three were fundamentally fanatics of a religious type, bent on the total reformation and purification of their societies with fire and blood. No price was too high, no intellectual convolution too embarrassing, no enormity too repulsive, if it contributed to the erection of the new paradise on earth. (The hallowed clichés, of course, used to justify the genocidalists are that they were acting out of good old "historical necessity"; after all, you "can't make an omelet without breaking a few eggs"!) But Mussolini was never that sure of himself, never that impressed with the possibilities of transforming human society overnight. Mussolini's prescription for the Italian people was in effect a regimen of strenuous exercise, not the amputations and lobotomies of his fellow dictators to the north and east. Thus Fascist "totalitarianism," although the term had been invented by Mussolini, never reached the nightmarish proportions of the Nazi and Bolshevik experiments. The Mussolini dictatorship emerged gradually over Italian life, and was not so different from what had gone before. As Adrian Lyttelton writes, "unfortunately the creation of the Police state in Italy was much assisted by the inadequacy of the guarantees for liberty provided under the parliamentary system. The Fascist regime was able to build upon established institutions and precedents." And even former members of the Aventine Secession could be forgiven, or at least ignored, if they kept away from trouble. Totalitarianism in Italy meant not an attempt at total control over every aspect and moment of society, but rather a refusal to recognize any preexisting limit on what the state might command. It was the arbitrary manner in which power could be and was used, rather than its repressive and all-pervasive nature, that could make life difficult in Italy. There was, for example, the matter of the professors' oath, a needlessly galling piece of heavy-handedness by which all Italian academicians employed by the state were given the choice of swearing allegiance to the fundamentals of the regime, or resigning their posts. Professors' oaths were certainly nothing new in Europe; two-score professors at the University of Bologna had been dismissed in 1861 for refusing an oath to King Victor Emmanuel. In any event, the professors of Mussolini's day accepted the oath almost unanimously (perhaps their perceptions of the regime were not quite so negative as it later became fashionable to proclaim). But despotism could also be enlightened: arbitrary authority permitted the introduction into Italian education of some long-needed reforms, many of which remained in effect after the regime had been overthrown.[14]

In a similiar manner, the Fascist government was able to move massively and effectively against that perennial plague of Sicilian society, the Mafia. The Prefect of Palermo, Cesare Mori, was given carte blanche to clean out the Mafia in 1926. He did his best, which was very good, and soon "broke the Mafia by the use of ruthless police methods, including torture. This was an achievement which undoubtedly won Fascism a good deal of popularity and prestige."[15] Alas, "the resurgence of the mafiosi quite naturally followed the collapse of the dictatorship."[16] For many years after Mussolini's fall, nostalgia for those Mafia-free days lasted among the peasant proprietors of Sicily who yearned for Fascist order and security.

MUSSOLINI AND PUBLIC OPINION

This brings us to the question of Mussolini's popular standing. Few, of course, any longer cling to the quaint and comfortable idea that all dictatorships are necessarily unpopular. Many dictators have in fact ruled with widespread popular support, at least during certain periods of their incumbency, and this is unquestionably the case with Mussolini, whatever his shortcomings and errors. The testimony of scholars, journalists, and other observers, Italian and foreign, is overwhelming on this point, and the following examples are only among the most notable. "The great majority of Italians," wrote Christopher Seton-Watson, "without embracing the Fascist creed, acquiesced."[17] As Maurice Neufeld puts it: "Not even Mussolini's bitterest political enemies and severest critics ever adduced substantial evidence to prove that the Fascist plebiscitary dictatorship did not enjoy the confidence of most Italians."[18] In Alberto Aquarone's view, by 1929 it was "incontestable that fascism could count on at least the passive support of great numbers of people in every social class."[19] However negatively phrased and cautious these statements, they are really quite impressive considering the seldom-violated postwar tabu against saying anything nonpejorative about the Mussolini regime. But there are more positive examples. According to Herbert Matthews, "the *Duce* really had enormous popular support in those days [the early 1930s]."[20] "By 1935," writes James Gregor, "the working masses of the peninsula, irrespective of the sacrifices they were obliged to bear, were supportive of the regime."[21] Indeed, the regime usually "had the country behind it," according to the venerable Federico Chabod.[22] After a decade in power, writes Renzo De Felice, Mussolini had actually created "a consensus."[23]

Certainly government and party propaganda had a role in generating this popularity, in choreographing this consensus, but the effects of such propaganda must have been fairly limited in a country with such a large number of functional illiterates and among a populace notorious for its political cynicism. Besides, modern students of propaganda are convinced that no regime, however determined and well-equipped, can complel a people to believe that which it knows or wants to be false,[24] a view whose accuracy has received its most recent confirmation in the eruptions of the Polish workers. It seems much more reasonable to attribute a good part of Mussolini's popularity to the fact that his regime provided, until close to the end, "stability, internal order, and external peace."[25] Nor should one overlook the attraction of Mussolini's personality for his people. In the *Duce* of fascism one could still discern the lonely boy of the Predappio hills, the isolated bad boy of the Faenza school: trusting no one completely, Mussolini had few close friends and few good advisers. Yet, whether engaging in balcony dialogues with the crowds in the Piazza Venezia or triumphantly touring the new towns of the reclaimed Roman Campagna, Mussolini showed that he had a sure understanding of millions of his fellow countrymen. His tastes, his prejudices, and his failings were theirs. The very resentments, the very psychological scars that he had accumulated over the years put him in touch with his people. When Mussolini spoke of a "Proletarian Italy" which must after so many centuries "rise up" and take for itself "a place in the sun," he tapped deep deposits of resentment and longing that previously had been exploited, however inadequately, only by the Marxists.

Thus the *Duce*, confident of his ultimate hold on his people, and with a characteristic blend of the Roman and the Machiavellian, could proclaim that "the world will not collapse, and still less the regime, if the great departments of state and the local authorities are, as has already happened, made the objects of discussion and criticism by knowledgeable people."

Mussolini's general popularity among the Italians was complemented by the approval and/or admiration he elicited from experienced and discerning foreign observers. In his classic study of Fascist Italy first published in 1935 and reprinted several times, Herbert Finer declared that "Mussolini has a profound knowledge of men, the richness and poverty of their character . . . his penetration is extremely subtle." Finer observed that the *Duce* knew how to talk to all manner of men: senators, peasants, students. He had, in fact, "a genius" for government. Finer also observed that Mussolini "reads assiduously, with a wider range than a professor. . . . I suppose no statesman since Gladstone has read so hard as Mussolini." Not only did the leader of fascism demonstrate familiarity with the ideas of men like Freud, Michels, Pareto, Shaw, Sorel, and Spengler, he had been in personal communication with most of them at one time or another. All this led John Gunther to remark that Mussolini was, to his knowledge, "the only modern ruler who can be genuinely termed an intellectual."

Mussolini's stock was also high among leaders of the Anglo-Saxon democracies. In 1933, Winston Churchill told his listeners that Mussolini was a good thing, not only for Italy: "With the Fascist regime, Mussolini has established a center of orientation from which the countries involved in a hand-to-hand struggle against socialism should not hestitate to be guided." Two years later Churchill expressed the conviction that Mussolini was a "really great man." And Austen Chamberlain, foreign secretary from 1924 to 1929, wrote: "The more one knows the Italian prime minister, the more one appreciates and loves him." On the other side of the Atlantic, admirers of Mussolini were abundant. Andrew Mellon, secretary of the treasury under three presidents, was one of them. Richard Washburn Child, the ambassador to Rome of Presidents Harding and Coolidge, was unbounded in his admiration for the Italian prime minister. Good relations between the regime and the United States Embassy in Rome continued during the presidency of Franklin Roosevelt, whose first two ambassadors, Breckinridge Long and William Phillips, both sent home positive assessments of Mussolini and his policies. In Washington, James A. Farley, United States postmaster general and chairman of the Democratic National Committee, and Hugh Johnson, the director of the NRA, (National Recovery Administration) were numbered among Mussolini's admirers, Johnson on at least one public occasion invoking the "shining name" of Mussolini. And President Roosevelt himself, writing to Ambassador Long, confided that, with regard to Mussolini, "I am much interested and deeply impressed by what he has accomplished."[26]

The political and legal structures of Fascist Italy would have received low marks from the authors of the *Federalist Papers.* But it is worth reflecting on the fact that the most effective and best-known piece of anti-Fascist literature to come out of those long years is Carlo Levi's *Christ Stopped at Eboli,* a chronicle of the difficulties faced by an opponent of the regime who is condemned to years of exile in a remote and very dull small town in the south. It is a sensitive and absorbing book, perhaps a masterpiece of Western literature. But it is whole worlds away from the Holocaust literature, not to mention *The Gulag Archipelago.* The heartbreak and horror recorded in those works resulted from the systematic degradation of the human person being incorporated as a policy of state, the destruction of millions of little people in the name of some cruel classist or racist utopia. These things did not exist under Mussolini.

· IX ·

FASCIST ECONOMICS

"Economic problems are political problems."

"In a reclaimed, cultivated, irrigated, disciplined
—that is, Fascist—
Italy, there is room and bread for
another ten million people."

Benito Mussolini

"Divergent as the different dictatorships appear in approach and in aim, they all agree on the basic formula: *the primacy of politics over economics."* Nowhere was this truer than in Mussolini's Italy. Fascists looked at the world in terms of struggle among nations. "The entire nation, faced by the impostures and imperialisms of 'bourgeois' and 'plutocratic' nations, found itself denied sustenance and place." For Fascists, Italy was a "proletarian nation." To improve this situation, to prevent the continued subordination of Italy in the order of the nations, to vindicate Italian claims too long ignored or despised, a buildup of national power was imperative. In the modern world the bedrock of national power is industrialization. That is why in the Fascist view, distribution (economic justice *within* the nation) was a secondary consideration. The interest not of this or that part, but of the entire nation, would and must be served by a program of rapid and sustained industrial buildup. "There in one common interest," Mussolini wrote right before the founding of the first *fascio*, "which overrides class struggle: the interest of production." Everything must be subordinated to this end. In a debate in the Chamber with the Communists in

1921 Mussolini declared: "We, like you, consider necessary a centralized and unitary state which imposes an iron discipline on all individuals; with this difference, that you arrive at this conclusion via the concept of class, and we arrive there via the concept of the nation."[1]

ECONOMICS AS POLITICS

Instead of a strong state bending every effort and harnessing every resource to a policy of industrial development, Italy's economic experience had been characterized by strife and stagnation. Giolitti's policy in labor disputes, even those with fundamental national ramifications, had been one of strict neutrality. Hence there were always strikes going on. Between 1901 and 1913 the annual number of workdays lost through strikes was never less than one million; often it exceeded three and approached four million. Even when they were not striking, many Italian workers did not work very hard because their Socialist evangels had convinced them that they were being exploited merely by being employed: hence by working less they would be exploited less. For a poor country like Italy all this was catastrophic.[2]

At the other end of the social scale, the wealthiest classes failed to fulfill their role as investors and savers; instead they squandered their money on conspicuous consumption and personal service. Thus, even on the part of Marxist observers, the most striking aspect of the economy of pre-1914 Italy was "the absence of any strong ideological stimulus to industrialization."[3]

By the fall of 1914, the Socialist approach to the national interest had become so clearly inadequate to Mussolini that he was willing to suffer explusion from his party as the price for failure to bring it around to his viewpoint. A few years later, watching the chaos and suffering that "War Communism" had created in Russia, Mussolini concluded that any attempt to impose collectivization on the Italian economy (as most Socialists in those days advocated) would result in disaster. (This shrinking from collectivization, even in the years of World War II, is another major reason why the Fascist regime never became thoroughly "totalitarian.")

So by the 1920s Mussolini and his Fascists (or most of them) were vehemently anti-Socialist and anti-Bolshevik. The Russian experiment could not and must not be attempted in Italy. These attitudes, plus the boisterous presence within its ranks of undeniably retrograde and brutally selfish elements, have led many to conclude that fascism must have been predominantly, if not entirely, a movement of reaction, and that its victory over the Socialists therefore constituted a real step backward for Italy. But these conclusions are simply wrong, the font of most of the confusion about the true (that is, *complicated*) nature of fascism. In the words of De Felice, fascism "had its life-giving humus above all in the industrial society of Milan." Among its aims was to transform the "picturesque" (impoverished) Italy so beloved of Anglo-Saxon visitors into a busy, productive, and mighty nation. "Produce, produce, produce," wrote Mussolini at the height of the war, "not only so that the Italy of tomorrow will be less poor than the Italy of yesterday, but so that Italy will be free." Production was power. What Mussolini and his followers were aiming at was a "development dictatorship," a dictatorship based on productive work. "The entire nation must become a wharf, a shipyard," proclaimed the *Duce*; therefore, "let us exalt work, production, those who save, those who work with their hands."[4] Eugen Weber has written that "Fascist doctrines and the Fascist temper are far from reactionary in themselves." On the contrary, the coming to power of the Fascists unleashed "the enthusiasm of reconstruction, the zest of going to work, in which many of the best energies of youth's urge to action found an abode." The goal of fascism in 1922 was, in summary, "not *counter*revolution but *another* revolution."[5]

CORPORATISM

In the quarter century between the founding of the first *fascio* and the murder of Mussolini, Fascist economic policies would undergo some important changes. Some observers have chosen to point to changes in policy and emphasis as proof that there were no fixed Fascist aims, that fascism was an ideological scarecrow stuffed with straw, the flimsy projection of one man's bloated ego. Typically, the same charges are almost never leveled against Lenin and his lieutenants, whose efforts to prove that all was always in strictest accord with the immutable Marxist canon were at times Kafkaesque. In explaining changes of policy in the economic realm, one has to keep in mind that Mussolini was never in total control of Italy, *especially in his own estimation*. The Fascist party shared power in an uneasy arrangement with several other power groups, including the throne, the Church, and the army. The party itself was a broad coalition of diverse elements. Then, Mussolini's pragmatism (and his innocence of theoretical economics) led him to experiment first with one policy, then with another, seeking to judge policy and doctrine by their results rather than forcing Italy to lie down in some Procrustean bed of nineteenth-century economic dogma. Mussolini was thus constantly performing a balancing act among the forces that upheld or were allied with his government, something in the style of an old-time American political boss, while simultaneously searching for a set of workable solutions to Italy's age-old problems of economic stagnation.

However winding the road, the quest remained the same, summarized in "two programmatic themes that were equally recurrent and insistent in Fascist ideology: (1) the collaboration of all 'productive' classes in the defense of the 'proletarian' fatherland in the service of (2) the maximum development of the nation's productive capacities."[6]

These ideas, goals and strivings constituted the seedbed of "corporatism."

"The central political idea of fascism," wrote Hannah Arendt, "is that of the corporate state." Fascist corporatism represented a modern application of two main corporatist traditions. One was that of Catholic sociology; the other, much more important, came from the national syndicalists, those Marxian heretics who had rejected both the control of the workers' movement by middle-class intellectuals and the validity of socialist internationalism. Corporatism, including Fascist corporatism, was first and foremost a response to the disintegrative tendencies of modern society, a search for a viable alternative to liberal capitalism and Marxist collectivism.

The liberal capitalist model sees society as an aggregate of individuals and groups whose primary concerns are of an economic nature. These individuals and groups will compete among each other for relative advantage. Competition and conflict within society is natural and beneficial, because it encourages the stronger and smarter to flourish and penalizes (perhaps with extinction) the less energetic and less gifted. The proper role of the state is limited to preventing this conflict from assuming openly violent forms, and to enforcing the rules of the game (so that, for instance, some group or combination of groups does not bring competition to an end). The "national interest," insofar as this concept is admitted at all, is understood in terms of permitting subsocietal units to define their own ends and pursue them by any means short of violence. Innovation is the greatest virtue, acquisition the ultimate reward.

In the classic Marxist formulation, the history of all hitherto existing society is the history of class struggles. These struggles take place between the economic exploiters, who are wicked, and the economically exploited, who are good. This epic contest between good and wicked will culminate, in a modern capitalist society, with a titanic confrontation between the only two important classes: bourgeoisie and proletariat. The confrontation becomes ever more violent, and ends with the final overthrow of the exploiters by the exploited, ushering in a new society that shall be nonexploitative (because classless) in that the foundation of economic inequality, the foundation of classes—private property—will be abolished. For Marxists, any society in which the proletarian revolution has not triumphed, any society still based on class divisions, is by definition an exploitative (wicked) one. The fundamental, the *only* political question for such a society is not its relations with other societies but the waging of the internecine struggle aimed at the final overthrow of the state and the class system on which it rests. Class collaboration in the national interest is an obscene pretense, a collaboration between the wolf and the lambs. The worker has no fatherland, he has only the class ally and the class enemy.

Liberals and Marxists agree that internal social struggle is natural and beneficial. Both subscribe to a belief in Progress (with a capital P) in which society moves forward and upward by means of profound and often sudden change. Conflict, innovation, the forming and breaking of patterns, the rise and fall of individuals, groups, and nations are inevitable and desirable *for Marxist and Liberal alike.*

In contrast to both these world views stands corporatism, "Fascism's most authentic contribution to the science of politics."[7] Corporatism was at the heart of Fascist thought, and undoubtedly the most attractive aspect of it for most Fascists.

Fascist corporatism was "a device to restore social cohesion." It rested on two fundamental perceptions: the destructive centrifugal tendencies inherent within modern society, and the urgent necessity of state direction if the arrested economy of Italy was to achieve any breakthroughs before the next round of international war broke out. Corporatism sought to overcome the atomizing trends of liberal capitalism and to avoid the stultifying bureaucratization of Marxist collectivism "by incorporating the individual into a rejuvenated Roman *civitas.* The New Rome, with its massive 'corporative' structure into which every individual would be fitted and in the service of which every person could find fulfillment and the release of his vital energy, would perfectly reconcile the individual with the state." The corporate state would be integrated, orderly, stable, organic, and planned.[8]

Various laws were passed in pursuit of these ideals, new institutions set up; eventually the Chamber of Deputies itself would be replaced by a Chamber of Corporations. Under corporatism, the nationwide contract replaced the provincial or regional contract. The system eventually produced "a trained corps of experts in the details of collective bargaining, mediation, contract interpretation, grievance procedures, social security, workers' education, protective labor legislation, prices, wages, incentive systems and payments, statistics of production, the vicissitudes of the labor market, and labor law."[9] Even so, the Fascist corporate state always remained less a highly articulated program than a sort of Sorelian myth, useful for indicating general directions, mobilizing energies, and justifying sacrifices. Like other Fascist conceptions, the corporatist ideal was subject to differing interpretations by persons with differing goals. To romantic radicals, corporatism was a necessary prelude to "true" socialism; for others, it was an assurance to the ablest of the entrepreneurs that Italy would not be the scene of a repetition of Bolshevik enormities. For many, it meant a system for protecting the man in the street from those constant revolutionary and anxiety-producing changes—upswings, downturns, depressions, permanent disruptions—produced by the market economy. And for thoroughgoing conservative statists like Alfredo Rocco, corporatism was a means to discipline the working classes and to direct the bourgeoisie—a modern variant of mercantilism.

Whatever the difficulties of interpretation and implementation, Mussolini really believed in this *via corporativa*; when he proclaimed at Turin in 1932 that "the twentieth century will be the century of fascism," he meant that the corporate solution would inevitably come to be preferred to the drastic cyclical crises of the market economy and the colossal destructiveness of Soviet police collectivism. Corporatism was the future, and it worked: "In ten years, comrades, Italy will be unrecognizable."[10]

CAPITAL AND LABOR

By the agreements of Palazzo Chigi (1923) and Palazzo Vidoni (1925), Fascist unions became the sole bargainers for labor, and the Confederation of Industry became the chief spokesman for business. The state undertook to supervise negotiations, arbitrate disputes, conduct labor exchanges, and expand the welfare services.

Labor was closely tied to the regime, since no one could hold high office in the Fascist unions who was not in good standing with the party. On the other hand, as long as it followed the general political line laid down by the government, industry was free to organize itself and choose its own representatives and work out its own bargaining position. Yet it would be a serious error to suppose from this that business "ran" the Fascist regime or even that it was independent of it. The policies followed by Mussolini were sometimes very helpful to big business, indeed were often designed to be just that, but being helpful to big business was not the purpose or the explanation of the regime. Before 1922, big business had provided useful financial support to fascism (especially when it began to become clear that fascism might come to power), but this relationship was based not on mutual trust but on mutual need (fascism for money, business for "insurance"). After 1922, the support given to the regime by the Confederation of Industry was at the best of times tentative, and with good reason: "capitalists were frequently pushed around—were made to pay heavy taxes, take workers they did not need, and pursue policies of which they did not approve." The great battle over the "quota novanta"—the effort to maintain the lira at a higher value than international market conditions would warrant—was carried on by Mussolini first for reasons of national prestige ("defend the lira"), and second to teach the industrialists and their financial experts who was boss.[11]

The changes of direction and emphasis in Fascist economic policy, from an almost Manchesterian liberalism in its early days to more and more state intervention, had little to do with the wishes of the great industrialists and very much to do with the search for an effective policy for increasing production. Paramount in Fascist economics was "the Fascist emphasis on economic and political independence, on the high emotional salience in which all these efforts were to be effected, on the quasi-military organization of society through the inculcation of 'moral incentives,' on the 'primacy of politics,' on a 'collectivist' rather than a 'liberal' social order. . . ." With the world depression and the foundation of the Institute for Industrial Reconstruction (IRI), "organized capitalism replaced market capitalism as the Fascist model of the economy." By the end of the 1930s, government intervention in the economic affairs of Italy was at a higher level than in any other country in the world outside the Soviet Union. Thus the "capitalists and financiers woke up to find that instead of a servant they had created a master."[12]

A few years ago, Roland Sarti did a great service for students of this subject by writing an illuminating study of the relationship between the Fascist regime and big business. One of Sarti's principal conclusions was that "it makes as much sense to say that Mussolini made use of the industrialists as it does that the industrialists manipulated Mussolini." Actually, fascism was so far from being a mere class dictatorship in the interest of the privileged that a distinguished Italian student of fascism has identified a fundamental weakness of the Mussolini regime precisely in this, that it was closely identified with no class or sector in the community in particular.[13]

Did fascism provide mere window dressing for capitalist domination or agrarian reaction (fascism is, typically, accused of both)? No; fascism's fundamental ideas were highly appropriate, or at least might be expected to be highly attractive, to any leadership group that perceived itself as directing a backward nation threatened by the imperialism of more advanced neighbors. A comparison of Fascist economic policies with the economic ideas of two other leadership groups—Nikolai Bukharin and his followers in Bolshevik Russia in the 1920s, and the rules of Japan during her period of rapid modernization, the so-called Meiji Era (1868–1912)—will illustrate this fundamental point.

Nikolai Bukharin (1888–1938) was eventually killed in Stalin's purges but had previously enjoyed a brilliant career in the Bolshevik party and regime; "by 1917, his reputation as a Bolshevik theorist was second only to Lenin's." Bukharin's vision was an economically modernized Russia. Like Mussolini, he believed that the accomplishment of such an enormous task required not a "distribution of wealth" (that is, a distribution of poverty) nor the destruction of the educated stratum of society, but rather the raising up of the lower levels of society in general through industrialization. In Bukharin's view, this required civil peace, cooperation among various classes, and the utilization of the talents and energies of all social strata. He recognized the key role that the agricultural sector must play in long-term economic modernization and advocated holding down unemployment in the cities by improving production techniques and living standards in the countryside. The Soviet economy would be characterized, in his vision, by "a large private sector, individual peasant farming, private accumulation, and the prevalence of market relations."[14]

The Japan of the Meiji Era was as far from Mussolini's Italy culturally as it was geographically. Yet the perceptions of the world shared by Mussolini and the Meiji leaders are strikingly similar. Ito Hirobumi, "Father of the Japanese Constitution," wrote: "In a country such as ours it was evident that it would be necessary to compensate for its smallness of size and population by a compact solidity of organization." The Meiji leaders were "convinced that their country was in danger of foreign attack" and consequently "ideas of social welfare were never allowed to divert policy from the chosen ends." Eventually the Meiji leaders "saw colonialism contributing to ever greater strength for Japan's rivals; and they became obsessed with the urgency of winning for themselves areas that might be available." In essence, Meiji Japan had developed the basic views and policies of fascism *avant la lettre.*[15]

In the astringent judgment of one respected observer of Fascist Italy at the time, "the safeguarding of property rights and the grinding down of real wages—this is the reality of Fascist labor policy."[16] There is some truth in this. Mussolini was, after all, following the classic formula for industrialization: encouraging investment in key sectors and holding consumption levels down, especially by forbidding strikes. This formula almost always works out, in the short and middle run, to the disadvantage of the working class, and Italy was no exception. Besides, the defeat of the Socialists in 1922 and the subsequent failure of Mussolini to win over the bulk of the Socialist working masses to his side after 1924 meant that the workers were, except for the Fascists' own labor leaders, outside the decision-making process, and outsiders are notoriously liable to suffer during periods of economic change. It was not the material poverty of individuals that disturbed Mussolini, it was rather the indignities to which the poor were subject, indignities that, he had come to believe by 1917-1918, were rooted in and indeed symbolized by the poverty and weakness of the nation as a whole. The secret of the poverty of the masses was not that they were proletarians but that they were *Italians*.

On the other hand, it is not clear on exactly what evidence one could make a case that the Italian working class in the 1920s could have entertained *realistic* expectations of something significantly better under a non-Fascist regime. All such expectations would have had to rest on the distributionist fallacy, that there was plenty of everything in Italy, it just wasn't in the right hands. True, a thoroughly pro-labor government might have decreed large increases in wages, but experience has shown often enough that such an action, especially when linked with reduction of working time for industrial workers in a modernizing society, leads to serious inflation which takes a heavy toll from the unorganized and the disadvantaged and, eventually, from the industrial workers themselves.

Fascists had never promised the workers an instant proletarian paradise. To the contrary, they had never made any bones about their belief in the need for belt-tightening all around if economic advances were to take place. Michele Bianchi (1833–1930), a syndicalist leader, a founding father of fascism, and one of the *Quadrumviri* of the March on Rome, was one of the most authoritative spokesmen of fascism in its early years. In 1919 he wrote in *Il popolo d'Italia*: "We must have the courage to say that if the economic conquests of the proletariat are not based on the rock of commercial and industrial prosperity, they can only be ephemeral." In other words, soak-the-rich was not going to be the order of the day. Even so, a full year before the March on Rome, Fascist labor organizations enrolled half a million members, including over a hundred and fifty thousand industrial workers.[17]

Besides, one should not confuse the *effects* of a policy with the *intent* of a policy; function is not purpose. It was no more Mussolini's purpose to punish the working class or permanently alienate it from his regime than it was Stalin's, under whom real wages fell by 50 percent in the early 1930s. Mussolini's big economic idea—derived from the experience of Caporetto and observations of post-1917 Russia—was that the key to all of Italy's economic problems was to be found not in better distribution but in greater production. Eventually a modernized, powerful, and productive Italy would be able to satisfy all the legitimate needs of all her citizens, including the working class. After 1922, moreover, workers received back part of their losses in real wages through government insurance, welfare, and recreation programs. Mussolini also took pains to see that housing was built and distributed to landless laborers in rural districts.[18]

Before the March on Rome, Mussolini had publicly and repeatedly eschewed all plans to carry out a wholesale nationalization of industry. The Bolsheviks had done that, and chaos had followed. Cooperation with private capital, not its liquidation, was the Fascist program. For many at the time, and even today, this provided more evidence for the thesis that Mussolini was nothing but a sold-out Socialist. Yet his position, that nationalization of industry is no panacea (indeed that it creates serious problems of itself), today is good socialist gospel from Birmingham to Bombay. The same position was also adopted, interestingly, during the 1970s as the official stance of the Italian Communist Party. Mussolini's enemies have loved to paint him in vivid colors as a crude reactionary, yet in perceiving in 1922 that economic modernization did not require wholesale nationalization, that it actually required *non*-collectivization, Mussolini appears to have been much more farsighted than his defeated detractors. Indeed, corporatist practice (if not corporatist theory) seems to be on the way to becoming the norm in most of the industrialized nations of Western Europe, and in the United States too.[19]

A much more vulnerable spot in the record of Fascist economics is the south. This area has been the despair of Italian statesmen since the days of Cavour. Massive and sustained economic investment was required here (which the Italian economy could not provide). The south also needed a radical assault on its antique and parasitical social structure. Mussolini did not implement such a program, with the notable exception of a fairly successful campaign against the Mafia. In general, the south was not in much better shape in 1940 than it had been at the time of the March on Rome. Two observations may be appropriate here. First, Mussolini claimed not to have invented a formula for the miraculous transformation of a historically depressed economy into a land of milk and honey, but rather to have ended the class struggle in the interest of national development. Second, four decades after the collapse of fascism, the Italian south is still the most depressed area in Western Europe. Social scientists like Gunnar Myrdal, renowned not only for their competence but for their humanitarianism, have provided new understanding into the frustrating complexities of regional poverty, the deep-rootedness of the culture of poverty. Even very wealthy nations like the United

States have failed, after repeated attempts, to eradicate poverty in areas of the nation where its causes seem to have little to do with the rise and fall of regimes.

ECONOMIC ACHIEVEMENTS

Fascism's lack of success in revitalizing the south brings us to the question of the regime's general balance sheet in the economic sphere. According to the hallowed principle that any stick may be used to beat a dog, Mussolini is accused, sometimes in the same paragraph, with being both the tool of the great industrial barons and with pursuing policies that retarded Italy's economic growth, without anybody being much disturbed by this paradox. As we have seen, the first part of the double accusation—that Mussolini was the puppet of the capitalists—has been subjected to severe criticism by reputable scholars. What about the second part, that as a consequence of Mussolini's policies Italy's "economic development was severely repressed," that the country endured "a slower pace of economic growth"? If these accusations are valid, they are not only damaging to the Fascist regime objectively but also subjectively, because Mussolini and his followers based their claim to the right to rule Italy, at least in part, on the promise that they knew how to turn the country into a modern—that is, an economically developed—society. This theme runs throughout Fascist manifestoes and party platforms, and the writings of official spokesmen and foreign admirers and apologists of the regime. As the *Duce* declared again and again, "increasing production increases the public welfare."[20]

What, then, did fascism actually do to the Italian economy?

For Mussolini, the foundation of a strong economy and a powerful nation was a healthy agriculture; for reasons of both internal and external politics he devoted a lot of money and attention to the rural sector. Years before he had come to power, Mussolini had been exposed to the view, the dream, of his father Alessandro and a whole generation of Romagnole Socialists: Italy—an abundant garden. The *Duce* of fascism was paraphrasing this deeply-held vision of his father when he declared that "in a reclaimed, irrigated, cultivated, disciplined (that is, Fascist) Italy, there will be space and food for another ten million people."[21]

Fascist agricultural policy rested on four main pillars: (1) a huge public works program to relieve rural unemployment and bind the various provinces together; (2) the drive to improve rural living standards in order to slow down the movement of population from the countryside to the cities; (3) an attempt to substantially reduce the importation of foodstuffs by increasing domestic grain production; and (4) a major effort to reclaim wasteland.

When Mussolini came to power Italy was afflicted with chronic unemployment among unskilled laborers, a woefully inadequate economic infrastructure, and a remarkably low degree of national integration. To combat all these problems simultaneously and especially to revivify agriculture, the regime early embarked on "a program of public works hitherto unrivaled in modern Europe."[22] The national highway system was doubled between 1921 and 1931, and the showpiece *autostrade* helped link the impoverished south more closely with the dynamic north.

Fascist policy sought to hold the peasant on the land, hoping thereby to avoid unrestricted urban growth and the unemployment and crime that go with it. This in turn required making rural life more appealing to those who lived in the countryside. Thus Mussolini worked "to shift the balance of state expenditure from towns toward the country. . . . Studies of rural economy and life received great encouragement. . . . The attempt to encourage the building of farmhouses rather than speculative construction in towns was praiseworthy. . . . The ministry of agriculture was revised and [placed] in competent hands." This was the type of policy advocated in Russia by Stalin's great adversary, Bukharin.[23]

Mussolini also wanted a major effort to make the nation self-sufficient in all-important wheat. The so-called *Battaglia del grano*, the Battle of Grain, got under way in 1925 and lasted until 1933. The campaign has often been dismissed as just another showy Fascist propaganda exercise. And indeed, the authors of the *Battaglia del grano* certainly did have serious propaganda purposes in mind. The struggle for national self-sufficiency in grain, especially wheat, was tied into the overall regime goal of national independence from foreign exploitation; the *Battaglia del grano* was a battle for national dignity. The country was covered with photographs of a bare-chested, perspiring Prime Minister Mussolini helping to gather in the abundant harvest. This "battle" approach to advances in various economic sectors would be adopted by many other regimes after World War II; Fidel Castro, no less, would allow pictures of himself performing heroic labors amid the sugar cane to be displayed all over the world.

But the Battle of Grain had serious economic dimensions as well. An Italy self-sufficient in wheat would save a great part of its scanty foreign currency reserves; wheat import costs had traditionally been second only to those of coal. The outbreak of the world depression, the worldwide movement toward economic autarky, and the gathering clouds of international conflict provided further cogent arguments in favor of making Italy more self-sufficient in basic foodstuffs. Some have criticized the *Battaglia del grano* because it involved putting lands into wheat crops that might have been used more productively for other purposes. This criticism seems invalid. Wheat production per acre increased by half between 1921 and 1938. "The total national crop, with a very slight increase in the amount of land put to wheat, was raised from 4.85 million tons in the period 1919-1923 to 7.59 million tons in the years 1935-1939, an amount sufficient for Italian demand."[24]

Above all else in Fascist agricultural policy, there was the reclaiming of the land, *la Bonifica integrale*. Indeed, reclamation was more than just a keystone of agricultural economics. It was, especially in the mind of Mussolini, the quintessence of Fascist national rejuvenation, the proof of a resurrection of Roman discipline, skill, and accomplishment, the pride and

A keynote of fascist agricultural policy was the reclamation of land. Here* Il Duce *is working alongside farmhands to celebrate the first harvest of wheat from the drained Pontine Marshes.

badge of the regime. It was also a real source of popular support. What the destruction of the peasantry was for the Bolsheviks, what the overthrow of the Versailles settlement was for the Nazis, land reclamation was for the Fascists.[25] Mussolini was, of course, from the Romagna, a classic home of land reclamation, and during his rule projects of this nature were truly massive. A law of 1928 provided for the reclamation of 5,700,000 acres of swampland, the equivalent of 7 percent of the total land area of the nation; 300,000 acres were reclaimed in the infamous Pontine Marshes alone. Expenditures on the reclaiming of the land rose from 182 million lire in 1926-1927 to 258 million in 1927-1928. To say this another way, the Mussolini regime spent nine times as much—in gold lire—on reclaiming wasteland between 1922 and 1936 as had been spent in the preceding half century. These reclamation projects included not only the draining of marshes (essential in itself), but also the construction of houses, social and civic centers, and roads in the reclaimed areas. All these attempts at restoration and regeneration in the long-neglected countryside, along with the extension of invalid insurance to farm workers, had many beneficial effects, notably a marked decrease in the death rate. Speaking at the inauguration of one of the newly-built towns in the reclaimed Pontine Marshes, Mussolini told the audience that "this is the war we prefer."[26]

AN INDUSTRIAL STATE

Yet in spite of the regime's pronounced solicitude for a healthy rural sector, approximately one million persons left the farm between 1922 and 1936 to seek a new existence in the growing cities, and left behind in the countryside fewer landless laborers and more tenants and smallholders. For the fact is that in 1936—despite the world economic depression, now in its seventh year, despite Italy's too well-known paucity of natural resources—Italy entered the ranks of the industrialized nations, as the proportion of the active population engaged in agriculture and related pursuits fell below 50 percent for the first time in her history. Developments in the urban industrial sector of the Italian economy, especially between the March on Rome and the Wall Street debacle of 1929, can only be described as impressive. From 1922 to 1929, industrial production actually doubled (using 1922 as a base of 100, the figure in 1929 was 204.5). Even greater advances were registered in particular key areas. For instance, electricity and metallurgy more than doubled; building activity quadrupled. Consider the steel industry, the backbone and symbol of a modern economy; in 1917, at the very height of the war effort, Italian steel production reached 1.3 million tons; by 1929 the figure was well over 2 million, or an increase of 50 percent. This generally increased tempo of Italian industrial life was reflected in some splashy but not insignificant international air exploits; Italian pilots set a record in a run from Italy to Australia in 1925, and twenty-four planes under the command of Italo Balbo (one of the leaders of the March on Rome) set another record on an Italy-Chicago flight in 1933.[27]

The distinguished economist Alexander Gerschenkron identified three key obstacles to Italian economic growth in the years before 1922: (1) political power was in the hands of an increasingly ineffective elite; (2) a prematurely aroused working class was making unrealistic and destructive demands on society; and (3) scarce resources were not concentrated on enterprises and areas which showed strength and viability.[28] It was exactly these three problems and obstacles that fascism had undertaken to attack.

The attack produced mixed results, and Fascist aspirations for economic development were achieved very imperfectly. Italy was a poor country when the Fascists took over, and unlike the new Bolshevik regime in Moscow, Mussolini did not repudiate the nation's massive foreign debts. Compromises with conservative forces, by which fascism had been able to come to power bloodlessly in the first place, often deflected or hobbled phases of the modernization effort. Government plans for the economy were not always the best quality nor executed in the wisest manner. During the 1930s, Italian industrial growth was severely hampered by the world depression and a growing Europe-wide movement toward autarky. With all these caveats, competent observers have nevertheless concluded that the foundations of Italy's vaunted "economic miracle" of the 1950s, when it entered the select ranks of the mass-producing, mass-consuming societies, were laid in the economic policies of the 1920s and 1930s. Years ago the Marxist analyst Franz Borkenau argued that it was fascism's "historic mission" to industrialize Italy. More recently, another Marxist scholar offered this summary of the effects of Mussolini's economic and social policies:

> *Under Fascist rule, Italy underwent rapid capitalist development, with the electrification of the whole country, the blossoming of the automobile and silk industries, the creation of an up-to-date banking system, the prospering of agriculture, the reclaiming of substantial agricultural areas through draining of marshlands, the construction of a considerable network of highways, etc. Italy's rapid progress after World War II . . . would have been unimaginable without the social processes begun during the Fascist period.*[29]

People often resist the idea that fascism was a revolutionary movement; perhaps this is because everybody knows that real revolutionaries, in order to usher in a better world, have to slaughter vast hordes of their fellow citizens, and the Fascist performance was woefully inadequate on that score. Whether or not fascism was a revolution, or a "real" revolution, is perhaps a matter of definition. What is less disputable is this: Fascism had effects on the Italian economy and, hence, indirectly on every aspect of the national life, effects that were notable, profound, and permanent.

X

ETHIOPIA

"As individuals, men believe that they ought to love and serve each other, and establish justice between each other. As racial, economic and national groups, they take for themselves whatever their power can command."

Reinhold Niebuhr

"Power creates its own legitimacy."

Henry Kissinger

"A truly pacifist people would soon disappear from history."

Gustave Le Bon

FOREIGN POLICY: THE 1920s

One of the primary convictions of fascism was that Italy had been deprived of her just rewards in the peace settlement of 1919. Hence Mussolini's advent to power raised a certain apprehension in the chancelleries of Europe. In his first address to the Chamber of Deputies as prime minister, however, Mussolini said: "Peace treaties, good or bad, once signed and ratified, must be carried out. A state which respects itself can have no other doctrine. But treaties are not eternal, they are not irreparable. They are chapters in history, not epilogues to history." However comforting this sound doctrine may have been to other European governments, its effects were soon completely offset by the alarming Corfu incident.

A boundary commission had been appointed to settle the thorny Albanian-Greek frontier. The president of the commission was an Italian, General Enrico Tellini, and the Greek press campaigned bitterly against his alleged partiality to Albania. In August 1923, General Tellini and several commission members were murdered on Greek soil, and Mussolini, who had so often and so vehemently criticized his predecessors for not protecting Italy's national dignity, had to act. Rome made several demands having to do with the apprehension and punishment of the culprits; most of the demands were accepted by the Athens government—but not all. As a result, a few days later an Italian naval force appeared off the Greek island of Corfu and demanded that its fortress surrender. Their demand was rejected, the fleet opened fire (not on orders from Rome), and several persons inside the fortress, including some civilians, were killed. What could have turned into a nasty situation soon blew over, due to a general willingness to back off. The Greeks offered a satisfactory settlement, and Mussolini set up a ten million lire fund to aid Greek refugees from Asia Minor.

Aside from this unsettling contretemps, Mussolini's early foreign policy enjoyed smooth sailing and several successes. (During the 1920s, Mussolini was foreign minister, as well as prime minister.) Rome signed the Washington Naval Treaty and adhered to the Locarno Pact.* The Fascist regime recognized the Soviet government (being one of the very first states to do so), and rebuilt Italian economic and military influence in Albania, which had been abandoned under Giolitti. Italy also obtained peaceful title to the Dodecanese Islands, and a favorable adjustment of the boundary of Italian Somaliland. Most importantly, the Fiume issue, which had helped feed the fires of early fascism, was settled peacefully and in Italy's favor (January 1924). For the rest, Mussolini's foreign policy was deeply influenced by his personal friendship with British Foreign

*Seven states, including Britain, Italy, France, and Germany, sent representatives to the Swiss town of Locarno. The Pact guaranteed the French-German and Belgian-German frontiers. Mussolini was chagrined because no mention was made of the Austro-Italian frontier, but Locarno-type "Big Power" diplomacy—as opposed to the League of Nations—was Mussolini's ideal, which he sought to have institutionalized through his ill-fated Four-Power Pact.

Secretary Austen Chamberlain,* while most of his energy was directed to the internal solidification of the regime and to negotiations with the Holy See.

Underneath a generally calm surface, however, powerful disruptive forces were at work. The British Labour Party was loud in its detestation of the Fascist government, while Paris was the center of anti-Fascist exile propaganda, and the bulk of the French press was openly hostile to Mussolini.

On a deeper level, Fascist and anti-Fascist Italians alike had long viewed their country as seriously disadvantaged, without rich natural resources at home or a compensatory colonial empire overseas. France and Britain had promised Italy colonial rewards in 1915, but failed to deliver after the war. Further, many Italians, including Mussolini, tended to visualize Italy as imprisoned in the Mediterranean, whose exits at Suez and Gilbraltar were in British hands, and in which Italian security was menaced by numerous foreign bases all around her: Corsica, Tunis, Malta, and Cyprus. Any serious Italian attempt to alter the status quo would place her on a collision course with Britain and France, the principal status-quo powers.

The most immediate obstacle to increased Italian security and prestige was France. During the 1920s, the Paris government sought, through its alliance systems (expecially the Little Entente of Czechoslovakia, Yugoslavia, and Romania), to maintain Eastern Europe and the Balkans; indeed France strove to exercise hegemony over the entire continent. No

*Austen Chamberlain (1863–1937), the half brother of Neville, had a distinguished parliamentary career lasting forty-five years, including the posts of chancellor of the exchequeur and secretary of state for India. He was foreign secretary from 1924 to 1929. The Locarno Pact was largely his work, and he received the Nobel Peace Prize for 1925. In 1925 Chamberlain wrote that "I thought Mussolini a strong man of singular charm . . . . I trust his word when given." Mussolini reciprocated Chamberlain's sentiments, and gave him an autographed photo (which he denied to Adolf Hitler).

Italian government, especially a nationalistic one, could countenance such a situation. To Mussolini, the Little Entente looked like a revived Habsburg Empire without the Habsburgs. One of his responses was an effort over many years to link Budapest, Vienna, and Tirana to Rome to counterbalance the all-powerful French, a policy that bore some fruit during the Ethiopian War.

Just as Mussolini's cultivation of friendship with Britain was in the Italian foreign policy tradition, so was opposition to French hegemony. The embodiment of Italian resentment of French pretensions had been Francesco Crispi, the first southern prime minister, who had served two terms in the 1880s and 1890s. Crispi reformed the prisons, attacked cholera, abolished the death penalty, protected emigrants, and extended the local suffrage. He also opposed Giolitti, suppressed the Socialists, and criticized his predecessors for servility to foreign powers. His farsighted project to divide the Sicilian latifundia into small farms on long leases was lost in the parliamentary labyrinth; his dreams of an African empire were drowned in blood at Adowa. Most of all, Crispi represented the anti-French and pro-German tendency in Italian foreign policy. Italy's colonial expansion—vital for survival in Crispi's view—required security for Italy on the European continent; thus he flaunted his friendship with Bismarck and stood firm for the Triple Alliance with Berlin and Vienna. Mussolini liked to identify his regime with many of these policies, and he believed Crispi to be of the same stature as Bismarck.[1] In the end, Mussolini would follow closely in the footsteps of his great predecessor, even to being driven from office for military defeat.

But that was all in the future. As the decade of the 1920s turned into the 1930s, Mussolini attempted to establish a revived Concert of Europe. He did not believe in the Versailles settlement, with its effort to impose total war guilt and heavy indemnities on Germany. The Allies had placed burdens on Germany which she found intolerable, and had at the same time left her powerful enough to challenge them one day. This was clearly a formula for future war. "How can we talk of European reconstruction," he asked in 1931, "if certain clauses of Peace Treaties, which have driven whole peoples to the edge of the abyss and moral despair, are not modified?" Mussolini did not believe in the League of Nations either; for him, collective security and the equality of all sovereign states was all dangerous cant, mere blather. Instead, Mussolini wanted to ensure that treaty revision—which for him, especially after the rise of Hitler to power, seemed inevitable—be carried out in a manner that was orderly and took into account the interests of all the major powers. Hence he presented his Four Power Pact, to bind Britain, France, Germany, and Italy together in a regular and organized search for mutual accommodation outside the debating halls of the League of Nations. Initially supported by Britain and acquiesced in by Germany, the Pact was vigorously opposed by the Little Entente, and also by the French. A watered-down version of the Pact was eventually signed but allowed to come to nothing. France, in seeking to freeze the status quo of 1919, guaranteed its eventual overthrow by force. The Four Power Pact idea was one of the last chances for Europe to head off Hitler, and the reception Mussolini's ideas had received in Paris offended him. Whether his plan would really have produced a peaceful revision in Europe is anybody's guess, but it certainly could not have produced anything worse than what eventually took place.

But if the Western Allies were unwilling to provide for evolution in the Versailles settlement, they were increasingly unwilling to defend it. Public opinion in Britain had to a large degree lost faith in the moral and intellectual foundations of the peace treaties; the British Labour Party was increasingly insisting on pacifism and unilateral disarmament. More important, the French army, principal victor in 1918 and chief guarantor of continental stability, opted after 1929 for a defensive strategy embodied in the Maginot Line. In the words of

Charles DeGaulle, France was "clearly withdrawing into a passive strategic policy which left Europe a prey to Hitler's ambitions."

A student of Machiavelli, Mussolini knew that this situation could not last.

AUSTRIA

The generalized unwillingness to defend fundamental points of the Versailles settlement, especially after Hitler was made chancellor in 1933, was soon brought home to the Italians in the most sensitive area possible: Austria.

The disintegration of the mighty Habsburg state had been Italy's chief gain from World War I, and an incomparable gain it had been. The continued independence of the successor state of Austria was Italy's guarantee that Teutonic military might would never gaze down from the Alps upon the north Italian plain. The destruction of Austrian independence through its annexation to Germany would mean, in a word, the destruction of Italian security. Everybody understood this; nobody understood it better than Mussolini. Thus the safeguarding of Austria was a cardinal point of his foreign policy.

Italian concern over Austria increased dramatically after January 1933, when Hitler took over in Berlin. Unlike some leading Italian Fascists, Mussolini disliked and distrusted the Nazis. He was put off by the bizarre sexual activities of many of Hitler's close collaborators; he considered Hitler's anti-Semitism excessive and likely to cause trouble for Italy overseas, to the extent that nazism should come to be regarded as a variant of Italian fascism. He recognized the implicitly anti-Latin thrust of Nazi racism. He even refused Hitler's request for an autographed photograph. Mussolini kept putting off his initial meeting with Hitler until June 1934, almost a year-and-a-half

Reviewing troops in 1933

after the latter's arrival in power. Even then, Hitler was not invited to Rome for a formal state visit; instead, he was restricted to a personal meeting with Mussolini at Venice.

The conference between the two dictators lasted from June 14 to June 16. The impression Hitler made on his host was utterly disastrous. Hitler arrived for his first talk with Mussolini clad in an old yellow raincoat, looking rather like Charlie Chaplin dressed up as Adolf Hitler. He talked too much and too loudly, hardly permitting Mussolini to get in a word (especially after Mussolini told him that persecution of the Jews was a mistake). Austrian Chancellor Engelbert Dollfuss (a protégé of Mussolini's) must go; Austrian Nazis must be given seats in the cabinet; the Nordic peoples were racially superior and Mediterranean peoples were clearly tainted, etc., etc. Mussolini later told his intimates that Hitler was some kind of "a buffoon." Two weeks after this unfortunate encounter, Mussolini was truly shocked to learn of the bloody purges Hitler was carrying out within the Nazi party, killing many of his intimate comrades of early days who had helped lift him to power. Hitler, said Mussolini, was "cruel and ferocious." The two men did not meet again for more than three years.

Far more important than these clashes in personality and style, what divided Mussolini and Hitler was the question of Austrian independence. To Mussolini, Hitler and his henchmen meant a drive for *Anschluss*, the unification of Hitler's Austrian homeland with Germany. No Italian government could possibly permit this. Even before Hitler had come to power, Mussolini was a pillar of strength to the Austrian Chancellor (prime minister) Engelbert Dollfuss. Totally committed to maintaining Austria's independence, Dollfuss was confronted by enemies at every hand. He outlawed the Austrian Nazi party in 1933 and crushed an armed rebellion of Vienna Socialists the next year. He made Austria a one-party state with a corporatist constitution. Dollfuss relied heavily on Italian support to uphold the independence of his country, a policy to which Mussolini was completely committed both for reasons of military strategy and because he felt a warm personal regard for Dollfuss. On July 25, 1934, while his family was visiting Mussolini, and he himself was preparing to leave for a meeting with Mussolini at a villa in Riccione, the forty-two-year-old Chancellor Dollfuss was shot in his office and left to bleed to death by a gang of Austrian Nazis intent on seizing power and proclaiming the *Anschluss*. German troops took up positions along the border. Mussolini choked with rage. He told Austrian Prince Stahremberg that Hitler was a "horrible sexual degenerate and a dangerous fool, the leader of a regime of murderers and pederasts. These Nazi butchers must be stopped." Mussolini mobilized Italian military units on the Italo-Austrian border, clearly signaling his intention to enter Austria from the south if German forces invaded from the north. Meanwhile, heartened by this vigorous underwriting of their position, Dollfuss's lieutenants quickly stamped out the Nazi revolt within Austria. The putsch failed, Hitler backed off, and the murderers of Dollfuss, who had fled into Germany, were handed over to the Vienna authorities.

All this might have seemed, on the surface, to have been a great success for Mussolini, whose strong action caused Hitler to step back and preserved the security of the Italian frontiers. But Mussolini was deeply troubled by the failure of the London and Paris governments to take any serious action when the Austrian crisis had been at its height. As early as 1925, Mussolini had been shocked to learn that certain circles in the British government were unconcerned with fate of the Austrian independence. He had never expected, however, to find himself in a situation where Italy might well have been at war with Germany, defending the Austrian state and the Treaty of Versailles—totally alone. "I cannot always be the only one to march to the Brenner Pass!" he exclaimed. He began to view the future with understandable apprehension, especially as the London government made clear it would enter into no treaty obligation to defend Austria, indeed that it considered Austria of no vital importance to Britain.

The next few months had more grim surprises in store for Mussolini. Hitler announced, in March 1935, the reintroduction of conscription. This was not only a blatant defiance of Versailles but a fundamental, visible threat to Anglo-French military security. Yet nothing was done; indeed, at the end of that fateful month British Minister for League Affairs Anthony Eden went to Germany and had a nice little visit with the Führer. (Eden would later play a leading role in the British imposition of sanctions against Italy in retaliation for her attack on Ethiopia, and his expressions of personal distaste and contempt for Mussolini, reported to Rome by Italian secret agents, helped prevent any subsequent Anglo-Italian rapprochement. Perhaps as much as any man, Eden* deserves the credit for the birth of the Rome-Berlin Axis.) A few weeks later, at the Stresa Conference, "the British representatives made it clear at the outset that they would not consider the possibility of sanctions in the event of Treaty violations" by Germany. This bracing revelation was followed in June by the announcement of an Anglo-German naval pact that permitted (again in violation of the peace treaties) Hitler to increase his maritime strength. Neither Paris nor Rome had been consulted by London in this "capricious and ill-considered decision." "Mussolini saw in this episode," writes Winston Churchill, "evidence that Great Britain was not in good faith with her allies, and . . . would apparently go to any length in accommodation with Germany."[2]

Thus, by the middle of 1935, the historic and continuing conflict of interest between Italy on the one hand and Britain and France on the other—which would in any event have been aggravated eventually by Mussolini's determination upon expansion—had been gravely exacerbated. French unresponsiveness to Mussolini's scheme for a Four Power Pact had been very irritating, but Western passivity during the recently attempted *Anschluss* and a general indifference to Hitlerian rearmament were positively alarming. Mussolini began to

*Exactly twenty years after the Italo-Ethiopian war, Prime Minister Eden would launch a British military invasion of Egypt, reminiscent in many ways of the earlier conflict—except that it was a total failure.

draw conclusions. Nevertheless, the victorious Anglo-Franco-Italian alliance of 1915-1918, though deeply fissured, was still standing by the end of the summer of 1935, when it was suddenly and irrevocably cracked wide open by the Italian invasion of Ethiopia.

IMPERIALISM

To describe the Fascists as imperialists would be among the most banal of truisms. Of course we are imperialists, they would respond. Fascism is about power. Empire—the control over human and material resources of other lands—is the open secret of the power of Britain, Russia, and America. The principal problem Fascists pledged themselves to address, once the Socialists had been put down, was that of the "stolen fruits of victory," the redemption of the promises of overseas territories made to Italy during World War I. Dictatorship was the means to the end of a strong foreign policy and a vigorous foreign presence; Mussolini's entire internal policy can be understood not unprofitably as a gearing up of national energies for eventual imperial expansion. (Here we come to yet another reason why there was never any need to introduce a really "totalitarian" regime under fascism: powerful groups in the country, like the army and the Church, and also many Liberals and syndicalists, were not opposed to imperialism *per se*, and would often support the Mussolini government in its external policies while rejecting or shying away from the internal.)

Fascist imperialism was fundamentally a more vigorous form of traditional Italian yearnings for colonial expansion, and these yearnings had two principal sources. The first was that of the Roman Myth, which had deep roots in the Italian consciousness. Every Italian schoolchild was steeped in the deeds of Roman days. After 1870, as Christopher Seton-Watson has written, "the possession of Rome generated dreams of an imperial mission in Africa, of making the Mediterranean *mare nostrum*, of showing that the Roman warrior mentality was not dead. Even Mazzini in his later writings admitted colonial expansion as a legitimate part of Italy's mission."

Mussolini himself was fascinated by Rome and *Romanità*. He spoke of them often, used the Roman eagle and wolf symbols, sprinkled his speeches with references to Julius Caesar, and spoke of a rejuvenated empire and a new Roman citizenry. Rome was his Sorellian Myth, a galvanizing and legitimizing principle, but it was also a font of national policy: in the reclaiming of the wastelands, the building of roads, and the concern to stabilize or increase the rural population, Mussolini was thinking and acting in the classical traditions of Republican Rome.

The contrasts between the myth of the Roman Empire and the reality of the Italian kingdom could hardly have been more distressing. Many Italians knew or suspected that they were looked down upon by other Europeans; many had been directly exposed to condescension or prejudice from tourists or as emigrants. Massimo D'Azeglio, the distinguished painter, novelist, aristocrat, and prime minister of Piedmont, had complained long before that "when a nation is the prey of anybody that takes it, when it allows all sorts of people from the ends of the earth to come to it and amuse themselves, just as hunters go where the game is most plentiful, then members of such a nation can be tolerated by foreigners, but cannot be considered their equals." Such feelings were widespread and enduring. Then there was the gnawing knowledge that, although Italy had been on the offensive in 1918 and numbered among the victorious powers, the part of her war experience that was best remembered in the West was the near-catastrophe of Caporetto. Patriotic Italians could only sigh or weep as they reflected that the world saw them not as the worthy descendants of the Romans but as a nation of organ-grinders and opera singers. Wounded *amour-propre* is perhaps the most powerful catalytic force in politics; its pervasiveness should never be underestimated.

A second principal source of traditional Italian imperialism was Italy's woeful lack of natural resources, and fascism fully grasped what was at stake under this rubric. An empire would provide the means necessary to fulfill the dreams of Fascist productionist economics, and would eventually make possible that improved standard of living for the urban working class that fascism was ever promising. In the meantime, the workers would have the satisfaction of being citizens of a country that was influential and respected: *civis Romanus sum*. Not incidentally, the pursuit of empire would further distract the urban masses from that preoccupation with the class struggle which they had so long imbibed from the teachings of socialism. Proletarian Italy would close ranks against the foreign monopolists. Even more important than these considerations was the concept of the empire as an outlet for surplus population. The population question, especially in the southern provinces (where superabundant labor had retarded the application of machinery to agriculture), had baffled or repelled Italian statesmen since before unification. Emigration had been a sort of answer to this problem, and the number of Italians leaving their country to find work overseas reached 900,000 in 1912 (which would be the equivalent, in the United States of the early 1980s, of six million people). But emigration entailed serious, if hidden, costs. It drained the nation of some of its most energetic young people. Italian immigrants were often abused, or even lynched. And it was humiliating to expose to the world the fact that Italy could provide neither bread nor space nor work for her children. As Dino Grandi, Mussolini's deputy foreign minister, asked bitterly in 1927: "Why should our race form a kind of human reservoir for the replenishment of the small or declining populations of other nations? Why should our mothers continue to bring into the world children who will grow up to be soldiers for other nations?" The Fascists looked upon artificial limitations of births as a sign of national decline. There could be only one solution: emigration not to foreign countries but to Italian colonies. Thus the failure to receive the expected colonial areas after the First World War was considered to be a devastating setback, and by no means only by Fascists. Amintore Fanfani would one day become a distinguished advocate of reconciliation between socialism and Catholicism in Italy, and would also become the first Christian Democratic prime minister to serve with Socialist support (1960 to 1963). He nevertheless expressed the belief of many when as a young student of economic history he wrote in 1936 that Italy needed an empire for her very continued existence. Thus when Mussolini declared that "it is in Africa, not in Europe, where we shall be able to find the solution to our national problems," he was expressing what for Italians of all persuasions was an obvious truth, and stood squarely in the tradition of Liberal Italy which had similarly justified the taking of Libya in 1911.

Also a consideration of fundamental importance, Fascist (as distinguished from Italian) imperialism could seek and find philosophical justification in those two schools of thought that had so deeply influenced Mussolini's own intellectual development—Marxism and syndicalism. Certain syndicalists had opposed Italian expansion into Libya in 1911; this was, however, not because they were against conquest *per se*, but because they thought that that particular war was not worth the effort involved. A firm conviction of syndicalists remained to the effect that the proletariat in a backward and disadvantaged nation could expect only continued exploitation and oppression, directly by their rulers, indirectly by more advanced foreign countries. The possession of colonies would further Italy's economic development, hence the eventual revolution and the triumph of justice. Roberto Michels, in his *L'Imperialismo italiano*, summarized the main syndicalist arguments in favor of imperialism: (1) Italy needed colonies for their natural resources; (2) Italy needed colonies as an outlet for her excess population; (3) Italy needed colonies because the colonial enterprise would bind the nation, in its various classes, together.

Syndicalist imperialism was only an application of fundamental Marxist teachings on the subject. In the authoritative view of Friedrich Engels, colonialism was the "brutal but necessary" antecedent to the universalization of capitalism (and therefore of the proletarian paradise). Thus superior civilizations—by which Engels meant industrialized ones—had the absolute and unquestionable right to take over political and economic control of inferior civilizations. Engels supported Prussia against the "half-civilized Danes," and later advocated German control over the backward Balkans and the inferior Slavs. Engels was even more enthusiastic about European expansion in overseas areas. For him, British rule in India had produced "the only social revolution ever heard of in Asia"; the French "conquest of Algeria [was] an important and fortunate fact for the progress of civilization." He also praised the Americans for taking California away from "the lazy Mexicans who did not know what to do with it."

These Marxist utterances of purest ray serene find their echo in many unexpected places, including the writings of the patrician twenty-first president of the United States. In a now-classic study of President Theodore Roosevelt's confident imperialism, his thoughts on the subject are neatly summarized: "The superior nations had the right to conquer in order that the world be stabilized; their very superiority and ability to control other peoples verified the right." Roosevelt justified his high-handed tactics in Panama on the grounds that "the Colombians had forfeited their right to civilized consideration because of their inferiority as a people; Roosevelt pronounced them 'not merely corrupt' but 'governmentally utterly incompetent.' Their inferiority was all the more unfortunate because their corruption and incompetence stood in the way of a great human achievement—the canal."[3] Three decades later the principal organ of the Jesuits, *Civilitá cattolica*, presented a variation on the above arguments by declaring its belief that a truly needy nation might legitimately appropriate underdeveloped lands not utilized or required by the owners.

Thus, Italian desires for a colonial empire seemed to find justification not only in Italy's admittedly serious economic problems, or in the actual practice of the British and the French (not to speak of the Dutch, the Portuguese, the Russians, the Americans, and the Japanese); a colonial empire for Italy was also supported by thinkers and writers of Marxist, Syndicalist, Rooseveltian, and Jesuit persuasions, certainly an impressive (if somewhat sinister) array.

If the Italians were to win and hold a new Roman Empire, then they must first be prepared; they must be schooled in Roman virtue. Part of this educational effort took the form of a sustained Fascist propaganda campaign. The face of Fascist propaganda of the 1930s seems very bellicose and arrogant to us now (meekness is not the hallmark of dictators), but that does not necessarily mean that its fundamental conceptions were entirely wrong and its aims totally base. Mussolini's propaganda, dramatizing Italy's contribution to the victory of 1918, quoting Napoleon on the valor of the emperor's Italian troops,[4] and suggesting that every peasant and every clerk could become—must become—a Roman soldier, certainly had its coarse, pompous, and quaint aspects, stemming in part from Mussolini's personal insecurities and in part from his acute consciousness that Italy was not very strong. But Fascist propaganda also had a *liberating* dimension. It sought to liberate the Italians from an *economic* poverty caused by the inadequacies of nature and the monopoly of the world's resources by other powers. It sought to liberate Italians from *spiritual* poverty, from their social distrust, lack of civic-mindedness, narrow *campanilismo*, and festering class and regional hatreds—all of which had been previously recognized (and still are) as curses of Italian society. It sought to raise Italian consciousness to something above petty envies and parish gossip. It sought above all to liberate Italians from their inferiority complex, the legacy of Custozza, Adowa, and Caporetto. In striving to rouse his countrymen to the defense of their nation's rightful place in the world, Mussolini was not acting very differently from a Winston Churchill or a Charles de Gaulle.

Every creed of nationalism is generally unattractive to people who live in other nations. Foreign well-wishers of Italy were disturbed during the 1930s by the growing Fascist emphasis on the infallibility of the *Duce* and the necessity for expansion. Even if he did make the trains run on time, Mussolini was ruining "their" Italy—picturesque and poor. His preachings on the inevitability of conflict in human affairs and on the nobility of the military virtues were peculiarly offensive to many. "War alone," said Mussolini, "brings up to its highest tension all human energy and puts the stamp of nobility upon the peoples who have the courage to meet it." This particular statement is often quoted to show the moral degradation of Mussolini and fascism. The values it expressed may perhaps have been degraded; they were certainly *widespread.* When Mussolini was a young man, William James had written: "Militarism is the great preserver of our ideals of hardihood, and human life with no hardihood would be contemptible. Without risks and prizes for a darer, history would be insipid indeed; and there is a type of military character which everyone feels that the race should never cease to breed, for everyone is sensitive to its superiority." And Theodore Roosevelt had declared that "all the great masterful races have been fighting races and the minute that a race loses the hard fighting virtues, then no matter what else it may retain, no matter how skilled in commerce and finance, in science or in art, it has lost the proud right to stand as an equal of the best." Friedrich Engels summed it all up succinctly: "Without force and without an iron ruthlessness nothing is accomplished in history." Undoubtedly many Englishmen and Frenchmen and Americans were quite sincere when they argued that the peace of the international order was the highest good, and maybe they were right. But it is perhaps not utterly impossible for us today to understand how Italians (and not only they) could view slogans about "perpetual peace" and "international law," about *Pax Britannica* and *La mission civilisatrice*, as essentially masks to cover a determination to preserve an imperial status quo favorable to Britain and France, a status quo in which nations like Italy were condemned to perpetual poverty and powerlessness.

Given the conviction of the Fascist (and many others) that an empire was essential to Italy's national well-being or even national survival, and given the clear recognition that the only plausible theater for Italian expansion was in Africa, the choice of Ethiopia as the target area was an obvious one. Ethiopia was the last available unclaimed area on the whole continent, in part because its topography was too forbidding and its inhabitants too warlike to have tempted the British or the French. Thus, unlike Tunisia or Egypt, Ethiopia (Abyssinia, as the Italians called it) could be the scene of Italian expansion without offering a direct challenge to any other European state. Further, Ethiopia separated the long-existing Italian holdings in Eritrea and Somalia,* and Italy's general primacy in the area had been recognized by London. The government in Addis Ababa had never been able to exercise real control over all the border provinces, and there had been a long history of armed clashes with Italian forces. Much more importantly, the Italians had a score to settle. Few could forget the humiliation at Adowa where, in 1896, 16,000 Italian and native troops had been utterly routed by 100,000 Abyssinian warriors, leaving behind 6,000 dead and 2,000 prisoners—perhaps the worst defeat of a European power in the history of colonialism up to the Russo-Japanese War. Adowa was never far below the surface of Italian political consciousness. In Churchill's words, "to proclaim their manhood by avenging Adowa meant almost as much in Italy as the recovery of Alsace-Lorraine in France."

Finally, the history and current condition of Ethiopia

*Eritrea and Somalia were both rugged, barren, and sparsely populated. Italy's control of these areas had begun in 1889. The Italians built highways, brought peace to the warring tribes, controlled pestilence and almost completely stamped out slavery. Today Somalia is an enemy, and Eritrea a rebellious province, of Ethiopia.

seemed to qualify it completely as one of those backward nations which, according to Marxist and Syndicalist thought, might be legitimately taken over by a superior civilization.

Ethiopia had been converted to Coptic Christianity in the fifth century, and then cut off from contact with Europe by the eruptions of the Mohammedans. During the eighteenth and nineteenth centuries, the land was drenched with the blood of tribal rebellions and civil wars. Menelik II, helped to the throne in 1889 by the Italians, caused the massacre of their troops at Adowa in 1896. One of his would-be successors, Joshua, a great slave raider and slave trader, was overthrown in 1916; his supporters were massacred in the streets of his capital city, their blood smeared over the faces of the victors. The London *Times* editorialized that "the spectacle presented by the one indigenous African state that has succeeded in retaining its complete independence is perhaps the best justification that can be found for the partition of the rest of Africa among the European powers." When Ethiopia first sought admission to the League of Nations, it was opposed by the British government on the grounds that Ethiopia practiced slavery and did not have full control over its own territory. Ethiopia's entrance into the League was also opposed by such nonimperial states as Norway, and by European Socialists generally; in their eyes, a land of blood feuds and civil war, of slavery and illiteracy, of abject poverty and unshakable indolence, a land without roads or schools, even without a currency, would be no adornment to an organization of sovereign states seeking permanent peace.

In 1930, Haile Selassie (whose name in Amharic means Power of the Trinity) became King of Kings and Conquering Lion of Judah. He was to prove one of the durable political figures of the century, appearing at John F. Kennedy's funeral in 1963 and retaining his throne until overthrown by a military coup in 1974. Born in 1891, a grandnephew of Menelik II, he was educated in part by a French priest, in whose language he became fluent. He was a provincial governor at the age of fourteen. Haile Selassie's coronation in Addis Ababa was attended by many European observers who found a capital city without paved avenues, sewers, or electricity, a city in which the policemen wore no shoes, and lepers wandered streets that also swarmed with prostitutes visibly suffering the effects of venereal disease.

For Mussolini personally, the conquest of Abyssinia would be, like the Conciliation of 1929, another colossal triumph in an area where his Liberal predecessors had met dismal failure. The founding of the empire would raise Mussolini up from the level of a successful politician to the rank of a leader who had fulfilled an historic mission. His glory would rival that of Cavour. For others of humbler station, for the landless peasants of the south, the broad and thinly populated expanses of Abyssinia would provide a limitless haven; many of the Italian soldiers embarking for East Africa in 1935 carried in their knapsacks a little bag of grain.

CONQUEST IN AFRICA

If many powerful factors converged upon the choice of Ethiopia as the locus of Italian expansion, the same is true with regard to the timing of that expansion. Some have suggested that the principal motive of the attack on Ethiopia in 1935 was to bolster Mussolini's popularity, in the manner of the tyrant described by Plato, "always stirring up some war or other, in order that the people may require a leader." Perhaps such motives did play a part in Mussolini's thinking on an unconscious level, but there is no evidence to suggest that Mussolini's popularity was in trouble in 1935, and there are plausible explanations for the timing of the invasion that have nothing to do with efforts to shore up an allegedly sagging regime. By 1935, a new generation had grown up since the March on Rome and it was time to test the results of Fascist efforts at re-Romanization. More important was the emerging threat from Hitlerian Germany, along with Mussolini's belief that in those circumstances neither Britain nor France would make any trouble over an Italian attack upon Ethiopia.

Mussolini's foreign policy had been relatively quiescent in the 1920s, owing both to his preoccupation with internal affairs, and to the superficial calm of the European situation. By the mid-1930s all had changed. At home, Mussolini was securely in control, while the order established at Versailles was rapidly disintegrating. In 1934 Mussolini had forestalled a Nazi attempt on Austria, and had gotten away with it because Germany was still weak. Strategists in Rome, however, believed that Hitler would be ready for war by the end of 1936. Therefore, the time to move against Ethiopia was 1935; the African war could be won and the Italian armies back guarding the Brenner Pass and Austria before Hitler was ready.[5]

Mussolini had also prepared the ground well with his European allies—or so he thought. Premier Pierre Laval had long ago made it clear to Mussolini that France would not oppose an Italian move on Ethiopia. As for the British, one of the "characteristic elements of Fascist foreign policy" had always been "a constant effort to find a stable agreement and friendship with England . . .";[6] to this end Mussolini had signed the Locarno Pact, even though it ignored Italian anxieties about the Brenner frontier. Besides, Britain had several times acknowledged Ethiopia to be in Italy's sphere of influence.[7] To Mussolini's way of thinking, there was an obvious and decisive difference between peace in Europe and peace in Africa; as he said, "Italy has a problem with Ethiopia, it does not have nor does it wish to have problems with Great Britain, with whom during the world war, and afterwards at Locarno and more recently at Stresa a level of cooperation was attained which is of undoubted value for European stability."[8] Indeed, Mussolini had left the Stresa Conference* in May, 1935 with "the clear conviction that Britain, which was fully aware of his military

*This gathering, in the little Piedmontese resort town, included representatives of Britain, France, and Italy. Mussolini was frustrated in his attempt to get a strong British commitment to Austrian independence, but he did succeed in having conference references to "peace in the world" changed to "peace in Europe," a perfectly obvious allusion to his Ethiopian plans.

preparations, attached little importance to Abyssinia."[9] It was simply inconceivable that the London government, occupied as it was with repressing pro-independence demonstrations in India, would take the side of a slave-holding feudal pseudo-state whose suitability for admission to the League of Nations Britain herself had contested in 1923, and turn against her long-time Italian ally, especially in view of Hitler's brazen announcement, that very spring, that Germany was rearming.

On October 3, 1935, Italian troops crossed the Ethiopian frontiers.

The Italian invasion proceeded on two fronts, from Eritrea in the north and Somalia in the south. Top command in the north was given to the former Quadrumvir of the March on Rome, General Emilio De Bono. De Bono, now sixty-nine years old, had been out of the regular army for many years, and was not known for his aggressiveness or audacity. His appointment, however, was necessary to make this not just an Italian but a Fascist war. For the same reason, Mussolini made sure that his sons Bruno and Vittorio both saw action in the campaign. The southern command was in the hands of Rodolfo Graziani, fifty-three years old in 1935, a soldier of personal panache and brutal methods of war. Graziani's forces, consisting of Italian and Somali troops, were ludicrously outnumbered; they were also starved for supplies, remote as they were from the centers of Ethiopian political and military power and so much farther away from Italy than was the Eritrean front.

The first Italian attack was launched from Eritrea. The invasion force consisted of Italian regular troops, Fascist militia, and Eritrean *askaris*. One corps of this invading force was commanded by General Ruggero Santini, who had fought in the ill-fated 1896 campaign. The town of Adowa fell to the Italians in the first days of the war, and General De Bono caused a marble monument to be erected in memory of the fallen of 1896. Right behind the advancing troops came the engineers building highways on the way to Addis Ababa across the rugged, roadless countryside. As they advanced, the Italians emancipated numerous slaves.

General De Bono, doubtful of his own competence to command such a large and important undertaking, was also a cautious and humane man, sparing of the lives of his men and careful of the Ethiopians to whom, as he believed, he was bringing the benefits of a higher civilization. De Bono prudently wished not to advance into unknown Ethiopian territory faster than his engineers could construct roads and telegraph lines. All the regular army commanders wanted time for methodical preparations, and from the strictly military point of view they were right. But their logistic formulas collided with Mussolini's political necessities: he desired as rapid a victory as possible, before the League of Nations should be rallied against Italy or before Italian public opinion grew doubtful about the wisdom of the war. The upshot was the removal of De Bono (and his promotion to the rank of Marshal) and the placing of the northern command in the hands of General Pietro Badoglio.* As it was politically essential that the war be concluded before the rainy season began in June, Graziani's southern offensive started in January and Badoglio's from the north in February. After three months of hard fighting, Addis Ababa fell on May 5. Although mopping-up operations continued for some time, after seven months the war was effectively over.

At the beginning of the war, European military experts had predicted a long conflict, lasting perhaps for more than two years. In comparison to the Russian campaign in Afghanistan in the early 1980s, Italy's situation in Ethiopia was far more precarious, in terms of distance from the fighting area, level of industrial development, and ratio of population. The Ethiopian fighting man, lacking European concepts of military discipline (and often European-type arms as well) was nevertheless very brave. The Ethiopians were, moreover, fighting a

*Born in 1871, Badoglio had served at Caporetto, and after the war was made army chief of staff. Under Mussolini he was ambassador to Brazil and then governor of Libya. At the successful conclusion of the Ethiopian campaign he was named viceroy and duke of Addis Ababa.

defensive war on terrain that only they knew, on an incredibly dusty landscape described as "lunar," where the temperature often reached 140 degrees Fahrenheit in the shade. Most of the time the Ethiopian high command pursued essentially guerrilla tactics of hit-and-run which, in such a large and rugged country, might well have been expected to prove fatal to the Italian campaign. It was no accident that Ethiopia alone of all countries on the African continent had preserved its independence for so long. True enough, the Italians had bomber planes (the Ethiopian air force was very small) and employed things like mustard gas which, though rarely fatal, could produce painful effects. The Italian troops were also accused of fighting a war of atrocity; for instance, headlines in New York and London shrieked about the Italian bombing of the hospital at Adowa (only there was no hospital at Adowa).

But neither poison gas nor alleged atrocities account for the rapid Italian victory. Rather, the explanation lies in two much more important factors. First, the Italian army employed modern military organization, excellent road-building techniques, and a mastery of tropical medicine; it enjoyed abundant logistic support from home, and was further armed with the general conviction that Italy represented the moral and technical superiority of a higher civilization. Second, there was Ethiopia's internal political weakness. Haile Selassie ruled over a sort of African Habsburg Empire; many ethnic groups within Ethiopia viewed themselves as oppressed. In the earliest days of the war, high-ranking officials such as Prince Gugsa, governor of strategic East Tigre, went over to the Italians for money. And once the inevitable defeat of Haile Selassie became obvious, many of the suppressed tribes rose against the emperor; in the spring of 1936 his retreating army was often attacked by fierce Galla warriors who mutilated their dead or captured foes.

Ironically, the rapid conquest of Ethiopia was to contribute to the undoing of the Fascist regime. The technical performance of Italian infantry, air, and engineering units endowed the Italians with a reputation for military might that engendered a dangerous sense of overconfidence in the regime and the nation as a whole. This military euphoria was coupled with the break-up of the old Anglo-Franco-Italian alliance of the Great War, a combination of circumstances that would soon cast the regime into an insuperable crisis.

Mussolini's well-founded expectations that the conquest of Ethiopia would be relatively free of international complications were soon shattered by what has been described as "the instinctive anti-Latin and pro-German character of British public opinion."[10] The League of Nations, under British leadership, imposed sanctions on Italy (after having failed to impose them on Japan for her invasion of Manchuria in 1931). They were strange sanctions: oil was not put on the list of goods to be denied Italy, and without imported oil the Italian war machine would have run dry. Nor was the Suez Canal closed to Italian ships en route to East Africa. Just enough was done to confirm Italian suspicions of British hypocrisy and confusion. Somewhat later, key officials in Paris and London worked out a deal that would have given huge areas of Ethiopia to Italy, while maintaining appearances through the preservation of an independent but fragmented Ethiopian state. Mussolini was of a mind to accept this compromise,[11] but the tremendous outcry sent up by the Labour Party (which believed both in unilateral disarmament *and* sanctions) against this so-called Hoare-Lavel Plan killed it, and so the war went on to its swift conclusion. Insult added to injury, the Emperor of Ethiopia was carried away to safety aboard a British man-of-war.

What were Mussolini and his advisers to make of all this? For the sake of a futile gesture on behalf of a semi-barbarous kingdom on the periphery of European consciousness—and perhaps to keep Italy in her proper subordinate station—the London authorities were willing to break up the alliance of 1918, even at the cost of unleashing Hitler or so it seemed in Rome.

The Western reaction to the Abyssinian affair was to prove

the fatal turning point of the Mussolini regime. Heretofore, although a dictatorship, Fascist Italy had still been a part of the Western camp,* firmly opposed to any revision by force of the Versailles settlement, and willing (as 1934 had shown) to take risks in resisting Hitler's revanchist desires. All that was now to be reversed by "the tomfoolery of the Western powers" which "finally drove Mussolini into the arms of Hitler."[12] The costs of this tomfoolery were to be incalculable—for Italy and for all the world. "By estranging Italy," growled Winston Churchill, "they had upset the whole balance of Europe and gained nothing for Abyssinia." Hitler's British biographer Alan Bullock has entered his view that "by insisting on the imposition of sanctions, Great Britain made an enemy of Mussolini and destroyed all hope of a united front against German aggression," a judgment pronounced in almost identical terms by other distinguished British commentators including Ivone Kirkpatrick, A. J. P. Taylor, and Denis Mack Smith.[13]

Fifty years before, the frustration of Italy's African ambitions had driven her into a German pact. History was repeating itself, with much more drastic consequences. With the Anglo-Franco-Italian front now broken, the way was open for Hitler and he soon acted: in March 1936 he remilitarized the Rhineland. This stroke, which utterly wiped out all the advantages France had gained from her vast sacrifices in World War I, was met by no action whatsoever. Clearly the day of Versailles was over, and Germany was about to reestablish that hegemony over Europe which she had exercised from 1870 to 1914. Italy, smallest of the great powers, would have to come to some kind of terms with this new order.

For the present, however, all was jubilation in Rome. The League sanctions had caused the entire nation, even prominent anti-Fascists like Benedetto Croce (who contributed his Sena-

*Fascist Italy, after all, had signed the Locarno Pact and had been invited to the Stresa Conference *as a matter of course.*

torial Medallion to the national gold collection to help finance the war), to rally around Mussolini in an ecstasy of indignation, and Italian mothers gladly donated their gold wedding bands to the cause. It was widely believed in Europe that the Ethiopian campaign, in a rugged country with no roads, no bridges, and no maps, against a warlike people, would require two full years. When it was brought to a triumphant conclusion in seven months, Italians were filled with pride. Proletarian Italy had stood up, defied the plutocracies in Geneva, and won. Ethiopia, unconquered for four thousand years, three and a half times the size of Italy, was now a dominion of Rome.

The Vatican had viewed the Abyssinian undertaking with mixed feelings; if the Italians should be defeated, the resulting blow to European prestige in all of Africa would hamper Catholic missionary efforts there. Even if Italy were victorious, she would inevitably be drawn closer to Berlin. But for the most part, Italian Catholics, lay and clerical alike, saw the venture as the advance of Catholic civilization into semibarbarous Ethiopia, and they rejoiced with the rest of the nation at the rapidity and totality of the victory.[14]

Mussolini's prestige surpassed even the heights to which it had soared with the signing of the Lateran Pacts in 1929. "He had avenged Adowa and wiped out the Italian's sense of inferiority. He had conceived the enterprise and launched it against the advice of his experts. He had personally supervised every move and seen to it that sufficient troops and material were made available to the commander-in-chief."[15] King Victor Emmanuel offered him the title of Prince (which he declined). His wife Rachele told him there would never be a better time to retire from politics. When, on May 9, 1936, Mussolini proclaimed from the balcony of the Palazzo Venezia the annexation of Abyssinia and the assumption by Victor Emmanuel of the title Emperor of Ethiopia, "he was," according to his biographer Kirkpatrick, "enjoying the unqualified admiration of the whole Italian nation."

Who could have seen on that day of glory and consummation that the road ahead led to the abyss?

· XI ·

HITLER

"Friendship is only a word.
I love no one."

Napoleon

With hindsight, it is clear that even though Mussolini was at the zenith of his popularity, after 1936 the regime was showing definite signs of trouble. There was Mussolini's physical decline and his loss of interest in domestic and party affairs; the almost complete disappearance of really first-rate men from the front ranks of state and party; the failure to invest large segments of youth—even Fascist youth—with that sense of mission and exuberance that had animated so many Fascists of the 1922 generation. There was also a continuing prevalence of monarchist loyalties among the officer corps. But all these things would have amounted to little—certainly not to the overthrow of the regime—had it not been for Italy's entrance into World War II on Germany's side.

The German connection would involve Italy in a disastrous military defeat that would destroy the Fascist regime, deliver the country to foreign invasion and civil war, and result in Mussolini's own violent death. Thus, Mussolini's step-by-step entanglement with Hitler after the Ethiopian war was the fatal mistake of his life.

THE ROAD TO BERLIN

It is easily assumed that an alliance between Mussolini and Hitler was inevitable, but this is just another example of the pit we can fall into when we read history backward. The obstacles to a German-Italian partnership were many and impressive, and it was to require five years after Hitler's coming to power to overcome them. Even then, Mussolini always remained a grudging and uncomforable ally, full of apprehension, resentment, and regrets. The chief impediments to a Rome-Berlin combination ranged from the personal to the ideological to the geopolitical.

To begin with, Germans of all ranks held negative attitudes toward Italy. True enough, Hitler had written in *Mein Kampf* of his desire for an alliance with Fascist Italy and there is no doubt that Mussolini was, perhaps alone among all men, one whom Hitler sincerely admired. Hitler liked to tell his companions that Mussolini had done a great service to all Europe by stopping Italy from becoming Bolshevik; indeed, had there been no March on Rome, had Mussolini not showed that the Communists could be beaten, even the Nazi movement itself would probably not have triumphed. Hitler copied Mussolini in many ways: party uniforms, the Roman salute, even Mussolini's title. And as Hitler imagined himself to be an authentic (if unappreciated) artist, he professed a great love of the cities of Florence and Rome. Nevertheless, disdain and dislike for Italians characterized even members of Hitler's entourage, and the Fuhrer himself shared some of these attitudes. In the first place, German military experts were skeptical of Italy's military value in a future war, and Hitler himself was convinced that the Italian army was poorly led by reactionary officers. Then, there was Italy's "desertion" of Germany in 1915, the memory of which remained fresh in the minds of many. The impatient treatment of German-speaking inhabitants of the Italian Trentino was another sore point with the race-conscious Nazis.

On the other side, Mussolini disliked Hitler personally and had a very low opinion of most of the leading figures of the Nazi regime. Indeed, the Nazis were disliked throughout the power structure of Italy; in their various ways the king, the general staff, and the Vatican all worked against entanglement with the Germans. The real animosity between King Victor Emmanuel and Hitler was notorious. The king's conceptions of international politics, civilized rule, and Italian dignity precluded any involvement with the Nazis, and his aversion for them was not alleviated when Hitler made his first official visit to Rome in May 1938. As a head of state, Hitler had been invited to stay at the royal palace. On the first night, when it was time to retire, Hitler asked that a woman be sent up to his room—a request that utterly scandalized Victor Emmanuel and threw the household into an uproar. When it was explained that the German chancellor had no licentious intentions, that he merely needed to watch a woman smooth down his bedsheets before he could rest properly, this only increased the incredulous distaste of the king and his court.

Ideological discordances between nazism and fascism were further irritants. The two movements shared certain convictions about communism and liberalism, but their overall world views diverged in crucial aspects. The essence of Italian fascism was nationalism; the essence of German nazism was racism. Mussolini envisaged Italy as a great empire, the respected and acknowledged equal of Britain and France; Hitler envisaged Germany as the cradle of the master race, holding millions upon millions of inferior beings in literal slavery. Indeed, the central Hitlerian idea was the conquest, depopulation, and colonization of Russia. Hitler's racial ambitions were first and foremost directed against Jews and Slavs, but the implications of his theories were obvious to many Italians, who reacted to them with a mixture of incredulity and apprehension.

Most of all, there was the question of Austria. Nazis of all ranks were outraged by Mussolini's stubborn and bellicose opposition to the *Anschluss*; indeed, up to 1939 Mussolini's

Italy was the only Western power to openly threaten Nazi Germany with military action (over the Dollfuss murder). For Italians, the benefits to their country of an independent Austria were obvious; so were the consequences of a German annexation. If Austria were to be swallowed up by Nazi Germany, if German military power were ever to reach Italy's northern frontier, then Italian foreign policy would be reduced to one single question: A German invasion, or a German alliance?

Yet by 1936, in spite of all obstacles, Italy and Germany were on the road to a possible alliance, or at least an active understanding. The British government had deeply offended Mussolini and all Italians by its actions during the Ethiopian war. More importantly, Mussolini was becoming convinced that the Western allies were not going to do anything to prevent Hitler's rearmanent or even his complete destruction of the Versailles settlement, including the state of Austria. Hitler meanwhile assiduously courted and flattered the *Duce*. When Galeazzo Ciano, Italian foreign minister and Mussolini's son-in-law, visited Germany in October 1936, his Nazi hosts made a great and successful effort to impress him with the power of the revivified Reich. But when the *Duce* himself came to Berlin in September 1937, all the stops were pulled out: "Never before in German history had Berlin witnessed such a display."[1] This visit to the German capital was fatefully decisive; Mussolini returned to Rome overawed by the colossal panorama of Germanic military and industrial might, which contrasted all the more dramatically with Anglo-French weakness and vacillation (the British Labour party would still be opposing conscription as late as May 1939). Mussolini would carry this impression of overwhelming German power to his last days. And Hitler had outdone himself in his flattery of the *Duce*, seeking to convince Mussolini that Italy need not fear this new German Goliath, painting for him a dazzling vision of an Italian hegemony over the Mediterranean and North Africa. So two months later the Rome-Berlin Axis was solemnized by the signing of the Anti-Comintern Pact.

Mussolini has often been criticized for failing to understand that a peaceful and stable Europe was more in Italy's interest than a German-dominated Europe. But this criticism is based on two faulty assumptions: first, that Europe before the Ethiopian war was stable, and second, that Mussolini wished for, or at least was prepared to see, a Nazi hegemony.

Post-1918 Europe had never been politically stable, despite fleeting appearances or frequent pronouncements to the contrary. Eastern Europe seethed with the hostility of the successor states to one another, to Germany, and to Bolshevik Russia. Moscow proclaimed and practiced a foreign policy of subversion. But the root of the matter was this: no German government of whatever complexion was going to permanently renounce Germany's status as a great, indeed, the dominant power on the continent, nor permanently accept the imposition of war guilt and reparations, especially as the results of a war that in the minds of many Germans had not been truly lost. Hitler's accession to power in 1933 did not represent a reversal of German foreign policy, but rather an exaggeration of it. The Nazi regime catalyzed, it did not create, a European situation made explosive by nationalist rivalries and economic depression. Finally, Hitler never made any secret of what he conceived to be his mission: "My program was to abolish the Treaty of Versailles. It is nonsense for the rest of the world to pretend today that I did not reveal this program until 1933, 1935, or 1937."[2] The ever more obvious unwillingness of the Anglo-French governments to resist Hitler's flagrant steps to dismantle the Versailles system, and their proclivity to grant to Hitler's threats concessions they never would have made to Stresemann's diplomacy,* accentuated the generalized feeling of crisis that had gripped Europe since 1914. Rome had to *deal*

*Gustav Stresemann (1878–1929) was Germany's foreign minister from 1923 to 1929. He sought to regain a respected position for Germany through conciliation of her former enemies and scrupulous observance of the Versailles Treaty. He won the Nobel Peace Prize in 1926.

with, it did not *bring about*, this state of affairs, and Mussolini's Four Power Pact, which just might have headed off Hitler, was scuttled by French conservatism.

But why was Mussolini so complacent about the prospect of a German-dominated Europe? The answer is that he, quite simply, was not. His frequently expressed personal distaste for Hitler and the vigorous opposition to the attempted *Anschluss* of 1934 show that perfectly well. Whatever the similarities in externals between fascism and nazism, Mussolini understood completely that a rearmed Hitlerite Germany was a major threat to Italy's position on the continent. But more than that, Mussolini's general foreign policy during the late 1930s has to be examined in the light of three considerations.

First, Mussolini did not understand Hitler. The *Duce* was not a professional diplomat, and he lacked a Talleyrand or a Mazarin to warn him of the dangers implicit in even his apparently most successful actions. Mussolini's foreign policy was essentially one of old-fashioned nineteenth century European imperialism; Hitler's foreign policy aimed at the enslavement or destruction of whole peoples. No matter how fulsomely or how often Hitler expressed his admiration for the *Duce*, Mussolini was never able to influence Berlin policy. Hitler was dynamic in a way that Mussolini and his Fascists had never been,[3] at least since 1922. Hitler always had the initiative with Mussolini; he always had plans that were more precise, more immediate, more plausible than anything Mussolini could cope with. Mussolini was forced to rely on the hope that if the Hitler connection ever became too hot to handle, Italy could always switch back to the old Franco-British alliance.

Second, Mussolini actively worked against Hitler until what seemed the last possible moment. The Italian move into Albania in April 1939 was calculated not only to further Fascist imperialism but also to stem the tide of German influence in the Balkans.[4] Like the timing of the Ethiopian invasion, the occupation of Albania was seen in Rome in fundamentally anti-German terms. Both, however, were misunderstood in the West and served further to isolate Mussolini. Nevertheless, the

Duce was so ambivalent toward his northern partner that when he accidentally learned about the impending German attack on neutral Belgium, he sent the Brussels government a warning (which was ignored). As Foreign Minister Ciano confided to his diary, "For Mussolini, the idea of Hitler waging war, and worse still, winning it, is altogether unbearable."[5]

Third, Mussolini, like everybody else, was completely surprised by the rapidity and extent of the German triumph in 1940. Before that time, Anglo-French mastery of the Mediterranean—a distasteful thing for any Italian government to contemplate—was the *actual* situation; German hegemony over Europe was only a *potential* one. The West stood for the status quo; Hitler stood for change. The West had rebuffed Italian colonial claims from Tunis in the 1880s up to Ethiopia in the 1930s; Hitler in contrast congratulated Mussolini on his East African victory and promised to regard the Mediterranean as an entirely Italian sphere. The substitution of a German hegemony in Europe for an Anglo-French one would require the completest sort of German victory and the completest sort of collapse, not only by France but by Russia as well. Who in 1939 imagined such a future? Who knew what Germany might look like, what her disposable power would be, after so great and so necessarily *costly* a victory? Would Germany really be able to *dominate* Europe? Hitler himself, even after the unexpected fall of France, tried to make peace with Britain. When Mussolini declared war on a France that was already crumbling, he was trying to salvage some advantages for his country out of the debacle; that, after all, is what political leaders are supposed to do. Taking advantage of the fall of France was not the same thing at all as wanting it. The destruction of the European order, which before 1914 Mussolini the Socialist had expected to be the work of the proletariat, was now being carried out by the *wehrmacht.* In his own grim words. "Better this happens with us than against us"—hardly a ringing endorsement of the Teutonic New Order.

Mussolini's involvement with Hitler was a capital mistake for him, but this is clearer now than then. Few—very few—of the men who exercised political power in the upheavals of those days emerged with honor and reputation intact. The tragic events that engulfed Mussolini, Italy and the world invite us to reflect upon the essential ambiguity and unpredictability of the human drama.

Italy's adherence to the Anti-Comintern Pact in November 1937, sealed the fate of Austria. Mussolini began to remark that if the Austrians wanted the *Anschluss*, things must be allowed to take their natural course. How could Mussolini continue to oppose Hitler's will in this matter, as he had done so effectively in 1934? Before the world, Britain and France had chosen to condemn Italy over Ethiopia, and stood by while Germany, in flagrant disregard for Versailles, girded herself for a new war. Even more to the point, Mussolini was now heavily committed in Spain's civil war.

Mussolini had intervened in the uprising against the Popular Front government in Madrid as a means of breaking out of his post-Ethiopian isolation; perhaps he could obtain the Balearic Islands as his reward, thus outflanking the French bases in Corscia and Tunis. Quite unexpectedly, the conflict dragged on and on, and began to assume the coloration of a global ideological confrontation. Stalin supplied the Madrid government and Italian anti-Fascists flocked to join the fray, while from the Vatican to the humblest rural rectory the Catholic Church viewed the struggle as nothing less than a deadly encounter between religion and bolshevism. By 1937 Mussolini had put 70,000 troops into Spain, along with a lot of equipment and aircraft (much to the delight of the Germans, whose eyes were upon Austria). Italy's large investment in the Nationalist side contrasted with the Anglo-French policy of weak support for the Loyalists. Thus emerged one more obstacle to any reconciliation between Mussolini and the Anglo-French leadership who had already shown, not only through League sanctions over Ethiopia, but also by the Anglo-German Naval Treaty, and the failure to react to German conscription and the march into the Rhineland, that their determination to oppose

Italian expansionism was exceeded only by their unwillingness to oppose German revanchism.

Yet to permit the Nazis to annex Austria must entail one of two results: either a future war against Germany on extremely disadvantageous ground (it would be the Caporetto situation again, only much worse)—or a German alliance. In exchange for Austria, Hitler would recognize the conquest of Abyssinia (in contrast to the British government, which had provocatively invited Emperor Haile Selassie to the coronation of Edward VIII).

And so the *Anschluss* was consummated. On the day Hitler entered Vienna (March 12, 1938) he said: "Tell Mussolini I shall never forget this, never, even if the whole world should turn against him." Nobody suspected what tragic prophecy lurked in those words of the elated Fuhrer. Typically (a bad omen) the first German officer to greet Italian border guards at the Brenner Pass was one Colonel Schoerner, who had won his *pour le mérite* at Caporetto.

In a speech to the Chamber, Mussolini tried to justify the loss of Austria. How could you defend the independence of a state when the majority of its citizens do not want to be independent, he asked? When something is going to happen anyway, the course of wisdom is to consent to it. This was very thin stuff. The *Anschluss* was a strategic catastrophe for Italy, and everybody knew it. Mussolini's popularity began to evaporate.[6] The only positive aspect of the whole affair, and it was certainly a slim one, was that Mussolini's personal intervention had helped save Austrian Chancellor Schuschnigg,* an honest if naive man, from brutal imprisonment or worse.[7]

So Mussolini had let Austria and Italy's northern frontier

*Kurt von Schuschnigg, forty-one years old at the time of the *Anschluss*, had been minister of justice between 1932 and 1934. He succeeded to the chancellorship upon Dollfuss's murder. His decision to hold a plebiscite on Austrian independence provided Hitler with an excuse to occupy the country on March 12, 1938. Schuschnigg remained in the Nazis' hands until 1945. He then settled in the United States, taught at St. Louis University, and died in 1977.

security go down the drain. What, then, did Paris and London do about this further deterioration of the balance of power? Nothing. Less than nothing. In fact, so far were these governments, erstwhile defenders of international morality, from raising any dust over the *Anschluss* that they were actually on the verge of handing Czechoslovakia—the very child and symbol of Versailles—over to the Nazis.

The so-called Sudeten Germans, living inside Czechoslovakia's western frontier, had long complained of mistreatment by the Prague government. When he came to power, Hitler began encouraging the Sudeten people to escalate their agitation and provoke "outrages." No sooner had Hitler swallowed Austria than he turned his complete attention to Czechoslovakia. The prize here, of course, was not the "liberation" of some German speakers on the wrong side of the border, but the destruction of a democratic Czechoslovakia, fruit of the Central Powers' defeat in 1918 and would-be protégé of the West. Bohemia thrust far into the vitals of Germany, her borders were girded by mountains, and the Czechs had a well-equipped army, backed up by a good munitions industry. This thorn in the Nazi side must be removed. Hitler's demands on Prague engendered resistance—at last—from London and Paris. War threatened. At the request of Prime Minister Chamberlain, Mussolini sent his Berlin ambassador to Hitler with a plea that Chamberlain's plan for a big-power conference be accepted. Hitler agreed, and Mussolini named Munich for the site of the meeting.

The Munich conference was, in effect, the actualization of Mussolini's Four-Power Pact—only several years too late. The statesmen of Munich agreed that Czechoslovakia had to hand over to Germany her predominantly German-speaking areas, leaving what was left of the country militarily defenseless. But had not the prime minister of Great Britain decribed the politically democratic and militarily puissant Czechs as "a far away people of whom we know nothing"?

On the other hand, Mussolini recouped his sagging popular-

Hitler and Goebbels with Mussolini and his son-in-law, Count Ciano, during Hitler's trip to Rome in 1938.

ity. He had starred at the Munich gathering by being able to speak everybody's language, while Chamberlain and Hitler could speak only their own. Mussolini had (apparently) saved his countrymen and all Europe from a conflagration, and he returned to Rome "perhaps more popular than he had ever been before."[8] Clearly, Mussolini's countrymen wanted peace. And in return for Mussolini's services, in November 1938 the British government recognized Victor Emmanuel as Emperor of Ethiopia. "Peace in our time," said the leader of the British Empire.

Within ten months the dreaded European war broke out.

Italy became Germany's ally because of Franco-British affronts, and because Mussolini believed that nobody was going to stop Hitler. Mussolini did *not* throw in his lot with the Germans in order to participate in the systematic extermination of ethnic groups, plans for which were in 1939 and 1940 a secret even from high officials of the Reich. Mussolini's alliance partner was the Hitler of Munich, not the Hitler of Auschwitz. None of what came later was foreseeable by Mussolini, any more than it was forseeable by Stalin, Chamberlain, Roosevelt, or by the Swedes who sold Germany iron ore all during the war.

The vulgar anti-Semitism that characterized the mentality of so many Europeans of his generation, including Socialists, was alien to Mussolini. Jews had played important roles in his life from his Socialist to his Fascist days, especially women like Angelica Balabanoff and Margherita Sarfatti.* In conversations with Emil Ludwig, Mussolini said that "anti-Semitism does not exist in Italy. Italians of Jewish birth have shown themselves to be good citizens, and they fought bravely in the war. Many of them occupy leading positions in the universities,

*The evidence indicates that during the 1920s (at least) Jews made up a larger proportion of the Fascist party than they did of the Italian population as a whole.

in the army, in the banks. Some of them are Generals. . . ." Mussolini often expressed his contempt for theories of biological determinism and backed up these expressions with real action, as when in March 1933 he instructed the Italian ambassador in Berlin to protest to Hitler about the treatment of German Jews.[9] Shortly after the assassination of Austrian Chancellor Dollfuss, Mussolini wrote in his *Popolo d'Italia* that if German racial theories were true, the Lapps would be the highest type of humanity. "Thirty centuries of history," he wrote, "allow us to regard with supreme indulgence certain doctrines taught beyond the Alps by descendants of people who were illiterate in the days when Caesar, Vergil and Augustus flourished in Rome." Biological politics directly contradicted Mussolini's beliefs in nationalism and the human will, and he explicitly condemned it in the *Enciclopedia italiana* in 1935.

But the Hilter alliance now made the introduction of anti-Semitic rhetoric and legislation into Italy inevitable. Anti-Semitism was unpopular among the cosmopolitan and tolerant Italians, especially because its official adoption was rightly seen as evidence of Mussolini's increasing subordination to Hitler. As late as February 1938, the Italian Foreign Office issued a statement that "a specific Jewish problem does not exist in Italy." Measures would be taken only against Jews who were "hostile to the regime." In the fall of 1938, nevertheless, came a spate of severe anti-Jewish legislation: any Jew who had immigrated to Italy since 1919 must leave the country within six months; Jews could no longer be state employees, teachers, or university students. Thus the sickness of official racism was introduced into a country where the Church had spoken thunderously against racialist theories, where Jews were a tiny minority of the population, and where anti-Semitism was historically of no importance.

In the style of Italian fascism, however, the bark was worse than the bite. A Jew was defined by the law not simply as someone of any Jewish heritage (as in Germany) but only as a person with two Jewish parents. Specifically *exempt* from anti-Semitic laws were Jews who had joined the Fascist party in its early days or who had been members during "the last half of 1924" (the dark days of the Matteotti crisis); also exempt were Jewish volunteers in World War I, wounded or decorated veterans, and those wounded in the service of the State or of fascism. These exemptions could be extended to family members as well, and also to families of Jews killed in military service or those who had "fallen in the Fascist cause." Jews who were deprived of their government posts could claim retirement compensation. In all these ways the regime showed its embarrassment. The plight of the Italian Jews did not become thoroughly perilous—no executions, no concentration camps, no extermination centers—until Mussolini was overthrown in 1943.

AN INTERVENTIONIST AGAIN

After Munich, the fateful minuet continued. In May 1939 Mussolini signed the Pact of Steel with the Germans. In spite of its menacing title, the pact did not contain an "automatic trigger," and neither signatory viewed it as likely to involve Italy in war in the near future. For Hitler, the purpose of the pact was to frighten France and Britain in the Mediterranean, freeing Germany for its attack on Poland. For Mussolini the pact was supposed to provide some leverage for his demands upon France for territorial concessions. At the signing, Mussolini told Hitler that Italy would not be ready for war before 1943. Hitler said that was all right, and Mussolini went ahead with his plans for an international exhibition to be held in Rome in 1942.

Yet in June 1940 Mussolini led his country to war against Britain and France. This was certainly one occasion in which it would have been better for everybody, Mussolini included, if his regime had truly been—as anti-Fascist publicists had so long portrayed it—nothing but the instrument of the throne, the Church, and big business, for indeed all these were profoundly opposed to any war, especially a war on the side of Nazi Germany. The responsibility for Italy's entrance into the war was Mussolini's, his alone.

It is difficult to see how, in the circumstances, he could have chosen differently. Since the German (and Russian) invasion of Poland in September 1939, Italy had been neutral, and neutrality was repugnant to Mussolini; he had, after all, built a career out of his opposition to Italian neutrality in 1914, and 1940 was like 1914 all over again: Europe's destiny was being played out; Italy could not merely sit on the sidelines and win nothing from anyone. Prime Minister Churchill, Premier Reynaud, and President Roosevelt had all addressed appeals to Mussolini to keep Italy out of the war, but at a meeting at the Brenner Pass in March 1940, Hitler had put subtle but unmistakable pressure on Mussolini to join in. Events seemed to be crying out to him to enter the war *now*, while there was still time to claim some booty and exercise some leverage. Russia was Germany's ally, thanks to the Molotov-Ribbentrop Pact which had enabled Hitler to unleash the war. Hungary, Romania, Bulgaria and Spain were all friendly to Germany. Poland had been easily conquered. So had Denmark, Norway, Holland, and Belgium. America was far away and neutral, caught up in the uncertainties of a presidential campaign. Then came the earthquake: the totally unexpected collapse of the French army—1870 all over again—and the flight of the British to the port of Dunkirk. Winston Churchill would soon be telling his countrymen that they must be prepared to fight German soldiers "on the beaches" of England. The temptation was too great for Mussolini; Italy must have a say in the new order that the Germans were clearly about to impose on Europe. The defeat of France and possibly Britain would entail a redistribution of their colonies—the solution to Italy's lack of natural resources. As in the days of the Austro-Prussian war, as in the days of the Triple Alliance, Italy would seek to satisfy her ambitions and compensate for her weaknesses through German military might. Thus, though his countrymen wanted peace, Mussolini declared war. Like Stalin, he believed in the probable permanence of German supremacy; like Stalin, he was willing to gamble on the reliability of Hitler's assurances. Stalin, who had already done so much to put Hitler in power in the first place,[10] would be saved from his folly by the immensity of his country and the severity of its winters. Mussolini would not be so lucky.

A LOSING WAR

That Italy was ultimately defeated is no profound mystery, fighting as she was against the combined populations and resources of the world's three mightiest empires. And certainly, World War II was hard on the military reputation of many countries. The collapse of the French army before inferior numbers in 1940; the evacuation of a stricken France by the British at Dunkirk; the ludicrous performance of the Red Army against gallant little Finland, and then the mass surrenders to the Germans in 1941 (In the summer and fall of 1941, anywhere from 2,000,000 to 3,000,000 Russian soldiers surrendered to the Germans); the capitulation at Singapore of 80,000 British troops to half that number of Japanese; all these unexpected disasters were a match and more for anything suffered by Italian arms. Units of the Italian army fought bravely and well in Russia and Tunisia, and most of the forces commanded by the victorious Rommel were made up of Italians. Yet in general, the performance of Italian armed forces in World War II amounts not to a mere defeat but to a debacle. In view of the fact that the Fascist regime, with all its emphasis on Roman discipline and military virtue, had been in power for close to two decades when the war broke out, Italy's war record requires some scrutiny.

In the first place, Mussolini must take responsibility for the indifferent training and poor equipment of Italian forces. Italian tanks, for instance, were completely inferior to those of the

British and the Germans. Mussolini's strategic conceptions, moreover, were in many respects old-fashioned or simply wrong. As an example, the Italian navy was a very good fighting force, or rather it would have been if it had possessed any aircraft carriers. But Mussolini thought that Italy's peninsular position in the middle of the Mediterranean Sea, with her outposts of Sardinia and Sicily and control of the coast of Libya, made her "one great aircraft carrier," to the enormous cost of the entire war effort.

Fundamental geopolitical and psychological aspects of the war worked to Italy's disadvantage as well. In World War I, the Italians were operating in a relatively narrow stretch of frontier against a traditional enemy, and in clear defense of the soil of the motherland. An effort of three and a half years, with enormous casualties, in a strategically disadvantageous posture, after many setbacks resulted in final victory.

In World War II, all was different. A great proportion of Italy's military stores had been consumed by the fighting in Ethiopia and Spain; *Italy had been at war almost uninterruptedly since 1935.* It was not so easy for a resource-poor nation, still to a large degree agricultural, to replace these expended munitions. This is especially the case since Mussolini, so often criticized for militarizing Italian society, had never embarked upon a full-blast armaments program like Stalin's or Hitler's, because it would have interfered with overall economic development. Mussolini was not prepared for war, he did not want war, certainly not in 1939; hence his declaration of neutrality. When Italy did enter the conflict, it was not because she was "ready" but because, as Mussolini told Ciano, it looked like Hitler was on the verge of an historic victory. Mussolini had intended to wage only a brief campaign against France, but the war unexpectedly went on, the conflict widened, and Italy's enemies multiplied. Thanks to Hitler's failure to make peace with Britain (or to defeat her), to Japanese policy on the other side of the world, and to Germany's totally unexpected assault upon Russia, the Italians found themselves fighting powerful sea-ruling empires. These far-flung battlefields—the African

Horn, the Ukraine, Libya, Albania, Greece—were as hard to supply as they were to identify with. The Italian navy, a force of considerable strength, was almost totally dependent upon Germany for supplies of fuel; Hitler's Russian campaign meant that precious little would be forthcoming from that quarter. Further, the Italians were fighting against the British and the Americans, nations most of them fundamentally admired, and of whose ultimate invincibility they were all too thoroughly convinced. Finally, all Italians had to face this dilemma: if the Axis lost, Italy lost; if the Axis won, Italy might eventually find herself a subordinate province of a nazified Europe. "What was the sense of showing bravery in a futile war for a bad cause?" (In contrast, the operations of Italian guerrillas in the north against the Nazi occupation of 1943-1945 were savage, persistent, and effective).

The general lack of enthusiasm for the war was reflected in the army, and aggravated by the fact that the Italian officer corps was something of a state within a state. This was the result of another one of those Mussolinian compromises whereby the Fascist regime had been brought into existence and kept in office. "The Fascist government bought the army's support by abandoning plans for reform and allowing the generals to run things as they wanted, under Mussolini's nominal control. The surrender of fascism to the military was to have fatal consequences for the regime; the Fascist state exalted preparation for war as the highest priority, and yet Mussolini's coordination of the armed forces was only nominal."[11] The officer corps had largely opposed the war from the beginning, never having liked the Axis nor trusted the Germans. Mussolini's main justification for entering the war had been to increase Italian territory, thereby counterbalancing the growth of German power. He had tried to get Corsica and Tunisia from the French, places that could have been turned into powerful bases for the defense of the Italian peninsula. But Hitler, eager to win the cooperation of the Vichy government, refused these demands, to the deep resentment of the Italian general staff. (The Germans would one day abandon Tunisia to the Anglo-American armies, thus exposing Sicily to invasion and Mussolini to overthrow.) There was, besides, very little intelligent cooperation and coordination of effort between the German and Italian high commands.

When Mussolini learned of Hitler's invasion of the Soviet Union, the preparations for which had been kept secret from him, he remarked to Ciano that he "wouldn't be sorry to see the Germans lose a lot of feathers." But the Russian attack marked the turning point of the whole war, concentrating German power and attention on the East and thus precluding any serious operations against the British in the Mediterranean or North Africa, areas absolutely vital to Italy. Two months after the attack on Russia had begun, Mussolini visited Italian troops on the Russian front. Hitler blandly informed him that German intelligence had misled the Fuhrer on the size and quality of the Russian forces, and on their determination. This chilling information came to Mussolini on top of the failure of his own invasion of Greece, which in turn had provoked the German invasion of the Balkans—a strategic castastrophe for Italy of inestimable dimensions. Then in the fall of 1941 Mussolini learned of the callous, even brutal, mistreatment of Italian workers in Germany. With no territorial gains to show, fighting on the side of an ally he neither liked nor trusted, in a war whose dimensions daily became more and more threatening, Mussolini nevertheless told Ciano that Italy could in no way opt out of the war and make a separate peace, because of the certainty of German vengeance.

On the diplomatic front the war had turned equally bitter for Mussolini. For example, no matter how hard he tried, no matter how often he reminded Franco of the aid he had rendered him during the civil war, Mussolini could not prevail upon Franco to undertake operations against Gibraltar, a traditional object of Spanish desire for centuries.

These grievous worries, hard work, and the knowledge that the responsibility for taking Italy into this losing war was his, took their toll of Mussolini; in October 1942 the *Duce*, who was nearing his sixtieth birthday, fell seriously ill. While he seemed to recover in time, his health was never again up to the strains of the war. The reverses in the field of battle must have been doubly devastating for him because, skillful propagandist that he was, over the years he had come to believe in his own pronouncements. Now the vaunted strength of Fascist and Roman Italy was being revealed as mainly headline hyperbole.

The increasing physical weakness of the *Duce* and the ever more obvious failure of the war should have suggested that it might have been time for a successor. But no successor had been prepared, or even annointed. No one could imagine fascism without Mussolini, a situation he himself had encouraged at least by omission. Thus, as men's minds turned more and more to the question "After Mussolini, what?" the answer began to emerge in all its simple clarity: *the king*. With all his faults, the king was the embodiment of legitimacy, a living link with the great days of the *risorgimento*, and (most crucially) the repository of the loyalty of most of the officer corps (whose oath was not to the *Duce* but to the sovereign). Had there been no king, no plausible alternative to Mussolini and to his disastrous war, perhaps all would have decided that there was nothing to do but rally around Mussolini for better or for worse, as the Germans had to rally around Hitler. The monarchy was the Achilles' heel of the Mussolini regime.

Mussolini believed that as a result of the Lateran Accords and the Ethiopian victory, he was politically invulnerable. True, the great problems confronting him in 1922—the Socialist opposition, the Roman Question, colonies, industrialization—all these had been solved, or were *being* solved. But along with the great problems had gone the passion. The *squadristi* of the early 1920s had grown old, along with their leader. Even many of those who still longed to see Italy play a great role in the world were not willing to play a German game, and the war aggravated their disenchantment.

An increase in venality accompanied the decrease in vitality. The crude avarice of many party leaders, high and low, whether they had once been true believers or had entered the party to get rich, offended many. All these negative elements were exacerbated by the bad war news, for which the responsibility was placed on Mussolini. Along with the roles of prime minister and party leader, Mussolini had insisted on filling the office of commander in chief of all armed forces. The error of this decision became all too apparent as the war began to go badly.

Under all this pressure the main, secret, fatal flaw of the Fascist regime was exposed. Mussolini had never been able to rest his regime on the foundations of his choice. His intention of uniting the bulk of the Socialist masses to his own Fascist party had been thwarted by the Matteotti Affair. Thus Mussolini had to rely, to a much greater degree than he would have wished, on the traditional power-holders of the kingdom: throne and army, Church and bureaucracy, landowners and bourgeoisie. That Mussolini found himself in this position, that he found himself in an unbreakable (from his side) alliance with fundamentally conservative groups, is the reason above all reasons why his regime never came to resemble the charnel houses of Hitler and Stalin. But it also meant that Mussolini was forced to rely for backing on many who had never really believed in or trusted him, and for whom he was merely the lesser of evils and the best of a bad lot. To the conservative forces of the nation, fascism, in its leadership and in its style, remained essentially plebeian and Mussolini would always at heart be a socialist revolutionary, a subversive, a red heart inside the black shirt. Meanwhile, the Socialists, having been defeated by Mussolini many times, remained (with some notable exceptions) sullen and unforgiving, or at least unenthusiastic. Thus the real Mussolini men were not "the nation," but only a third part of the nation. This situation was all right as long as the sun was shining, but under the growing gloom of

Hitler and the war, Mussolini's supporters grew increasingly demoralized and confused, while Mussolini's enemies and false friends began to prepare for changes.

Even in the light of all this, the situation might have still been stabilized if, after the initial phase of their Russian campaign, the Germans had managed to gain some real successes. But by the middle of 1942 (certainly by the end of it), it had become apparent that Hitler had failed both in the West and in the East. The Allies now made a decision that sealed the fate of Mussolini. Containment of the Germans on the Russian front and the clearing of the last Axis forces out of North Africa meant that an invasion of Hitler's "Fortress Europe" was only a matter of time. Had the Anglo-Americans determined in 1943 to invade Europe in Norway, Normandy, or Greece (and all of these potential sites had their fervent advocates and sound recommendations), it is quite conceivable that the Mussolini regime would have survived until the end of the war. Indeed it is conceivable that Mussolini would have been able to make a separate peace that would have preserved Italian territorial integrity and at least the outward continuity of the Fascist regime. Instead, Italy—the "soft underbelly" of Europe—was selected for a knockout blow. In his history of the Second World War, Winston Churchill explains that Italy was chosen as the site for the invasion of Europe for three main reasons: (1) successful Allied landings in Italy would reverse the pro-Axis political trends in the Balkans; (2) the Italian fleet would be eliminated, freeing British naval units for operations in the Atlantic and the Pacific; (3) the loss of their major European partner would demoralize the Germans (thus, a sort of mirror-image of the Austro-German Caporetto strategy of 1917). This strategic decision of the Allies was doubly disastrous for Mussolini. Not only had the unpopular and unsuccessful war neutralized most of his domestic political support, there was in Italy no space into which Fascist armed forces, faced with a successful invasion could retire and retrench.

Practically every square inch of Italian territory was vulnerable to Allied naval and/or air attacks. The Gaullists had their African empire from which to carry on the struggle. Stalin gave up 500,000 square miles to the German invaders (an area four times the size of Italy), along with two and a half million men and 18,000 tanks. But Italy had no space.

The strategic situation of the Italians in the spring of 1943 was grim. Wagering on a German hegemony in Europe, Fascist Italy had entered the Anti-Comintern Pact. With her continental frontier thus presumably secured, Italy was free to pursue colonial conquest in North and East Africa. Hitler's failure, however, to conclude the war in the West before attempting the subjugation of Russia had been a monumental mistake. The myth of the invincible German army had been shattered; German and Italian troops were now being pushed back everywhere. The entrance of the United States into the war meant that while no one could be certain *when* the war would end, all could see *how*.

The salvation, or at least survival, of the Axis therefore depended on the termination of the Russian campaign. This was true above all for Italy (over 100,000 Italian troops had been killed in the siege of Stalingrad), because only if the Russian war were terminated or at least reorganized on a defensive footing could sufficient men and matériel be transferred to North America and the Mediterranean to counter the "soft underbelly" plans of the Allies.

It was with this purpose—to convince Hitler that the Eastern hemorrhage must be stanched—that Mussolini journeyed to his meeting with the Fuhrer at Salzburg in April 1943.[12] Whatever else, the fate of fascism depended on Mussolini's ability to bring about such a revolution in Axis strategy. On his way to the fateful encounter, Mussolini spent a lot of time on the floor of his railway compartment doubled up with stomach cramps.

But Hitler said no. He was totally consumed by his passion to remove for all time the "threat from the East." Russia's losses were colossal; the tide would turn, and Germany would crush the Russians and defeat the British and the Americans as well. There would be no strategic revolution. Nor could there be any wholesale transfer of Italian troops from Russia and the Balkans to the defense of the homeland. Instead, Hitler promised Mussolini that the soft underbelly would be defended on the southern shores of the Mediterranean. The indomitable German troops fighting there would turn Tunis into the "Verdun of Africa." (Hitler apparently forgot how easily Verdun, scene of the bloodiest battle of World War I, had fallen to the Germans in 1940.)

Germany and Italy tried unsuccessfully to supply Tunis by air. "One sees clearly," lamented Mussolini, "the importance of control of the sea." On May 12, 1943, the First Italian Army, under command of Rommel's successor, General Giovanni Messe, surrendered. Two hundred thousand German and Italian prisoners were taken, and Churchill would compare the decisiveness of the battle of Tunis to Stalingrad.

And so from Salzburg Mussolini returned to Rome, his mission unaccomplished. The war was lost, the gamble had failed, the regime was doomed, and Mussolini faced his supreme crisis.

XII
THE END

"I am convinced that
I will die in my bed."

Benito Mussolini

"And a man's enemies will
be those of his own house."

Matthew X.36

THE GRAND COUNCIL

Things began to visibly break apart for the regime early in 1943. In the early spring, for the first time in nearly twenty years, there were major strikes in the industrial centers that the government was able to end only with great difficulty and many concessions. Everywhere there was nervousness and uncertainty about the health of the *Duce*, and above all, about the course of the war, which was clearly being lost. In May the Afrika Korps surrendered, ending Axis resistance in North Africa and opening the way to Italy itself. The blow fell on July 10; 160,000 Allied soldiers under the command of Generals Alexander, Patton, and Montgomery landed in Sicily. Mussolini had to do something dramatic, and very soon.

A few days after the invasion of Sicily, Mussolini announced a meeting of the long-dormant Grand Council of Fascism, for a confidential airing of discontents and ideas at the highest level. Mussolini hoped to have very good news for the Grand Council, news that would extinguish smoldering opposition among some of its members to his continued leadership. At yet another meeting with Hitler, this time at Feltre, Mussolini intended to explain to the Nazi leader the military untenability of Italy's position. He would then obtain Hitler's permission for a separate Italian peace with the Allies. Hitler's southern flank would thereby be neutralized and free the Germans to concentrate against the menace on the Eastern Front. But Mussolini's plan failed; he was able to get hardly a word in, being instead subjected to another of Hitler's endless hysterical monologues, filled with promises of new weapons—super-secret weapons that would turn the tide of the war in a day. Hitler's astrologer had told him all would be well, wait and see. In these circumstances, Mussolini now had to face the Grand Council.

Dino Grandi, one of the founding fathers of fascism and former ambassador to London, had been openly circulating a resolution he intended to lay before the Grand Council criticizing Mussolini and calling for the king to assume all military command. On the day of the scheduled meeting Rachele told her husband not to attend, but instead to have all the malcontents arrested.[1] Not for the first or the last time, Mussolini ignored his wife's shrewd advice.

The meeting of the Grand Council was long and exhausting. In his opening speech Mussolini acknowledged the growing unpopularity of the war, but pointed out that the masses never had their hearts in any war, including those of the *risorgimento*. If necessary, the government would move north and make a stand in the Po Valley. Then Grandi made an impassioned address blaming all of Italy's troubles on Mussolini's personal dictatorship. He introduced his motion calling upon the king to take over direction of the military. Support for this motion was widespread within the Council, and included most of the influential party leadership: Acerbo, Bottai, Federzoni; Mussolini's son-in-law, Ciano; and the surviving leaders of the March on Rome—De Bono and De Vecchi—along with others. After the vote, Mussolini grimly surveyed his fellow Fascists: "You have provoked the crisis of the regime."

In later testimony it appeared that many who voted for Grandi's resolution did not understand its implications, as if they could publicly rebuke Mussolini and not harm the regime from which they themselves had benefited. Many also denied believing that their votes would cause the fall of the *Duce*. And despite his chilling words about the "crisis of the regime," there seems to have been a lack of clarity also in Mussolini's mind about what all this would mean for the future. (The large German military and diplomatic contingent in Rome also failed to appreciate the implications of the Grand Council vote.) The morning after the Grand Council session he received the new Japanese ambassador, asking him to put pressure on Hitler about disengaging from the disastrous Russian front. Then he toured bombed sections of Rome and distributed money to the victims. Later he was supposed to report to the king.

The vote of the Grand Council, however, had set many wheels in motion. Unknown to Grandi (not to say Mussolini), the king had been conspiring for a long time with certain generals and high police officials, with the object of getting Mussolini out of power and Italy out of the war. Victor Emmanuel made up his mind to move against Mussolini after the July 19 air raid on Rome; hence the Grand Council vote was a heaven-sent pretext for him. If not for the action of that body, the king would have had to move directly against Mussolini on his own authority and perhaps provoke a countercoup, or even a civil war with fascist party elements.

The afternoon of the day after the Grand Council meeting (that is, on Sunday, July 25) Mussolini was preparing for his regularly scheduled audience with the king. Rachele, once again, smelling something in the air, implored her husband not to go; once again he ignored her and went out to Villa Savoia to see his sovereign. The hot July afternoon was heavy and oppressive, as before a thunderstorm. During the audience, the manner of the king betrayed his embarrassment at the deed he was about to commit. Biting his nails, he informed Mussolini that he could no longer be prime minister. "I am your only friend," the King said to Mussolini, who was then arrested by *carabinieri.* Without protest, Mussolini allowed himself to be taken off in an ambulance, first from one barracks to another, then from one island to another aboard a naval vessel, until finally, on August 28 he found himself under heavy guard, at a resort hotel high up on the Gran Sasso in the Abruzzi, fifteen miles from the provincial capital of Aquila. During all these days of captivity he displayed an unusual stoicism, talking quietly to his guards, reading a life of Christ, and translating Carducci's poems into German. "Thus ended," wrote Winston Churchill, "Mussolini's twenty-one years' dictatorship in Italy, during which he had raised the Italian people from the Bolshevism into which they were sinking in 1919 to a position in Europe such as Italy had never held before."[2]

THE PRISONER

Mussolini had paid the price of being a leader in a losing war; in this his fate was no different from that of the Kaiser, the Tsar, the Habsburg Emperor, the Turkish Sultan, or the parliamentary politicians of the Third Republic. His German and Japanese allies would soon follow him.

Nevertheless, the ease with which Mussolini was overthrown reveals a great deal about his regime. Clearly his rule was not based on force alone, because force did not save him when he became unpopular. The basis of Mussolini's long rule had been the acquiescence of the Italians, which he had obtained by undeniable successes. When the successes stopped, so did the acquiescence—and the regime fell.

Until the war, Mussolini was the Statesman of Munich, the Conqueror of Ethiopia, the Conciliator of the Church, the Guarantor of the Social Order. There was no movement to replace him, nor did there exist a potential replacement, from any quarter, who could possibly have hoped to rally anything like nationwide support. There was no important group in

Italy that Mussolini had not tried to please: churchmen, professional soldiers, veterans, patriots, industrialists, landowners, monarchists, all had their emotional and/or financial stake in the regime. For the proletariat there was industrial peace, summer camps for children, and impassioned rhetoric about the destiny of Proletarian Italy. For the peasantry, there was improved housing, land reclamation, promises of new lands in Africa, and the impressive and effective symbolism of a bare-chested prime minister helping with the wheat harvest. (Can we image a Giolitti or a Salandra engaged in such sweaty activity? or a—a *Lenin*?)

True, by 1943 the war had cost Mussolini much, perhaps most, of his popularity. Nevertheless there was no popular clamor for a particular successor. It is essential to always keep in mind that Mussolini was removed from power *during a losing war, by a narrow military conspiracy, with the sanction of a monarch who had been a public collaborator of Mussolini's for twenty years.*

In light of all this, Mussolini's almost total lack of preparation for resistance to a possible coup becomes all the more crucial. The Italian police had never been penetrated by the Fascists; in fact, the head of the police in Rome during 1942-1943 had been working out elaborate plans of action for the eventual fall of the regime. The *carabinieri* (para-military police) were also outside of Fascist control, never having been directed by men whose primary loyalty was to the *Duce.* Above all, the officer corps of the regular armed forces after twenty years of fascism still swore its oath not to Mussolini but to the king.

The Germans had long been suspicious of the Royal House and the regular Italian army, and several important personages of the Reich had been urging Mussolini to form a special bodyguard. And so the "M Division" had eventually come into being, with the purpose of giving pause to any disloyal generals or policemen who might contemplate moves against the regime. The creation of the M Division began in April 1943. It consisted of from eight to twelve thousand men, mostly veterans of the Fascist Militia units from the Russian front, carefully screened for their political reliability. The Germans made an impressive contribution of thirty-six Tiger tanks to this force, along with some artillery and instructors. The M Division was supposed to be in a state of readiness by the end of June. The availability of this force would almost certainly have prevented, or at least postponed, the coup.* But shortly before the crucial day, the M Division was inexplicably placed under command of the regular army and ordered to move outside of Rome. When the coup occurred, telephone lines had been taken over by the army, and it was impossible to recall the M Division in time.

But why didn't the Fascist party rise? Surely, among the self-servers and opportunists who had weaseled into the ranks during all those years there must still have been many thousands of true believers, or those who at least were smart enough to understand that the fall of the regime would mean no good for them. There was the Fascist party militia, but during the war it had become disorganized; many of its members were well above military age, and many good Fascists were in the armed forces on various fronts. The coup took place on a Sunday, when party and militia offices were closed. Telephone lines, especially between Fascist Militia headquarters in Rome and the M Division, were in the hands of sympathizers of the coup. Besides, the radio announced that Mussolini had *submitted his resignation* to the king as a consequence of the vote of the Grand Council, which, after all, was supposed to be the ruling body of fascism; and nobody could get in touch with the *Duce* to see if all this were indeed true. For twenty years the existence of the monarchy had permitted the Mussolini regime

*In the same manner, the presence of a few thousand politically reliable troops in Petrograd in October 1917, would have profoundly altered the destiny of the whole human race.

to act as if everything were normal and constitutional. Now (1943) the existence of the monarchy permitted the removal of Mussolini by a military coup to also appear normal and constitutional. Within a few minutes of Mussolini's arrest, army units were visibly occupying Rome. Nearly one thousand prominent Fascists were placed under arrest or drafted. A rising against the king to save Mussolini (on whose orders?) would have meant civil war between Party and Army, something the aging, confused, all-but-leaderless cadres of the party would have found morally, as well as physically, impossible. And the *Duce* himself issued no call, sent no word. Tired of power, knowing when the game was up, Mussolini made no attempt to stir a revolt. On the day after the coup, Badoglio wrote Mussolini of the existence of plots against his life and said that all was being done for his protection. Mussolini replied in writing that "I desire to assure Marshal Badoglio ... that there will be no difficulties on my part and I will continue to cooperate in every way." Clearly, Mussolini had absolutely no idea how old, how widespread, and how hostile to him personally the conspiracy actually was.

In some quarters of the city of Rome the news of Mussolini's resignation was greeted literally with dancing in the streets. Many supposed that now the war would soon be over. Alas, these naive sentiments were soon dashed. As Mussolini's successor as prime minister the king named Marshal Badoglio, who announced that Italy would continue loyally in the struggle at the side of her German comrades. Badoglio had been heaped with honors by Mussolini (he was, inter alia, "Duke of Addis Ababa"), but his reputation had been tarnished by the fiasco of the Greek invasion. During 1942 Badoglio entered into private (treasonous) negotiations with the British. Thereafter his labors were directed not toward strengthening Italy's war effort but to undermining the regime, and this should be kept in mind in any evaluation of the frequently poor performance of the Italian army. The excuse of the king and Badoglio for overthrowing the man who had done so much for them was that in casting Mussolini down they would spare Italy an Allied invasion and prevent the country from becoming a mere German satellite. They failed utterly in both endeavors. On September 3, the British Eighth Army landed on the Italian mainland. Badoglio, having solemnly assured his German allies that Italy would continue in the war, capitulated to the Anglo-Americans on September 8, 1943. German army units in Italy had been greatly strengthened during Badoglio's tenure. They were immediately ordered by Berlin to take over the country and met hardly any resistance from Badoglio's forces. On September 9, learning that German troops were in the outskirts of Rome, the king and his new prime minister fled the capital, leaving the inhabitants of the city to deal with the Nazis as best they could. (It was this ignominious act, perhaps, more than the long alliance with Mussolini, that would cost Victor Emmanuel his throne after the war. One of the troubles with being a king is that once in a great while you have to know how to act like one, at least in public; Victor Emmanuel failed completely.) Ensconced in a small southern town, totally in the power of the Allied armies, the king and the Badoglio "government" declared war upon Germany.

Had Mussolini not been removed from power, the worst that probably would have happened to Italy was that she would have been defeated by the Anglo-Americans after a more-or-less protracted struggle. But as a result of the coup, Italy found herself not only the scene of a major military campaign, but also with the northern half of the country now occupied by the vengeful Nazis. Moreover, there would now be *two* Italian governments, each of them the puppet of a foreign power, neither of them trusted much by anybody. And so the country was cast into the abyss of civil war.

While Badoglio carried on this destructive farce, Mussolini was being taken from confinement to confinement, so that would-be rescuers would not be able to make effective plans. While on this melancholy sojourn, Mussolini, a veteran of prison life, transcribed his thoughts. Among them:

"Of all the so-called totalitarian states that emerged after 1918, the Turkish one seems to me the strongest."

"Women have never exerted even minimal influence on my policies. Perhaps this was unfortunate. Often, thanks to their sensitivity, women are more farsighted than men."

"Once a pope, the earthly representative of God, called me 'a man sent by God.' Those were good days!"

"In my life I have never had a friend."[3]

Completely passive, as if relieved of a great burden, Mussolini still worried about his reputation before history, and about the fate of those who had served the regime. "It is impossible that everything has collapsed. When I look back on all the tasks, all the achievements, all the labors and hopes of the past twenty years I ask myself if I have been dreaming. Was everything an illusion? Everything superficial? Didn't anything have substance? Will those who died in the service of fascism—and they are so many—will they be respected?"[4]

These reflections were suddenly cut short. One of the conditions of the armistice between the Badoglio government and the Allies had been the handing over of Mussolini to the Allies. Before this could be complied with, on September 12, literally from out of the blue, a party of German commandoes descended by glider on Mussolini's mountain prison. In command of this operation was Captain Otto Skorzeny of the Waffen SS. Hitler had summoned Skorzeny the day after Mussolini's arrest and told him to begin work on plans to rescue the *Duce*, saying that "I cannot and will not fail Italy's greatest son in his hour of need."

Mussolini's guards had orders to shoot him if there was a rescue attempt, but no one wished to carry out these instructions. Mussolini was soon flown by his rescuers to Munich (his family had been brought there from Forlì on Hitler's orders) and then to a meeting with Hitler in the latter's East Prussian headquarters. On September 23 he was back again at Forlì, charged by Hitler with the task of setting up a new Fascist government to help the German war effort, in opposition to that of the king and Badoglio in the south. This was a crushing assignment for Mussolini, unwillingly brought back from his Elba. Indeed, it was his death warrant. But after his interview with Hitler he saw there was "no chance of his being allowed to go into peaceful retirement." Despite a fearsome weariness and a total understanding that the war was irrevocably lost, Mussolini had no choice. His failure to serve the new Fascist state would be interpreted as lack of faith in the inevitable German victory. If he refused Hitler's directive, an Italian puppet state would be set up under some other Fascist hierarch, who would combine a fawning admiration for the Germans with none of Mussolini's prestige. If German policy in north Italy were to be mitigated at all, Mussolini would have to do it. "He saw himself," writes Kirkpatrick, "as a buffer between his own people and the barbarian Germans" who otherwise "might exact a terrible vengeance" for the acts of the king and Badoglio. In these circumstances began the last chapter of Mussolini's life, the saddest chapter of all, leading swiftly to a lonely and brutal death.

THE REPUBLIC OF SALÒ

The new regime was named the Italian Social Republic. The new state was doomed from the start, dependent for support upon a Germany which every day moved closer to total defeat. But the days of the regime were made more difficult because from the very start the Germans treated it as a puppet and tool, not an ally. There was, to begin with, the question of where the capital of the new Fascist state should be located. Mussolini had of course wanted to locate it in Rome, returning in triumph to the city that the pusillanimous king had abandoned. Besides,

Mussolini feared that if Rome were left uncontested in the hands of the charismatic Pius XII, this could lay the foundation for a postwar revival of the Pontifical States, the undoing of the *risorgimento* and the *conciliazione*, the unraveling of Italy itself. But the Germans insisted that Mussolini place his capital somewhere far to the north of Rome. So on October 10 Mussolini left the Romagna, where he had been staying since his return from Germany, for the Lake Garda area and established his headquarters in the town of Salò, from which the Social Republic derived its *de facto* title. Whatever prestige the new government possessed in the eyes of its nominal subjects was not augmented by its location in this obscure and minuscule capital, so far from Rome, so close to the German border.

The constitutional bases of the new state were laid down at a Fascist Republican Congress held in November 1943 in the city of Verona* where many, especially among the young men, were known to be still loyal to the *Duce*. The Manifesto adopted by the Verona Congress was based on a draft by Mussolini—a Mussolini freed at last from the conservative coalition that had been the condition and the limitation of his power, the Mussolini of San Sepolcro, with the old dream, the Grand Coalition of Fascists, Socialists, and Catholics. The Verona Manifesto proclaimed that "the Republic is based primarily upon labor." It called for the abolition of capitalism, struggle against the "world plutocracies," and the establishment of a European economic community. Catholicism was made the official religion, all others being permitted. Civil liberties were guaranteed so that, for instance, no one could be held for more than seven days without judicial approval.

The Manifesto was patently an attempt by the ex-Socialist *Duce* to win over the large and vital northern working class, an ambition that had been thwarted in 1915 and in 1924. Not only

*Forty years before Mussolini's Bersaglieri regiment had been stationed at Verona, this "dear Venetian city."

was Mussolini's old-time socialism reasserting itself; Mussolini was filled with rage against the industrialists who, in his eyes, were eagerly awaiting the arrival of the "Anglo-Saxons." But plans for real participation by labor unions in the affairs of factory and republic were blocked: the Germans were shocked at Mussolini's radicalism, and they were much more interested in mobilizing north Italy's resources for the war effort than in encouraging proletarian activism behind the lines. The mass of the workers, on the other hand, generally remained indifferent, where they were not stirred to actual hostility by the reviving Communist party. Thus Mussolini's vision of a Social and Fascist Republic, the vision of 1919, was slowly drained of life by the Nazis on one side and the Communists on the other.

Mussolini at Salò was starting from scratch; he needed to build a new party, a new administration, and above all a new army. His Republic had no real capital, was in imminent danger of invasion, and under the military control of a very skeptical ally. The only really valuable resource the Salò Republic possessed was Mussolini himself. Nevertheless, within a few months, there were approximately 250,000 members enrolled in the new Fascist Republican party. Typically, Mussolini refused any salary as president of the Republic: "What do I want with all that money?"[5]

The central issue and chief problem of the new state was the nature of and control over the armed forces. The *Duce* was anxious to build up an army right away, to recoup some prestige for fascism, to show that the Salò Republic was real, and to wipe out the humiliation of the July 25 coup and Badoglio's switching sides in September. The Badoglio government was supplying important military units for the Allied side; Mussolini must do no less for Germany.

In the beginning, Mussolini wanted the new armed forces to be a party-in-arms, based on the Fascist Militia, and thus presumably immune from the pressures to which the soldiers of the monarchy had been subjected. But the man in charge of these matters was Marshal Rodolpho Graziani, commander of the southern front in the Ethiopian war and the only man of any real prestige to rally to Mussolini's republic. Graziani's plans for the new army were quite different. He envisioned a small force, all volunteers, young, German-equipped, and nonpolitical; eventually this army might grow to twenty-five divisions, perhaps 300,000 men. Mussolini was attracted by Graziani's plans, but they were vigorously opposed by the Facist Militia, which wanted to build or at least shape the armed forces itself. Much more importantly, the Germans did not care for Graziani's scheme at all. They had been totally stunned by the Badoglio coup and feared its repercussions within Germany and the satellite states. They blamed it for serious losses in Russia caused by the necessity of pulling troops off the line there to be sent into Italy. They were shocked and appalled to learn that treasonous activities within the Italian army had been hatching for years before July 25. Would Graziani, they asked, one of these professional officers (a caste for which Hitler in particular had deep contempt), be able to resist some future temptation to make himself the man on horseback, or even a second Badoglio? And underneath all this was the seldom-spoken but never-absent German recollection of Italy's previous "change of sides" in 1915. Fearing yet another betrayal, the Germans did everything they could to hamper the erection of anything like a sizable regular army at the disposal of the Salò government. In Germany there were 600,000 Italian prisoners of war—the basis of a good army—but the Nazis would not let Salò officials recruit among them. In addition, a furious competition for available manpower raged among the cadres of the new Salò army, the party militia, and the various police formations; German labor recruiters also were busy enticing men to leave northern Italy for work in German factories. Even the regular German army was recruiting its own Italian units, and the SS was busy pursuing its plans for a special Italian division. Many men were drafted by the Salò government and they responded, but they found neither barracks nor equipment ready for them, so they began to drift away. In this maelstrom of competition and inefficiency, at least one good lesson that had been derived from the experiences of July 25 was applied: every member of the armed forces of the Social Republic would swear a personal oath of loyalty to the *Duce*.

The Republic of Salò had from the beginning an atmosphere of unreality that only deepened with the passing months. Mussolini was virtually a prisoner of SS guards, selected for him by the Germans specifically for their inability to speak either Italian or German. His telephone calls were monitored. He had to go and listen to more maniacal ravings by Hitler, who every week became less and less in contact with reality. Domestic life was not much of a consolation: he lived in a villa not only with Rachele, his children (except for Edda and Bruno), and his grandchildren, but also with his daughters-in-law who quarreled incessantly. Mussolini sought some relief from all these political and familial difficulties in the violin ("when I play the world slips away from me"), often spending whole evenings playing Beethoven or Verdi for his appreciative SS "protectors." There were also visits to Clara Petacci, who was staying at a nearby villa. Clara had been imprisoned by the Badoglio government after the coup, but had soon been liberated by the Germans. She and her unscrupulous relatives found themselves a house conveniently close to the *Duce*. Rachele Mussolini had learned about the affair between her husband and Clara only on the evening of the coup, from the wife of a gardener at Villa Torlonia who had imagined that she had known about it all along. Donna Rachele seethed with the knowledge that Clara was in Salò, and that her husband was visiting her. There was one memorable session when Rachele drove in a rage to Clara's house. A stormy confrontation between the two women ensued, and Mussolini himself had to be summoned to arrange, with much difficulty, a bristling truce. Another time Mussolini told Clara that he was not coming to see her again, but she cried piteously and their rendezvous continued, in their constricted and gloomy world, in Clara's damp villa.

Disappointments and failures abounded on every side. The Italian Social Republic had naturally received diplomatic recognition from Germany and Japan, and also from Romania, Bulgaria, Slovakia, and Croatia. But Mussolini was consumed with anger because the Vatican would not recognize his regime; the Church would render to Caesar, but not to Marc Antony. Mussolini spent many hours scheming to force a change in this intolerable situation. He watched the "traitorous bourgeoisie" in the south greet their American and British conquerors with open arms. Meanwhile, the heavy Fascist investment in Spain proved totally sterile; not only had Franco continued to refuse to enter the war with an attack on Gibraltar, in a final act of ingratitude he failed to even send an envoy to Salò.

Germany made matters even worse by annexing the southern Tyrol (part of Italy's gains from the First World War), parts of Venetia, and Italian areas on the other side of the Adriatic. These moves provoked the deepest outrage among all Italian patriots against the Germans, and, by implications, against their captive allies at Salò. Such gross violations of Italian sovereignty and sensitivity took place over the vehement protests of Mussolini, and were "perhaps the most bitter personal shock which the *Duce* had thus far sustained."[6]

More anguish was to come. Hitler demanded that the traitors of the Grand Council, those who could be located, be punished. This would establish the "credentials" of the Salò government with Berlin, and show to anybody in Germany who might be contemplating a putsch against Hitler what to expect. Mussolini himself blamed the king more than the Grand Council, but Hitler wanted blood vengeance, especially the blood of Galeazzo Ciano. The Nazis were acidly critical of Mussolini for being too close to his family. Such unmasterful weaknesses could not be tolerated. If Salò would not punish at least some of the traitors of July 25, then Berlin would, employing its own inimitable methods. So Ciano (who after the coup had stupidly gone to Germany) and several other formerly important Fascists were condemned to death. Edda Mussolini

Ciano pleaded with both Mussolini and Hitler for the life of her husband, offering to turn over his diaries if only he would be spared. But Mussolini was under too much pressure from Berlin; "sentiment and *raison d'état* have sharply collided in my soul." So Ciano was shot, and Edda fled with her children to Switzerland.

While this cruel drama was being played out in the north, in Allied-occupied Italy the Sforza Law of July 1944 promised the death penalty to those found guilty of "having betrayed the Fatherland", and other condign punishments to "those who have contributed to maintaining the Fascist regime in power." Many acts going as far back as the 1920s were repudiated *ex post facto*. Mussolini's enemies were firmly in control in the south, and the defeat of the Salò Republic would surely unleash a real orgy of anti-Fascist vengeance.

But without doubt the most bitter experience Mussolini suffered during the dark year and a half of Salò was watching the north of Italy being consumed by the flames of civil war. In the early fall of 1943, the leaders of Italy's burgeoning Communist party reached a fateful decision: in order to rally Italy's masses to the Communist-dominated guerrilla movement (the "partisans"), the Salò regime and its German allies would have to be provoked into taking drastic reprisals against the civilian population. This was the unleashing of Communist terrorism, with a program of systematic assassination of local Fascist leaders; in late November 1943 alone, twenty-eight were killed. The Republic never had enough manpower to cope with the guerrillas, and strong measures against deserters from the Salò army helped to swell the partisan ranks. But it was the Germans who played most completely into the hands of the Communists. German troops—the cruelest being SS men from the south of Tyrol who could speak Italian—took fearful revenge against the partisans, their sympathizers, and even mere suspects. Whole villages were burned with all their inhabitants locked in their homes. The Germans also organized an intense roundup of Jews (which was often sabotaged by local Fascist authorities). Mussolini's attitude toward his German allies became ever more embittered. Once, when he heard a radio report that Badoglio's troops were doing well in some action against the Germans, he shocked his companions by expressing his deep satisfaction: "After all, they are Italians." And many captured partisans were saved from execution by Mussolini's pardon. (One of these was Ferruccio Parri, who later served as prime minister of Italy.) Yet the savage terrorist war went on, and many thousands died in the obscure and merciless encounters of those days.

In the first months of the Salò Republic, Mussolini continued his habits of hard work. German liaison officers were impressed by his twelve-hour days with only short lunch breaks. But as the grim months went by, Mussolini became restless, often seeming despondent. He was bowed down by the awareness that the war was lost, eaten up by the brutality of the civil war, tormented by the execution of Ciano and the break with Edda, worried about his place in the history books. Caught between an increasingly vicious Nazi occupation and an increasingly murderous guerrilla campaign, Mussolini's position was a cruel one. Both his earlier Socialist roots and his later nationalist convictions would, in other circumstances, have found him helping the partisans rather than the foreigners. Mussolini's nominal power at Salò came at a very high price. He was tired, more tired than he had ever been, but for the first time in his life he had trouble sleeping. He ate less and less. He seemed uninterested in governmental affairs. He spent long hours every day reading newspapers, especially critical accounts of himself published in Rome. He buried himself in books, with this usual eclectic diet of authors: Plato, Hemingway, Tolstoy, Sorel. He chopped wood in the garden to keep fit. He brooded on the existence of God, asking several persons if they were believers, and requesting priests of his acquaintance to pray for him. Even the demonstration of tens of thousands of admirers—as enthusiastic as it was unexpected—that greeted his unscheduled visit to Milan in December 1944, failed to shake him out of his fatalistic resignation. And so the days passed, while the Allies fought their way painfully up the Italian peninsula, raced across northern France, and closed inexorably in on Berlin from the east.

THE LAST ACT

As the Allied armies inched closer and closer, Mussolini made up his mind what he would do. Right up until the last days, he had the opportunity to fly to Switzerland or Spain, but he repeatedly refused these options. It was his intention to gather about him several thousand loyal Fascists, retreat to the Alps north of Brescia, and make a last stand "for history." Before leaving, Mussolini had to try to make sure than there would be no massacre of Fascists by the partisans once they had taken control, and that the diplomats accredited to the Salò government would be treated in accordance with international law. Negotiations to these ends took place between Mussolini and partisan delegates in the presence of the Cardinal Archbishop of Milan, in the latter's palace. The meeting broke up when Mussolini learned to his consternation that the Germans were already evacuating Italy without informing his government. Mussolini left Milan with a handful of supporters (and the faithful Clara) for the city of Como, where 4,000 Fascist militiamen were supposed to gather in order to accompany him to the Alps. When Mussolini arrived at Como, however, the militia was not there. Before having left for Como, Mussolini sent Rachele a farewell letter. He apologized for the harm he had done her; he advised her to flee with the children to Switzerland, with whose government Mussolini had had mutually beneficial relations for years, or else to surrender to the Allies rather than to the Italians. He assured her that their son Bruno in heaven would help them. But when Rachele received this letter she immediately drove to Como. There her husband told her to ask to be handed over to the English (Churchill would deal manfully with them; "in some respects he is like my father"). Rachele said goodbye to her husband for the last time. In Como, Mussolini had made friends with some of his guards and gave one of them his gold watch. He told them that the British Empire would not long survive the war, and that the principal beneficiary of the world conflict would turn out to be Stalin's Russia.

The militia still had not arrived, so the *Duce* and his little party left for the north. (Several thousand militiamen did eventually reach Como, but Mussolini was gone and the city had fallen to the partisans, so the militia dispersed.)

Mussolini and his party had left Como in the company of over two hundred well-armed German troops who were racing for the Austrian border. Challenged along the road by a handful of partisans armed with shotguns, the Germans agreed to hand over the Italians in their convoy in exchange for permission to proceed. And so Mussolini, along with Clara, found himself in the hands of Communist guerrillas.

The Como partisans were ordered by the guerrilla command in Milan to bring Mussolini alive to that city. Communist boss Palmiro Togliatti, however, unilaterally countermanded this order. Mussolini, along with the documents he had with him,* must not be allowed to fall into the hands of the American army, for then he would be put on public trial and make many embarrassing disclosures. He might even one day return to power. So the order went out for Mussolini to be immediately killed.

Then Mussolini and Clara were taken out in a car by a partisan colonel, a man whom Mussolini had once pardoned. On a lonely road near the hamlet of Dongo, the party got out of the car. The partisan colonel then machine-gunned Mussolini

*For several weeks before his abortive meeting in the Archbishop's palace in Milan, Mussolini had been assiduously selecting documents to bring with him to his Alpine retreat for possible use at some future trial.

to death, along with Clara, who at the last moment threw herself between the executioner and her beloved. Mussolini's last words had been "Shoot me in the chest."

Eventually the bodies were transported to Milan, where they were subjected to obscenities and outrages from onlookers. On April 29, Mussolini's body, with that of Clara and others, was strung up by the feet and displayed in the Piazzale Loreto. And in those same days, the lives of hundreds of clerks, priests, and other obscure persons were taken to satisfy the demands of what is called proletarian justice.

Prime Minister Churchill, upon hearing of the murder of Mussolini, reviled "the treacherous and cowardly method" of the execution.[7] He demanded to know how this had been allowed to happen, ordering the British Army to investigate the entire affair.

Nothing much came of the Churchillian indignation, nor does anyone know what happened to the treasure Mussolini had with him when he was captured; works of art, gold bars, American, British, French, and Italian currency. Most of this is believed to have found its way into the coffers of the Italian Communist party. Several persons involved in the execution of Mussolini, especially those who were knowledgeable or curious about what happened to the "treasure of Dongo," met premature deaths.

■ ■ ■

EPILOGUE

"The 20th Century will be the century of Fascism."

Benito Mussolini

By any standard, Mussolini was one of the most remarkable men of his time. But what is his significance for the world today?

This is not an easy question. On the one hand, Mussolini's legacy would be clearer if his rule had lasted longer. His power was based, as we have seen, on a series of compromises and accommodations. In part, these were tactical necessities for attaining office; in part, they reflected Mussolini's strategy of national development: to harness rather than to massacre the ruling classes. (He had derived this strategy from studying both the writings of the national syndicalists and the convulsions gripping Bolshevik Russia in the early 1920s.) The Fascist party itself, ostensibly the main support of the regime, was a mixed bag. Nationalism was fascism's dominant note, hatred of Marxists and an urge to industrialize its principal expressions. But right after the March on Rome the party became flabby with too many converts of convenience. It must be remembered that Mussolini's premiership turned into a dictatorship partly as the result of an accident.

Hedged in by these ambiguities and concessions, balked in his plans for a national Grand Coalition, Mussolini was forced to proceed slowly in pursuit of many of the transformations that he desired to effect in Italy. It was precisely because the March on Rome had not ended the traditional fragility of the Italian state that it was all the more necessary to proclaim the state's paramount position—"totalitarianism." After several years of radical experiments with the Russian economy, Lenin was forced to introduce his New Economic Policy (NEP), a compromise between ideology and reality. Mussolini's Fascist state was a sort of twenty-year NEP. Before Mussolini had half finished his work, the weakness of the flesh and the might of the Allies had overtaken him. The Fascist regime died, so to speak, a premature death. Nobody knows how it would have evolved given another ten to fifteen years (Mussolini would have been only seventy in 1953).

On the other hand, Mussolini remained in power too long for fascism's reputation or his own. Suppose he had been assassinated in 1929 (he was the object of at least four assassination attempts in the 1920s), when Fiume was settled, industrial production on the upswing, massive strikes an unhappy memory, public finances in decent shape, and the Vatican recently reconciled. Or what if he had been killed in a plane crash in 1936 (he was an amateur pilot), just after establishing the dominion of his nation over the fierce Abyssinians? Certainly the equation of fascism with nazism, which has caused so much confusion, would not have occurred. Instead, Mussolini lived to see Europe overshadowed by the swastika, and he wasn't lucky enough to be shoved, like Stalin, onto the winning side. Our view of Mussolini is therefore dominated, and hence woefully distorted, by Italy's defeat in World War II, and Mussolini's own collapse of will following the fateful Grand Council meeting of July 1943. And just as Cromwell's foes, triumphant at last, dug up his bones and hanged them at Tyburn, Mussolini's enemies covered his corpse with curses and spittle, a macabre exercise carried on in spirit to this day, to the emotional gratification of some but to the intellectual enlightenment of no one. All these spectacular events, occurring at the end of the thirty-year career of Mussolini, impede our understanding of his previous dynamism and attraction, completely obscuring the salient fact that Mussolini was removed from power not by an uprising of the many but by a conspiracy of the few, most of all the king, who had opened to him the road to Rome and received from him the crown of Ethiopia.

Mussolini's dictatorship provides cautionary tales for constitutionalists, tales of the intellectually and morally corrosive effects of too much power exercised over too many years. Dictatorship encourages and magnifies the personal peculiarities of the dictator. Many of Mussolini's shortcomings were, of course, those of the Italian people (for example, the conception of politics as an arena in which to settle scores and expect betrayal), and of the born-and-bred Socialist (for example, an iconoclastic contempt for the accumulated experience of the race). Even Mussolini's most particular psychological flaws did not always produce negative effects, especially in the early years of power. The lonely boy of Predappio, the rejected student of Faenza who could not make friends, set for himself as dictator the goal of having as large an audience and as many collaborators as possible. He would win over the Socialists, he would win over the Catholics; the elections of 1924 must register truly overwhelming approval of him.

Perhaps Mussolini's most serious personal flaw, from a political point of view, was his inability to recognize and trust good men. His regime was not unique in the gradual elimination of men of principle from high office; every dictatorship becomes in time a bacchanal for sycophants. If, as de Gaulle observed, old age is a shipwreck, this is as true of regimes as of men. Nevertheless, by appointing such conniving second-raters as Ciano to the Foreign Office, Starace to the Party Secretariat, and Badolglio to the General Staff, Mussolini cut himself off more and more from sound or even loyal advice, as another world war approached. At the same time the very nature of dictatorship deprived him of the bracing effects of public criticism. Thus there was no one to prevent Mussolini from coming, like every skillful propagandist, to believe in his own propaganda (though his dream of a twentieth-century Roman Empire dominating the wine-dark sea was hardly more illusory than the Franco-British policy of confronting Mussolini in Ethiopia rather than Hitler in the Rhineland). Nor was there anyone to oppose him effectively when, attempting in 1940 to relive the glorious days of 1915, he made his fateful wager on a Hitler victory.

Yet it is clear that the real failings of Mussolini are not rooted in personal psychology but in international politics. During the 1920s, and for most of the 1930s, he gave his countrymen civil and religious peace and economic advance. It was only in the late 1930s that things began to go really wrong, in a world dominated more and more by Adolf Hitler. Mussolini joined, not for unintelligent reasons, what turned out to be the losing side. That is the heart of the matter. If Mussolini had only stuck to his original intention of not joining Hilter's war, he would be considered by many today, as he was for so many years before 1939, a statesman of exceptional talent.* Even with Italy's calamitous participation in World War II, a deposed Mussolini might have returned to power through a free election, many years later, in the manner of Juan Perón. The prospect did not seem so farfetched to the Italian Communists in 1945; that's why they killed him.

*Undoubtedly perceptions of Mussolini's political abilities and personal attractiveness were enhanced by his high office. But there is simply too much testimony from too many persons of worldly experience over too many years to permit the facile conclusion that Mussolini was just a facade.

Certainly Mussolini was progressively handicapped by being surrounded, like all dictators, by yes-men (although he read the foreign press avidly). But suppose that Italy had been a democracy (or something similar) in the 1930s. Would its foreign policy necessarily have been directed down a safer path in 1938–1940? Did democratic Britain, did democratic France, pursue between the wars a foreign policy that can be called exemplary, or even sensible? Who, precisely, let the Nazi demon out of the bottle anyway? Was it Mussolini, with his Four Power Pact scheme to lock Germany into a new Concert of Europe and provide a mechanism for orderly change? Or was it the Mussolini who threatened Hitler with war in order to prevent the *Anschluss*? If Italy's erstwhile allies had been more sympathetic toward her perfectly understandable desire for colonies, if they had grasped the necessity to protect Austria, if they had chosen to make their stand not in Ethiopia but on the Rhine if. . . .

But the failure of the Western Allies to contain Hitler was to usher in a profound historical change—the final decadence of the classical European state system and the subordination of Europe to the Russian and American superpowers. In the light of these developments, Mussolini's pursuit of the dream of a new Roman Empire became daily less relevant. He completely failed to grasp, until just before the end, what was happening to the world. He was not the only one. As late as 1945 Winston Churchill would be prepared to maintain the British raj in India with military force; the French would pursue their vision of *la mission civilisatrice* through the rain forests of Indochina and across the sands of North Africa, right into the 1960s.

In the last analysis, democrats really do not require lessons on the pitfalls of autocracy, and anti-democrats never profit by them. Advocates of constitutional government would do well instead to reflect on the reasons why fascism came to power in Italy in the first place. Naturally such reasons are numerous and complicated, and their totality may be beyond our understanding, or even our knowledge. But some of the causes of the triumph of fascism stand out clearly, like firebells in the night. Alfred Cobban observed, many years ago, that where the doctrine of class war has been widely accepted a dictatorship of some kind becomes almost inevitable,[1] and we have seen how seriously enfeebled the pre-Fascist Italian political system was by the size and nature of the Italian Socialist party. Their revolutionary messianism and dogmatic pedantry, their identification of the politics of envy as a crusade for justice, led them to continue and expand the Italian tradition of political violence. The never-ending Socialist preaching of hatred for bourgeois values and the rules of the parliamentary game, the raising of utopian expectations, the readiness to resort to violence and to promise greater violence in the future, the covering of every aspect of existing society with execration, the total contempt for property, work, the family, the law, the state, religion, patriotism, the army, the nation—all this, day in and day out, decade after decade, could not fail to sap the vitality of any society. Nor would it fail one day to provoke a reaction as savage as it was predictable, to which the Socialists, due to their self-intoxication with the Leninist model, could not respond effectively.

Yet, while many profound students of the subject have identified Italian socialism as the prime cause of the success of the Fascists, it is at least doubtful that this destructive variety of socialism could have emerged in anything other than a political system that was already suffering from serious maladies. The triumph of fascism represented, above all else, the failure of liberalism. The inadequacies of the Liberal State in economics and foreign policy were real enough, but were also in part a matter of perception and expectation. A healthy and well-integrated society could have survived these disappointments. But the failures of classical liberalism had also to do with philosophy, psychology, and theater. Italian Liberals stood, in effect, for the loosening of ties between the individual and his family, his province, and his church, without offering anything in substitution except bloodless abstractions like Progress and Reason, and a thoroughly unheroic and pedestrian monarchy and parliament. Liberalism, in its at least partial rejection of traditional Italian society, gave indirect sanction to the socialism which was eating the vitality of the nation, while at the same time it sought to impose a system of politics on a society which did not exist and could not come into existence.

One of the proudest achievements, for instance, of European liberalism was the institution of widespread suffrage and competitive elections. These presented an opportunity, rather than an obstacle, to fascism. The process of popular elections is designed to give effect to the wishes of a majority based on consensus. In a country divided into ferociously egocentric minorities, however, nobody ever really wins any election; what results instead is the frustration of mutual checkmate. By 1922, much of Italy was exhausted by an endless round of inconclusive elections, carousel cabinets, and corridor intrigue. This is never a desirable state of affairs; in the super-agitated atmosphere of postwar Italy it was insupportable, especially for those millions of veterans who had imagined that their wartime sufferings were but the labor pains of a bright new society. Postwar liberalism continued to stand for politics as usual, with an underlying attitude of *enrichissez-vous*. A generation that wanted sagas was handed ledgers instead. It cannot be far from the truth to say that Mussolini came to power because the longings of so many of his countrymen for dedication, sacrifice, and comradeship were mocked by the mediocrity, selfishness, and sectarianism of the politicians.

In contrast, Mussolini and his Fascist movement offered a feeling of real participation to many for whom the methods and rituals of parliamentary government had become dry and meaningless. Within fascism, while there were those who saw in it an opportunity to settle old scores, live without hard work, and indulge in bullying, chest thumping, and graft, there were others who were determined to create a united and renewed people, disciplined, civic, and austere at home, brave, powerful, and respected abroad. In his emphasis on community and the state, in his rejection of individualism and competition, Mussolini was clearly tapping into the deep needs of many of the Italian people, employing a political psychology whose insights have become commonplace in the 1980s.

Thus, the experience of pre-Fascist Italy, especially in the crucial period between the end of World War I and the March on Rome, strongly suggests that the centrifugal and disintegrative tendencies of liberalism are the greatest source of peril to political democracy. Liberty *and* Community—that is the challenge.

Mussolini could not have come to power but for the grotesque inadequacies of his opponents—true enough. And once in office he made good use of an effective political police and an apparently monolithic party; nor did he forebear to employ those political artifices which have characterized dictatorship since ancient Athens.

Yet let us not confuse surface with substance. Mussolini satisfied the yearnings of his countrymen for domestic order, international respect, and economic development. This is the key to his twenty-year tenure of power.

His most important accomplishments in office were undoubtedly the reconciliation of Church and State, and the industrialization of Italy. As for the first, the Lateran Pacts are still in force more than half a century after their signing; even the Communists voted for the incorporation of the Pacts into the new republican constitution of 1946. And the Catholic party—the Christian Democrats—which settled down to decade upon decade of uninterrupted power after 1945, is of course the now somewhat overripe fruit of the national Catholic Action organization that existed on Mussolini's sufferance. Mussolini did more to establish the political power of the papacy in Italy than anybody since Gregory the Great.

Equally in Mussolini's debt are the Italian Communists. He

gave them their patron saint, Antonio Gramsci, safely sheltered in Italian prisons from Stalin's purges. More than that, Mussolini helped to imbue a whole generation with the idea that liberal capitalism was old-fashioned and based on unattractive aspects of human nature. Many Italians who wrote essays for Fascist Youth competitions in the 1930s would find, after the collapse of the Fascist experiment, a prudent and comfortable refuge within the ranks of the Communist party. The passage from the "extreme right" to the "extreme left" was made with ease because, of course, these points are not opposites but neighbors. The true extreme contrast in politics is between those who believe in constitutional limitation and those who worship the omnicompetence of authority. Adolf Hitler knew that former Communists made the very best Nazis.

Mussolini showed himself to be in a real sense the "Italian Bukharin,"[2] his policies conforming to the currently much-vaunted "central principles of Bukharinism—class collaboration, civil peace, and balanced evolutionary growth."[3] (Like Mussolini, Bukharin was killed by the Stalinists.) At one time it was fashionable to criticize Mussolini for having slowed down economic modernization through his policies; this was a euphemism for saying that he should have been more radical, more Stalinist. Today we know better the economic (and other) costs of too-radical economic change, and Mussolini's concern to improve agriculture and hold down urban gigantism seems uncannily contemporary. The essence of the matter is this: Mussolini showed that a poor country, overpopulated and underendowed, can become an industrial society *without Stalin's cataracts of human blood*. Indeed, under the rubric of repression, Mussolini must take a back seat not only to such virtuosi of homicide as Stalin and Hitler, but also to the bush-country Berias who have adorned the political landscape of our day, from Haiti to Uganda to Cambodia. There are those, of course, who argue that the unbloody nature of Mussolini's regime was not owing to his conscious policy—Mussolini was always wrong—but to the "humanity of the Italian people." Quite apart from the intriguing implication that the regimes of Hitler, Stalin, Mao, and Amin were so gory because the Germans, Russians, Chinese, and Ugandans are inhuman, or subhuman, or whatever, this position completely ignores the utterly ferocious conduct of the Italian partisans during the years 1944 and 1945.

It is with this aspect of his regime—modernization of the economy without destruction of society—that we arrive at perhaps the paramount significance of Mussolini: the new combination of ideas and symbols that his regime represented.

Mussolini had always believed that this was a world of struggle. The teachings of Alessandro and his experiences growing up in the Romagna had shown him that. Before 1914, Mussolini the Marxist perceived the struggle as preeminently between classes; World War I convinced him that the real, the decisive struggle was instead between nations. The "aristocracy of the trenches" thus replaced the "vanguard of the proletariat" as Mussolini's future elite.

If Mussolini was the last political leader to proclaim a vision of an Italy powerful and influential, if the fires of nationalism have been extinguished or at least banked in Italy, yet those flames blaze and roar in our time across Asia, Africa, and Latin America. The *Communist Manifesto* has informed us that "the history of all hitherto existing societies is the history of class struggle." Yet contemporary research on voting patterns, from pre-civil war Pennsylvania to present-day Canada, Holland, and Switzerland, suggest strongly that class divisions within society are always blurred or overshadowed when ethnic and/or religious tensions develop. And the bloody clashes between such fraternal Marxist states as Russia and China, China and Vietnam, Vietnam and Cambodia, are only the latest evidence of the validity of that key insight of the Fascists: that in the crucial hour the struggle among the peoples supersedes the struggle between the classes.

But the nationalism of Mussolini was of a special kind. He

had been early and thoroughly imbued with the Socialist teaching that inequality indicates iniquity, and that made him a rebel all his life; before 1914 a rebel against exploitation and subordination within his country, after that time a rebel against exploitation and subordination *of* his country. Mussolini learned to identify himself with his country; its humiliations and unfulfilled aspirations became his—and vice versa. The phrase "Proletarian Italy" perfectly captured the combination of socialism and nationalism, the red heart within the black shirt, the explosive evocation of multiple resentments. "Proletarian Italy" was his Faenza experience writ large: the Italian people must no longer be forced to eat at the international "poor table."

This is why the nationalism of Mussolini reminds us less of nineteenth-century France than of twentieth-century China, Egypt, or Mexico. It is the nationalism not of celebration but of confrontation, and much of the nationalism of today's Third World is an intensification of this type. It is perhaps not so easy for Americans—with their history of military security and economic abundance, with their tradition of optimism (admittedly somewhat frayed these days), their conviction that every problem has its reasonable solution—to understand the anxiety and the envy of those peoples whose experiences have been radically different, whose status is a matter of dispute, whose destiny is not manifest but obscure. But this is the very stuff of politics over most of the planet. And ever since 1917, the irrelevance of Marxist theory to backward economies has become embarrassingly more obvious all the time. Economic development requires not distribution of wealth but creation of wealth, not the proletarian revolution but the *bourgeois* revolution. In the Third World of the 1980s this translates into the necessity for an authoritarian elite to break through the hard crust of tradition, ignorance, and disorganization, to impose planning, order, and discipline. And thus we see that all over the non-European world, from the Japanese militarists of the 1930s to the Brazilian militarists of the 1980s, from the Argentina of Peron to the Ghana of Nkrumah, regimes have appeared which adhere, consciously or unconsciously, to the fundamental Fascist formula: the redress of national grievances through massive and sustained economic development, requiring collaboration among all social strata, unquestioned authority of the state in all areas of social life, and the monopoly of political leadership by an aristocracy of patriotism.[4]

Sometimes Third-World fascism comes complete with a charismatic leader and mass party. Often it is the military which propagates and imposes Fascist ideas. In other cases, fascistic attitudes and concepts may be so diffuse in a society that they are not the distinguishing monopoly of any one party or sector but permeate the whole atmosphere. Consider Latin American "populism" of today. One authority has identified it as "the major force in Latin America." The Populists posit "a community of interest among all groups within the nation"; they reject the class struggle in favor of an all-out defense of the nation against the "anti-nation." Populists want economic "development with a minimum of social conflict," and the "central agency charged with achieving these goals [is] the state." In sum, "Populist ideology [is] at its base nationalist, statist, and elitist," with an "implicit corporatist image of sociopolitical organization."[5] Any Italian Fascist would have felt comfortable with these aspirations and assumptions.

Indeed, the penetration of fascistic ideas into all parts of the globe has prompted one influential student of world radical movements to write that "the major expressions of revolutionary politics in the remainder of the twentieth century will most likely evidence at least some of the species-traits of fascism."[6]

And so we come to the last and perhaps the greatest of the Mussolinian paradoxes. He who was an anachronism in Europe has become a prototype in the Third World: a politician so utterly defeated, coldly murdered, and universally castigated is now identified as a harbinger and prophet of the principal political current of our time.

Mussolini's shadow is a long one.

CHRONOLOGY

1861	17 March	Kingdom of Italy proclaimed
1866	June–August	Austro-Prussian War; Italy obtains Venetia
1870	September	Occupation of Rome
1882	May	Italy enters Triple Alliance
1883	29 July	Birth of Mussolini
1896	1 March	Battle of Adowa
1902	July	Mussolini travels to Switzerland
1904	December	Having returned from Switzerland, Mussolini enters the army
1906–1908		Mussolini teaches school
1909	February–September	Mussolini in the Trentino
1910	January	Mussolini founds *La lotta di classe* at Forlì
1912	July	Congress of Reggio Emilia
	December	Mussolini becomes editor of *Avanti!*
1913	October	Mussolini is an unsuccessful Socialist candidate for parliament

1914	August	Germany invades Belgium
	20 October	Mussolini resigns as editor of *Avanti!*
	15 November	First issue of *Il popolo d'Italia*
	24 November	Expulsion of Mussolini by Milan Socialist party
1915	May	Italy enters World War I
	September	Mussolini in the army
1917	February	Mussolini wounded
	October–November	Battle of Caporetto
1919	23 March	Founding meeting of fascism in Piazza San Sepolcro, Milan
1921	May	Mussolini elected to Chamber of Deputies
1922	27–28 October	March on Rome
1923	August	Corfu Incident
1924	January	Italy obtains Fiume
	February	Exchange of ambassadors with Bolshevik Russia
	April	Fascist electoral landslide
	June	Aventine Secession begins
1925	3 January	The "I am responsible" speech
	December	Italy adheres to Locarno Pacts
1929	February	Signing of the Lateran Pacts
1931	September	Japan invades Manchuria
1934	25 July	Murder of Austrian Chancellor Dollfuss
1935	March	Hitler announces conscription
	April	Stresa Conference
	June	Anglo–German naval treaty
	3 October	Italy invades Ethiopia
1936	March	Hitler remilitarizes Rhineland
	7 May	Fall of Addis Ababa
	July	Start of Spanish Civil War
1937	July	Japan attacks China
1938	March	The *Anschluss*
	September	The Munich Conference
	November	Introduction of anti-Semitic laws

1939	March	Fall of Madrid
	May	The Pact of Steel
	August	Molotov–Ribbentrop Pact
	September	Germany invades Poland from the west, Russia from the east
1940	June	Fall of France
1941	22 June	Germany invades Russia
	December	Mussolini declares war on the United States
1943	May	Rommel abandons Africa
	10 July	Invasion of Sicily
	25 July	Arrest of Mussolini
1943	October	The Salò Republic
1945	28 April	Death of Mussolini

NOTES

NOTE TO THE PREFACE

1. Renzo DeFelice, *Mussolini il fascista* (Turin: Einaudi, 1966), vol. I, p. 476n; J. Meisel, *The Genesis of Georges Sorel* (Ann Arbor: Wahr, 1951), p. 220n; P. Melograni, "The Cult of the Duce," *Journal of Contemporary History,* XI (October 1976), p. 233; Renzo DeFelice, *Mussolini il duce* (Turin: Einaudi, 1974), p. 39n; D. Mack Smith, *Italy: A Modern History* (Ann Arbor: University of Michigan, 1969), p. 441; L. Salvatorelli and G. Mira, *Storia d'Italia nel periodo fascista* (Turin: Einaudi, 1957); John Gunther, *Inside Europe* (New York: Harper & Row, 1938), p. 197; DeFelice, *Mussolini il duce,* p. 543; John P. Diggins, *Mussolini and Fascism: The View from America* (Princeton: Princeton University, 1972), p. 257; Alan Cassels, *Mussolini's Early Diplomacy* (Princeton: Princeton University, 1970), p. 314; Mario Toscano, *Designs in Diplomacy* (Baltimore: Johns Hopkins University, 1970), p. 330.

NOTES TO THE INTRODUCTION

1. A. James Gregor, *The Fascist Persuation in Radical Politics* (Princeton: Princeton University Press, 1974), p. 411.
2. Renzo De Felice, *Mussolini il fascista* (Turin: Einaudi, 1966), vol. 1, p. 462.
3. Gregor, *Fascist Persuasion,* p. 139.
4. Albert O. Hirschman, in Dankwart Rustow, ed., *Philosophers and Kings* (New York: George Braziller, 1969), p. 355.

NOTES TO CHAPTER I

1. S. B. Clough, *Economic History of Modern Italy* (New York: Columbia University, 1964), p. 168.
2. Denis Mack Smith, *Cavour and Garibaldi, 1860* (New York: Cambridge University, 1954), p. 443.
3. Christopher Seton-Watson, *Italy from Liberalism to Fascism* (London: Methuen, 1967), p. 17.
4. Maurice E. Neufeld, *Italy: School for Awakening Countries* (Ithaca: Cornell University, 1961), p. 20.
5. Alexander Gerschenkron, *Economic Backwardness in Historical Perspective* (New York: Praeger, 1962), p. 72.
6. Benedetto Croce, *A History of Italy, 1871-1915* (Oxford: Clarendon Press, 1929), p. 45.
7. Denis Mack Smith, *Italy: A Modern History* (Ann Arbor: University of Michigan, 1969), p. 123.

NOTES TO CHAPTER III

1. Margherita Sarfatti, *Life of Benito Mussolini* (New York: Frederick A. Stokes, 1925).
2. Renzo De Felice, *Mussolini il rivoluzionario* (Turin: Einaudi, 1965), p. 40.

3. Herman Finer, *Mussolini's Italy* (New York: Universal Library, 1965), pp. 58-59.
4. A. James Gregor, *Young Mussolini and the Intellectual Origins of Fascism* (Berkeley: University of California, 1980), Chapter 6.

NOTES TO CHAPTER IV

1. Mussolini, *Opera Omnia,* (Florence: La Fenice, 1951-1963) VII, p. 182.
2. Ernst Nolte, *Three Faces of Fascism* (New York: Holt, Rinehart and Winston, 1966), p. 172.
3. Mussolini, *Opera Omnia*, IX, p. 176.
4. Mussolini, *Opera Omnia*, X, p. 111.
5. A. James Gregor, *Young Mussolini and the Intellectual Origins of Fascism* (Berkeley: University of California, 1979), Chapters 4 and 5.

NOTES TO CHAPTER V

1. Domenico Settembrini, *Fascismo controrivoluzione imperfetta* (Firenze: Sansoni, 1978); Edward R. Tannenbaum, *The Fascist Experience* (New York: Basic Books, 1972).
2. Renzo De Felice, *Mussolini il rivoluzionario* (Turin: Einaudi, 1965), pp. 730-735.
3. Mauice F. Neufeld, *Italy: School for Awakening Countries* (Ithaca: Cornell University, 1961), p. 547.
4. Settembrini, *Fascismo controrivoluzione imperfetta*, p. 125n.
5. A. C. Jemolo, *Church and State in Italy 1850-1950* (Oxford: Blackwell, 1960), p. 183.
6. Gaetano Salvemini, *The Fascist Dictatorship in Italy* (New York: Fertig, 1967), p. 49; see also De Felice, *Mussolini il rivoluzionario*, p. 426.

7. Salvemini, *Fascist Dictatorship*, p. 50.
8. Adrian Lyttleton, *The Seizure of Power: Fascism in Italy 1919-1929* (New York: Scribner's, 1973), p. 46.
9. Lyttleton, *Seizure*, p. 51.
10. Ernst Nolte, *Three Faces of Fascism* (New York: Holt, Rinehart, Winston, 1966), p. 151.
11. A. James Gregor, *The Fascist Persuasion in Radical Politics* (Princeton: Princeton University, 1974), p. 176.
12. See the party program of November, 1921 in Charles F. Delzell, *Mediterranean Fascism*, 1919-1945 (New York: Harper and Row, 1970).
13. Gregor, *Fascist Persuasion*, p. 20.
14. Gregor, *Fascist Persuasion*, p. 178.
15. Renzo De Felice, *Mussolini il fascista* (Turin: Einaudi, 1966), vol. 1, chapter 3.
16. De Felice, *Mussolini il fascista*, vol. 1, p. 306.
17. Richard A. Webster, *The Cross and the Fasces* (Stanford: Stanford University, 1960), p. 77.

NOTES TO CHAPTER VI

1. Renzo De Felice, *Interpretations of Fascism* (Cambridge, Mass.: Harvard University, 1977), p. 150.
2. Renzo De Felice, *Mussolini il fascista* (vol. 1) (Turin: Einaudi, 1966), pp. 476-477n.
3. *ibid.* 376.
4. Benito Mussolini, *Opera Omnia* (Florence: La Fenice, 1951-1963), XIX, pp. 17-23.
5. Ernst Nolte, *Three Faces of Fascism* (New York: Holt, Rinehart and Winston, 1965), p. 214.
6. Denis Mack Smith, *Italy* (Ann Arbor, Michigan: University of Michigan, 1969) p. 374.
7. Ivone Kirkpatrick, *Mussolini: A Study in Power* (New York: Hawthorn, 1964), p. 203.
8. De Felice, *Mussolini il fascista*, p. 396.

9. Nolte, *Three Faces*, p. 214.
10. Giuseppe Rossini, "Fascism between Legality and Revolution," in Roland Sarti, ed., *The Ax Within* (N.Y.: New Viewpoints, 1974), p. 17.
11. Alberto Aquarone, *L'organizzazione dello stato totalitario* (Turin: Einaudi, 1965), pp. 17-21 and 25-27.
12. Roland Sarti, *Fascism and the Industrial Leadership in Italy*, 1919-1940 (Berkeley: University of California, 1971).
13. Alan Cassels, *Fascist Italy* (New York: Crowell, 1968), p. 64; Laura Fermi, *Mussolini* (Chicago: University of Chicago, 1961), p. 271.
14. De Felice, *Mussolini il fascista*, p. 532.
15. Adrian Lyttleton, *The Seizure of Power: Fascism in Italy 1919-1929* (New York: Scribner's, 1973), pp. 127-129.
16. De Felice, *Mussolini il fascista*, p. 537.
17. *ibid.*, pp. 440, 581ff.
18. Lyttleton, *Seizure of Power*, p. 144.
19. De Felice, *Mussolini il fascista*, p. 588; Mack Smith, *Italy*, p. 380; Kirkpatrick, *Mussolini*, p. 212; Herbert W. Schneider, *Making the Fascist State* (New York: Howard Fertig, 1968), p. 90; Edward R. Tannenbaum, *The Fascist Experience* (New York: Basic Books, 1972), p. 46.
20. Luigi Sturzo, *Italy and Fascismo* (New York: Harcourt, Brace, 1926), p. 175.
21. De Felice, *Mussolini il fascista*, pp. 600-602; Lyttleton, *Seizure of Power*, p. 95.
22. Mussolini, *Opera Omnia*, XX, pp. 307ff.
23. Lyttleton, *Seizure of Power*, p. 232ff.
24. Cassels, *Fascist Italy*, p. 46.
25. Lyttleton, *Seizure of Power*, p. 238.
26. Mack Smith, *Italy*, p. 382; Herman Finer, *Mussolini's Italy* (New York: University Library, 1965), p. 234.
27. Lyttleton, *Seizure of Power*, p. 238.
28. De Felice, *Mussolini il fascista*, p. 704.
29. *ibid.*, 688.
30. *ibid.*, 653.

31. Finer, *Mussolini's Italy*, p. 323.
32. Sturzo, *Italy and Fascismo*, p. 221.
33. Piero Melograni, "The Cult of the Duce", *Journal of Contemporary History* XI (October, 1976).
34. Hannah Arendt, *The Origins of Totalitarianism* (New York: Harcourt, Brace, 1951), p. 303n.
35. Robert Conquest, *The Great Terror* (New York: Macmillan, 1968), p. 335; C. W. Cassinelli, *Total Revolution* (Santa Barbara: Clio, 1976), p. 117.
36. Tannenbaum, *Fascist Experience*, p. 141.
37. H. Stuart Hughes, *The United States and Italy* (New York: Norton, 1965), p. 59. The role of socialism in the breakdown of the Italian parliamentary system was "major" in the analysis of Juan Linz. *The Breakdown of Democracy* (Baltimore: John Hopkins University, 1978); Domenico Settembrini writes: "On revolutionary socialism rests, not only the dual responsibility of engendering fascism and infecting it with totalitarianism, but also the responsibility of having made its decisive victory possible." "Mussolini and the Legacy of Revolutionary Socialism, *Journal of Contemporary History* XI (October, 1976), p. 245. Of all the factors that made the March on Rome possible, says Angelo Tasca, "most important were socialist feebleness and mistakes, which were the direct cause, not of fascism, which appeared in every country after the war, but of its success in Italy." *The Rise of Italian Fascism, 1918-1922* (New York: Fertig, 1966), p. 159; Maurice Neufeld condemns the "dialectical hallucinations of the maximalist and communist bigots." *Italy: School for Awakening Countries* (Ithaca: Cornell University, 1961), p. 268; for Denis Mack Smith, the Socialists "positively refused to collaborate against Fascism... and in so doing they made a [Fascist] victory almost inevitable." *Italy* (Ann Arbor: University of Michigan, 1969), p. 327.
38. Nolte, *Three Faces*, p. 217.

NOTES TO CHAPTER VII

1. D. A. Binchy, *Church and State in Fascist Italy* (London: Oxford, 1941).
2. A. C. Jemolo, *Church and State in Italy, 1850-1950* (Oxford: Blackwell, 1960), p. 247
3. Renzo De Felice, *Mussolini il fascista*, vol. II. (Turin: Einaudi, 1968), pp. 438-439.
4. Richard A. Webster, *The Cross and the Fasces* (Stanford: Stanford University, 1960), p. 111.

NOTES TO CHAPTER VIII

1. Elizabeth Wiskemann, *Fascism in Italy* (London: Macmillan, 1969), p. 64.
2. Renzo DeFelice, *Mussolini il fascista*, (Turnin: Einaudi, 1966), Vol. 1, p. 473.
3. A James Gregor, *The Fascist Persuasion in Radical Politics* (Princeton: Princeton University, 1974), p. 270.
4. Giuseppe Prezzolini, *Fascism* (London: Methuen, 1926), p. 4.
5. Adrian Lyttelton, *The Seizure of Power: Fascism in Italy 1919-1929* (New York: Scribner's 1973), p. 379.
6. Richard A. Webster, *The Cross and the Fasces* (Stanford: Stanford University, 1960), p. 45.
7. Lyttelton, *Seizure of Power*, p. 183.
8. Mussolini, *Opera Omnia*, XXI, p. 425.
9. Samuel P. Huntington and Clement Moore, eds., *Authoritarian Politics in Modern Society* (New York: Basic Books, 1970), p. 29.
10. Herman Finer, *Mussolini's Italy* (New York: Universal Library, 1965), p. 390.
11. Renzo De Felice, *Mussolini il fascista,* vol, II (Turin: Einaudi, 1968), p. 355.

12. Gregor, *Fascist Persuasion*, p. 233; In Stalin's Russia, "the mass party was a loose association of the successful and the would-be successful; and the Party apparatus, although its functions of exhortation, example, and positive education were important, was only one among many control agencies, and was clearly less powerful than the political police...." C. W. Cassinelli, *Total Revolution* (Santa Barbara: Clio, 1976), p. 144.
13. Mussolini, *Opera omnia*, XX, p. 251.
14. R. C. Simonini Jr., *The Universities of Italy* (Washington: AAUP, 1955).
15. Lyttelton, *Seizure of Power*, p. 199.
16. Anton Blok, *The Mafia of a Sicilian Village*, 1860-1960 (New York: Harper Torchbooks, 1974), p. 189.
17. Christopher Seton-Watson, *Italy from Liberalism to Fascism*, (London: Methuen, 1967), p. 707.
18. Maurice Neufeld: *Italy: School for Awakening Countries* (Ithaca, N.Y.: Cornell University Press, 1961), p. 396.
19. Alberto Aquarone, *L'organizzazione dello stato totalitario* (Turin: Einaudi, 1965) p. 159.
20. Herbert L. Matthews, *The Fruits of Fascism* (New York: Harcourt, Brace, 1943), p. 259.
21. A. James Gregor, *Italian Fascism and Developmental Dictatorship* (Princeton: Princeton University, 1979), p. 206.
22. Federico Chabod, *History of Italian Fascism* (London: Weidenfeld and Nicolson, 1961), p. 84.
23. De Felice, *Mussolini il fascista,* vol. II, p. 379.
24. Jacques Ellul, *Propaganda: The Formation of Men's Attitudes* (New York: Vintage 1973), *passim*, esp. chapter II.
25. Seton-Watson, *Italy from Liberalism to Fascism,* p. 707.
26. Arthur Schlesinger, *The Age of Roosevelt: The Coming of the New Deal* (Boston: Houghton Mifflin, 1959), pp. 153-154; John P. Diggins, *Mussolini and Fascism: The View from America* (Princeton: Princeton University Press, 1972), p. 279.

NOTES TO CHAPTER IX

1. Sigmund Neumann, *Permanent Revolution* (New York: Praeger, 1965), p. 158; A. James Gregor, *The Fascist Persuasion in Radical Politics* (Princeton: Princeton University Press, 1974), p. 176; Benito Mussolini, *Opera Omnia* (Florence: La Fenice, 1951-1963), XII, p. 250; Domenico Settembrini, "Mussolini and the Legacy of Revolutionary Socialism", *Journal of Contemporary History*, XI (October, 1976), p. 241.
2. Alexander Gerschenkron, *Economic Backwardness in Historical Perspective* (New York: Praeger, 1962), pp. 85-86; Shepard B. Clough, *Economic History of Modern Italy* (New York: Columbia University, 1964), p. 59.
3. Clough, *Economic History*, pp. 59-60; Gerschenkron, *Economic Backwardness*, p. 86.

4. Mussolini, *Opera Omnia*, XIX, p. 187.
5. Ernst Nolte, *Three Faces of Fascism* (New York: Holt, Rinehart, Winston, 1966), p. 221; Eugen Weber, *Varieties of Fascism* (Princeton: Van Nostrand, 1964), pp. 140-141; Edward R. Tannenbaum, "The Goals of Italian Fascism", *American Historical Review*, LXXIV (April, 1969), p. 1204.
6. Gregor, *Fascist Persuasion*, p. 178.
7. Alan Cassells, *Fascist Italy* (New York: Crowell, 1968), pp. 55-56.
8. Cassells, *Fascist Italy*, pp. 55-56; Dante Germino, *The Italian Fascist Party in Power* (Minneapolis: University of Minnesota, 1959), p. 5.
9. Maurice F. Neufeld, *Italy: School for Awakening Countries* (Ithaca: Cornell University, 1961), p. 430.
10. Mussolini, *Opera Omnia*, XXV, p. 147 and XXII, p. 246.
11. Clough, *Economic History*, p. 238; Renzo De Felice, *Mussolini il fascista* (Turin: Einaudi, 1968). Vol. II, p. 282; Adrian Lyttelton, *The Seizure of Power: Fascism in Italy 1919-1929* (New York: Scribner's, 1973), p. 360.

12. Gregor, *Fascist Persuasion*, p. 16; Adrian Lyttelton, *The Seizure of Power*, p. 360; Alfred Cobban, *Dictatorship* (New York: Scribner's, 1939), p. 129.
13. Alberto Aquarone, *L'organizzazione dello stato totalitario* (Turin: Einaudi, 1965); see also Federico Chabod, *History of Italian Fascism* (London: Weidenfeld and Nicolson, 1961), p. 53.
14. Stephen F. Cohen, *Bukharin and the Bolshevik Revolution* (New York: Knopf, 1974).
15. Nobutake Ike, "War and Modernization," in Robert F. Ward, ed., *Political Development in Modern Japan* (Princeton: Princeton University, 1968), p. 190; W. G. Beasley, *The Modern History of Japan* (New York: Praeger, 1963), pp. 131 and 135; C. E. Black *et al.*, *The Modernization of Japan and Russia* (New York: Free Press, 1975), p. 139.
16. Carl T. Schmidt, *The Plough and the Sword* (New York: Columbia University, 1938), p. 127.
17. Renzo De Felice, *Mussolini il rivoluzionario* (Turin: Einaudi, 1965), p. 509; Aquarone, *L'organizzazione*, p. 115.
18. Maurice F. Neufeld, *Poor Countries and Authoritarian Rule* (Ithaca, N.Y.: Cornell University, 1965), pp. 152-153; Paul Corner, *Fascism in Ferrara* (London: Oxford University, 1975), p. 286n.
19. Domenico Settembrini, *Fascismo controrivoluzione imperfetta* (Florence: Sansoni, 1978); See Samuel H. Beer, *British Politics in the Collectivist Age* (New York: Knopf, 1966) and Andrew Shonfield, *Modern Capitalism* (New York: Oxford University, 1965).
20. A. F. K. Organski, "Fascism and Modernization", in S. J. Woolf, ed., *The Nature of Fascism* (New York: Vintage, 1969), pp. 37, 32; Paul Einzig, *Economic Foundations of Fascism* (London: Macmillan, 1933); Alfredo Rocco, "The Political Doctrine of Fascism", *International Counciliation*, 26 (October, 1926); Luigi Villari, *The Fascist Experiment* (London: Faber and Gwyer, 1926); Mussolini, *Opera Omnia,* XII, p. 50.

21. Mussolini, *Opera Omnia,* XXIII, p. 216.
22. Christopher Hibbert, *Il Duce* (Boston: Little, Brown, 1962), p. 52.
23. George S. Hildebrand, *Growth and Structure in the Economy of Modern Italy* (Cambridge, Mass.: Harvard University, 1965; Lyttelton, *Seizure of Power*, p. 353.
24. Neufeld, *Italy*; Clough, *Economic History*, p. 242.
25. Nolte, *Three Faces.*
26. W. G. Welk, *Fascist Economic Policy* (Cambridge, Mass.: Harvard University, 1938), p. 187; Mussolini, *Opera Omnia,* XXV, p. 185.
27. Clough, *Economic History*, p. 246; Rosario Romeo, *Breve storia della grande industria in Italia* (Rocco San Casciano: Cappelli, 1968), p. 102.
28. Gerschenkron, *Economic Backwardness.*
29. Roland Sarti, *Fascism and the Industrial Leadership in Italy, 1919-1940* (Berkeley: University of California, 1971); Shonfield, *Modern Capitalism,* pp. 177-178; Gregor, *Fascist Persuasion*, p. 193; Mihaly Vadja, "Crisis and the Way Out: The Rise of Fascism in Italy and Germany", *Telos*, 12 (Summer, 1972), p. 13.

NOTES TO CHAPTER X

1. See Benito Mussolini, *Opera Omnia* (Florence: La Fenice, 1951-1963), XXVIII, pp. 232-237; XX, pp. 149-151.
2. Winston Churchill, *The Gathering Storm* (Boston: Houghton-Mifflin, 1948), p. 139.
3. David H. Burton, *Theodore Roosevelt: Confident Imperialist* (Philadelphia: University of Pennsylvania, 1968), p. 128.
4. Mussolini, *Opera Omnia*, XXIX, p. 86.
5. Elizabeth Wiskemann, *The Rome-Berlin Axis* (London:

Collins, 1966), pp. 57-58; Ivone Kirkpatrick, *Mussolini: A Study in Power* (New York: Hawthorn, 1964), pp. 310-311; George W. Baer, *The Coming of the Italian-Ethiopian War* (Cambridge: Harvard University, 1967), p. 41; Renzo De Felice, *Mussolini il duce* (Turin: Einaudi, 1974), p. 418.

6. Renzo De Felice, *Mussolini il fascista* (Turin: Einaudi, 1968), vol. II, p. 440.
7. Baer, *The Coming*, pp. 3-6.
8. Mussolini, *Opera Omnia*, XXVII, p. 116.
9. Kirkpatrick, *Mussolini*, p.303; Baer, *The Coming*, chapter 6.
10. Wiskemann, *Rome-Berlin Axis*, p. 71
11. De Felice, *Mussolini il duce*, pp. 719-721.
12. Hajo Holborn, *The Political Collapse of Europe* (New York: Knopf, 1951), p. 144.
13. Churchill, *The Gathering Storm*, p. 187; Alan Bullock, *Hitler: A Study in Tyranny* (New York: Harper and Row, 1962), p. 340; Kirkpatrick, *Mussolini*; A. J. P. Taylor, *The Origins of the Second World War* (New York: Fawcett, 1978), p. 107; Denis Mack Smith, *Italy: A Modern History* (Ann Arbor: University of Michigan, 1969), p. 449.
14. De Felice, *Mussolini il duce*, pp. 624 ff; Baer, *The Coming*, *passim*.
15. Kirkpatrick, *Mussolini*, p. 331.

NOTES TO CHAPTER XI

1. Ivone Kirkpatrick, *Mussolini: A Study in Power* (New York: Hawthorn, 1964), p. 351.
2. Alan Bullock, *Hitler* (New York: Harper and Row, 1962), p. 315.
3. Elizabeth Wiskemann, *The Rome-Berlin Axis* (London: Collins, 1966), p. 186.
4. Wiskemann, *Rome-Berlin Axis*, p. 151.

5. Hugh Gibson, ed., *The Ciano Diaries 1939-1943* (Garden City, N.Y.: Doubleday, 1946), entry for November 20, 1939.
6. Wiskemann, *Rome-Berlin Axis*, p. 131.
7. Wiskemann, *Rome-Berlin Axis*, p. 132.
8. Wiskemann, *Rome-Berlin Axis*, p. 161.
9. Kirkpatrick, *Mussolini*, p. 371.
10. Bullock, Hitler, pp. 253-254; S. Halperin, *Germany Tried Democracy* (Hamden, Conn.: Archon, 1946), pp. 95-100, 179, 319; Golo Mann, *The History of Germany since 1789* (New York: Praeger, 1968), p. 414.
11. Adrian Lyttelton, "Italian Fascism", in Walter Laqueur, ed., *Fascism: A Reader's Guide* (Berkeley: University of California, 1976), p. 136.
12. See the illuminating description of these events in F. W. Deakin, *The Brutal Friendship: Mussolini, Hitler and the Fall of Fascism* (New York: Harper and Row, 1962), pp. 259-275.

NOTES TO CHAPTER XII

1. Ivone Kirkpatrick, *Mussolini: A Study in Power* (New York: Hawthorn, 1964), p. 550.
2. Winston Churchill, *Closing the Ring* (Boston: Houghton Mifflin, 1951), p. 51.
3. Mussolini, *Opera Omnia*, XXXIV, pp. 286-294.
4. Mussolini, *Opera Omnia,* XXXIV, pp. 278 and 290.
5. Christopher Hibbert, *Il Duce* (Boston: Little, Brown, 1962) p. 43n. I am very much in debt to Hibbert for many of the details of the *Duce*'s life which follow.
6. F. W. Deakin, *The Brutal Friendship* (New York: Doubleday, 1966), p. 616.
7. Winston Churchill, *Triumph and Tragedy* (Boston: Houghton Mifflin, 1953), p. 528.

NOTES TO THE EPILOGUE

1. Alfred Cobban, *Dictatorship: Its History and Theory* (New York: Scribner's, 1939), p. 250.
2. Domenico Settembrini, *Fascismo controrivoluzione imperfetta* (Florence: Sansoni, 1978).
3. Stephen F. Cohen, *Bukharin and the Bolshevik Revolution* (New York: Alfred A. Knopf, 1971), p. 333.
4. See Anthony James Joes, *Fascism in the Contemporary World* (Boulder: Westview, 1978).
5. James Malloy, "Authoritarianism and Corporatism in Latin America: The Modal Pattern", in James Malloy, ed., *Authoritarianism and Corporatism in Latin America* (Pittsburgh: University of Pittsburgh, 1977), pp. 10-11.
6. A. James Gregor, *The Fascist Persuasion in Radical Politics* (Princeton: Princeton University, 1974), p. 394.

SELECTED BIBLIOGRAPHY

In preparing this book I have relied most heavily on the following: Mussolini's collected works *Opera Omnia* (Florence: La Fenice, 36 volumes, 1951–1963); Renzo De Felice's magnificent multivolume biography (not yet completed): *Mussolini il rivoluzionario* (1965), *Mussolini il fascista*, vol. I (1966), *Mussolini il fascista*, vol. II (1968), and *Mussolini il duce* (1974), published in Turin by Einaudi; the works of A. James Gregor of the University of California, especially *The Ideology of Fascism* (New York: Free Press, 1969), *The Fascist Persuasion in Radical Politics* (Princeton: Princeton University, 1974), and *Young Mussolini and the Intellectual Origins of Fascism* (Berkeley: University of California, 1979).

The following have also been supremely valuable: Alberto Aquarone, *L'organizzazione dello stato totalitario* (Turin: Einaudi, 1965), Adrian Lyttleton, *The Seizure of Power: Fascism in Italy 1919–1929* (New York: Scribner's, 1973), Ernst Nolte, *Three Faces of Fascism* (New York: Holt, Rinehart & Winston, 1966), and Domenico Settembrini, *Fascismo controrivoluzione imperfetta* (Florence: Sansoni, 1978).

Very helpful studies of Mussolini's foreign policy are: George W. Baer, *The Coming of the Italian–Ethiopian War* (Cambridge: Harvard University, 1967), Ivone Kirkpatrick, *Mussolini: A Study in Power* (New York: Hawthorn, 1964), Esmonde M. Robertson, *Mussolini as Empire Builder: Europe and Africa, 1932–1936* (New York: St. Martin's, 1977), and Elizabeth Wiskemann, *The Rome–Berlin Axis* (London: Collins, 1966); on Mussolini's relation with Hitler, F. W. Deakin's *The Brutal Friendship* (New York: Harper, 1962) is indispensable.

On the economy of fascism see: Shepard Clough, *The Economic History of Italy* (New York: Columbia University, 1964), Paul Einzig, *Economic Foundations of Fascism* (New York: Macmillan, 1933), A. James Gregor, *Italian Fascism and Developmental Dictatorship* (Princeton: Princeton University, 1979), Salvatore La Francesca, *La politica economica del fascismo* (Bari: Laterza, 1973), Maurice Neufeld, *Italy: School for Awakening Countries* (Ithaca: Cornell University, 1961), Rosario Romeo, *Breve storia della grande industria in Italia* (Rocco San Casciano: Cappelli, 1967), Roland Sarti, *Fascism and the Industrial Leadership in Italy, 1919–1940* (Berkeley: University of California, 1971), Carlo Schmidt, *The Plow and the Sword* (New York: Columbia University, 1938), and William G. Welk, *Fascist Economic Policy* (Cambridge: Harvard University, 1938).

For Church–State relations, see D. A. Binchy's classic *Church and State in Fascist Italy* (New York: Oxford University, 1941), A. C. Jemolo, *Church and State in Italy 1850–1950* (Oxford: Blackwell, 1960), and Richard A. Webster, *The Cross and the Fasces* (Stanford: Stanford University, 1960).

Interesting personal glimpses of Mussolini may be obtained from: Emil Ludwig, *Colloqui con Mussolini* (Verona: Mondadori, 1950), P. Monelli, *Mussolini: The Intimate Life of a Demagogue* (New York: Vanguard, 1954), Rachele Mussolini, *La mia vita con Benito* (Verona: Mondadori, 1948), and

Margherita Sarfatti, *Life of Benito Mussolini* (New York: Frederick A. Stokes, 1925).

Also very useful studies on various aspects of Mussolini's life and regime: Federico Chabod, *History of Italian Fascism* (London: Weidenfeld and Nicolson, 1961), Paul Corner, *Fascism in Ferrara, 1915–1925* (London: Oxford University, 1975), Herman Finer, *Mussolini's Italy* (New York: Universal Library, 1965), Christopher Hibbert, *Il Duce* (Boston, Little, Brown, 1962), Roberto Michels, *First Lectures in Political Sociology* (New York: Harper, 1965), Giorgio Pini and D. Susmel, *Mussolini: L'uomo e l'opera* (Florence: La Fenice, 1953), Giuseppe Prezzolini, *Fascism* (London: Methuen, 1926), Luigi Salvatorelli and G. Mira, *Storia d'Italia nel periodo fascista* (Turin: Einaudi, 1964), Herbert W. Schneider, *Making the Fascist State* (New York: Fertig, 1968), Edward R. Tannenbaum, *The Fascist Experience* (New York: Basic Books, 1972), Angelo Tasca, *The Rise of Italian Fascism, 1918–1922* (New York: Fertig, 1966), and Eugen Weber's small and very helpful *Varieties of Fascism* (Princeton: Van Nostrand, 1964).

On the subject of fascist or fascistic regimes and movements outside the European context, see A. James Gregor, *The Fascist Persuasion in Radical Politics* (Princeton: Princeton University, 1974), and Anthony James Joes, *Fascism in the Contemporary World* (Boulder: Westview, 1978).

INDEX